Making Headlines

100 Years of The Vancouver Sun

Making Headlines

100 Years of The Vancouver Sun

By **Shelley Fralic**

With research by Kate Bird

THE VANCOUVER SUN

SERIOUSLY WESTCOAST

Published by *The Vancouver Sun*

Pacific Newspaper Group, a division of Postmedia Network Inc.

200 Granville Street,

Vancouver, B.C., Canada, V6C 3N3

vancouversun.com

Library and Archives Canada Cataloguing in Publication

Fralic, Shelley, 1953-

Making headlines : 100 years of the Vancouver

Sun / by Shelley Fralic, with research by Kate Bird.

Includes bibliographical references and index.

ISBN 978-0-919776-40-1

1. Vancouver Sun (Firm)--History. 2. Newspapers

publishing--British Columbia--Vancouver--History.

I. Bird, Kate II. Title. III. Title: 100 years of the Vancouver

Sun. IV. Title: One hundred years of the Vancouver Sun.

PN4919.V363V36 2012 071'.1133 C2012-904187-4

Editing by Bev Wake

Design by Joseph Llamzon and Peter Merrison
Creative Services, Pacific Newspaper Group

Indexing by Iva Cheung

Printed and Bound in Canada by Friesens

MIX
Paper from
responsible sources
FSC® C016245

Printed on FSC certified paper, which is
acid-free and ancient forest-friendly
and has been processed chlorine-free.

TABLE OF CONTENTS

1997 drawing of the Sun Tower by Robin Ward. *Vancouver Sun*

A 100th birthday is not only a time to reflect, it is also a time to look forward, to the next 100 years.

And while *The Vancouver Sun* has endured as B.C.'s paper of record for the past century, it isn't an overstatement to say we've seen more changes in our industry in the past decade than we did in the nine that preceded it. And the change is far from over.

It has been challenging to adapt to the information and digital revolutions, but it has also been tremendously exhilarating. The explosion in news and information and the new digital tools at our disposal have brought us the largest audience we've ever had.

Today what defines *The Vancouver Sun* is not the medium, but the content. It's not about the platform, it's about the news.

What will remain constant in the years to come is our dedication to joining with British Columbians in the communal conversation — be it political, cultural, economic, scientific or social. The writers, photographers, designers and editors who have so defined this newspaper over the years will continue to create the content the community seeks to reflect itself, to remain engaged in the public discourse.

One hundred years ago, the proprietors of the first *Vancouver Sun* said their goal was that "readers should feel that *The Sun* is their paper and that it has an individual meaning to every citizen of British Columbia."

Today, whether it's on paper, mobile, tablet or the Internet, we look forward to proudly upholding that legacy into the next century.

Kevin Bent
Publisher, *The Vancouver Sun*

Vancouver Sun reporter and photographer atop the Sun Tower in 1946. *Vancouver Public Library 26911*

It has been said, and it is true, that a daily newspaper is the first rough draft of history.

But it is so much more than that.

Since the first edition of *The Vancouver Sun* rolled off the presses 100 years ago, on Feb. 12, 1912, we have chronicled not only the ever-evolving story of Vancouver and B.C., but the universe around us.

We have published through The Great Depression and every world war, through the industrial age and the moon landing, through global triumph and local tragedy, through the golden era of Hollywood and the digital revolution, through the city's race riots and hockey riots, the tragedy of missing women and the glory of the 2010 Olympic Games, our century-long legacy an unmatched and priceless archive of the explosive demographic, social and cultural shifts around the globe and right here in our own backyard.

As journalistic obligation dictates, we have informed and entertained, analyzed and provoked, delivering to doorsteps a daily hand-picked menu of breaking news and erudite opinion, of cheeky humour and political commentary, of stunning photography and artistic criticism.

And while dutifully comforting the afflicted and afflicting the comfortable, we have also endeavoured to fulfill our duty to readers as an active partner in the community, encouraging literacy initiatives through Raise-a-Reader, funding programs for needy children with our Vancouver Sun Children's Fund, and promoting health and fitness with our annual Vancouver Sun Run.

As our nameplate unabashedly declares, we are, proudly, Vancouver.

This, then, is the celebratory story of a newspaper and its city, a decade-by-decade centennial compendium, from the sinking of the *Titanic* just two months after hawkers hit city streets with our first edition through the patriot games that were the 2010 Winter Olympics.

That we have weathered and survived unprecedented change – from morning-to-evening-to-morning publication, from picket lines to changing mastheads, from manual typewriters and hot metal to offset printing and digital delivery, from relentless market competition to the game-changing Internet explosion – is best credited to an unwavering constant: knowing that the value of our currency has always been found in those who carry the press passes, in the reporter with the notebook and the nose for news, and the photographer with the lightning shutter and the eye for detail.

Our reputation was built not only on enterprise and a scrappy personality but on a stellar stable of columnists and reporters, artists and editors, cartoonists and photographers, for our story is also the story of newspapering greats like legendary saloon reporter Jack Wasserman and editorial cartoonist Len Norris, city columnists Denny Boyd and Pete McMartin, photographers Ralph Bower and Glenn Baglo, sports writers Archie McDonald and Cam Cole, and female trailblazers Simma Holt and Patricia Graham.

It has been both humbling and thrilling to have borne witness to this newspaper's history, to have ridden the exhilarating roller coaster, as I have, for 33 years as a *Vancouver Sun* reporter and editor, and it is no less a privilege to be able to tell the story of what this newspaper has meant to each of us, and to our city.

The first editorial published in *The Sun*'s debut edition 100 years ago promised its 20,000 readers that it would strive to uphold journalistic standards while never losing sight of its purpose: "What we do want is that our readers should feel that *The Sun* is their paper and that it has an individual meaning to every citizen of British Columbia."

Our mandate is no less compelling or committed today, for even as newspapers find themselves adapting to publishing in the ephemeral dimension that is the digital age, the readers' appetite for trustworthy and contextual news and information remains as strong as it ever was.

This, then, as we welcome *The Vancouver Sun*'s rise into its second century, is the edited version of that first rough draft of history.

Shelley Fralic

THE VANCOUVER SUN
PUBLISHERS
PRINTERS and
BOOKBINDERS

ORDER Now VANCOUVER SUN
VANCOUVER HOME NEWSPAPER

THE 1910s

The 1910s:
The Sun rises over Vancouver

When the first edition of The Sun rolled off the presses on the morning of Monday, Feb. 12, 1912, it entered a crowded market, as Vancouver had its fair share of newspapers chronicling the many challenges facing a region fraught with growing pains.

Dailies of the day were typically founded by men who used them, flagrantly, to espouse their own political and religious ambitions and beliefs, thus ensuring their perspective became part of the public discussion. It was printing press politics, as editorialists fervently opined on issues of the day, such as taxes and growth, resource exploitation, provincial and civic governance, immigration, trade and local services.

The Sun's owner, John P. McConnell – known as Black Jack – was no different. His new paper debuted with an editorial noting its intention was to provide a Liberal voice in opposition to the conservative editorial positions promulgated by the rival News-Advertiser, another morning newspaper with a small circulation, and The Province and The Vancouver World, which owned the evening market.

About 20,000 people bought a copy of The Sun's first issue, which amounted to one out of every six Vancouverites. They were greeted by a front-page drawing of an angel with dragonfly wings, carrying leaflets promising a newspaper that would be Reliable, The Latest and Best-Informed, Just Out, Smart and Up-to-Date.

McConnell's new paper was printed at the Burrard Publishing Company Limited building at 711-713 Seymour Street, and when newsboys hit the streets hawking that first edition, it was a 24-page broadsheet with two, 12-page sections. It cost five cents.

PRECEDING PAGE: In 1917, *The Vancouver Daily Sun* **moved into new offices on the 100-block of West Pender Street.** *Courtesy of Jane Gray*

The Vancouver Sun's first building at 711-713 Seymour Street can be seen (with the semi-circle sign) in the lower right-hand corner of this 1912 photo. *Vancouver Public Library 6651*

The Sun

VOL I. NUMBER 1.   VANCOUVER, MONDAY, FEBRUARY 12, 1912.—TWENTY-FOUR PAGES.   FIRST SECTION—PAGES ONE TO TWELVE

THE WEATHER
Vancouver and lower mainland—Southerly light wind, dry and settled.

ONE MAN INJURED WHEN POLICEMEN BREAK UP MEETING

Sunday Free Speech Fight Marked by Temperate Attitude of Those Belligerents.

AQUATIC ORATOR TAKEN WHILE USING MEGAPHONE

James Hawthornthwaite Delivers Fiery Speech to Night Gathering at Theatre.

YOUNG LIBERALS TO COME TO RESCUE OF THEIR PARTY

Plan Revival of the Association That Two Years Ago Joined the Older Body---May Form a Social Club as Well---"New Blood From the East" Are Eager to Get Into Fray in British Columbia.

CHINESE TONGS MAY BATTLE IN SAN FRANCISCO

Chief of Police, Fearing Trouble, Warns Leaders of Warring Clans.

GUN FIGHTERS HAVE BEEN BROUGHT TO CITY

Truce May Be Patched Up to Allow Celebration of the Celestial New Year.

LEAVE CHURCH TO CAPTURE BURGLAR

Portland Minister's Wife Leads Congregation in Apprehension of Thief in Parsonage.

LUMBERMEN PRESENT VIEWS IN OTTAWA

Matters of Importance to the Industry Submitted to Government's Consideration on Saturday.

GERMANY IS AFTER CENTRAL AFRICA

Expansionists Commence Campaign for Partition of Portuguese Colonies.

BELIEVED VESSEL IS LOST WITH ALL HANDS

Son of John McLaren, Former Chief of Police, Vancouver, Was Aboard.

FEATURES OF THE NEWS.

ACQUISITION OF LAND WILL COST CITY A HUGE SUM

Over Million Dollars Will Be Expended for Appropriation of Property.

IS AN INCREASE OVER THE LAST YEAR

Parks Department Will Obtain About $500,000 for Securing Open Spaces.

WORLD NEWS IN TABLOID FOR BREAKFAST TABLE READERS

CITY.

PROVINCIAL.

NEW WESTMINSTER.

GENERAL.

UNITED STATES.

MARINE.

FINANCIAL.

The first edition of *The Sun*, published Feb. 12, 1912.

Good morning B.C.

The Olde English font type that announced *The Sun*'s name – the word Vancouver wouldn't be incorporated into the nameplate for another five years – topped a lineup of stories that reflected not only the bustling trade and commerce of the west coast harbour, but the move by politicians and city leaders toward the modernization demanded by a burgeoning population straining the town at its seams.

The Sun's first pages were jammed with text-heavy stories, introduced by multiple layers of headlines and subheads. There was little in the way of photography or visual relief, a design deficiency common to the era. While a single issue cost a nickel, home delivery by carrier was a steal: 10 cents a week or $5 for a year in advance. Such would be the zeal of its young carrier force, *The Sun* reported, that a police complaint was received from citizens objecting to "the noise caused by newsboys shouting their wares on the streets."

Above the fold of the big broadsheet's debut issue, where top stories are traditionally placed in a hierarchical manner to convey their importance, the all-capital headlines included "YOUNG LIBERALS TO COME TO RESCUE OF THEIR PARTY" and "ONE MAN INJURED WHEN POLICEMEN BREAK UP MEETING," a story that was followed by a detailed accounting of a dust-up at a local free speech event.

Other front-page choices reflected the social, ethical and political touchstones of the day: wire stories declared "CHINESE TONGS MAY BATTLE IN SAN FRANCISCO" and "GERMANY IS AFTER CENTRAL AFRICA." There was an item about the lumber industry, another about land appropriation by the city and yet another about the sinking of a vessel in local waters.

John P. McConnell and his daughter, Edith, in 1926. *Courtesy of Robin Denton*

The story of Black Jack

John P. McConnell was already active in the newspaper business when he launched *The Sun* at age 37, his journalistic ambitions whetted in Toronto, where he wrote unsigned commentary for *Saturday Night* magazine and gained a name for using his rich vocabulary to pull no punches. McConnell had even wanted to call his new paper the *Vancouver Globe*, given he'd once worked at the influential *Globe* in Toronto, but he was talked out of it by a staffer.

In Vancouver, "Black Jack" McConnell had worked as a special travelling correspondent for *The Province* in 1905 and 1906, where his reports included an Aug. 12, 1905 dispatch from horseback while visiting the Nicola Valley coal mines. The full-page piece started with a descriptive scene setter: "At last the diamond hitch is thrown on the last pack, the last coat is slung in its latigo, spurs are adjusted and each man swings into the saddle."

Both journalist and businessman, he was also a part owner of *The Morning Sun* and weekly *Saturday Sunset* newspapers with his brother-in-law Richard Ford, but was actively seeking an outlet for his own voice, telling *The* *Province* in 1907 that it was time Vancouver had a weekly journal "devoted more to comment and current events . . . entirely different from that covered by daily papers."

When McConnell's attempts to take control of other papers in which he had interests failed, the only answer, as he explained in that first edition of his new *Sun*, was to publish a new morning paper. "The necessity for a paper to consistently advocate the principles of Liberalism had been making itself felt for some time. There was no paper in the city that could be considered as consistently Liberal and it was felt that the first step toward rehabilitating the party in British Columbia should be the establishment of a daily newspaper." The $80,000 business investment necessitated the importation from San Francisco of a printing press that had been damaged by fire but rehabilitated.

The April 12 masthead indicated various levels of editorial jurisdiction: president F.C. Wake, who was a lawyer transplanted from the Yukon; McConnell as managing editor; news editor John Gerrie; Richard Ford as managing director; and advertising manager William Carswell.

Other staffers in those early days included city editor Arthur Burns, marine reporter Bert Coleman, sports writer Wilbur Bryan, telegraph editor John Linkie, financial editor Bradford Hyer and cartoonist Graham Hydre.

The page-six masthead of the April 12 edition carried a "declaration" from circulation manager Cecil Quilliam that "the average paid circulation from February 12 to March 12, 1912, was 15,295." A note to "correspondents" advised readers of a universal letters to the editor tenet that "No letters will be published in *The Sun* except over the writer's signature . . . All manuscripts submitted are at the writer's risk."

Like father, like daughter

Underscoring the theory that the journalism gene may well be hereditary, and hinting at future *Sun* dynasties, McConnell's daughter Edith would be a columnist and women's page editor at several Vancouver papers, including *The Sun*, for 40 years. She was best known for her column *Let's Go Shopping*. While Black Jack upheld his rapscallion reputation by marrying four times, Edith married Ivan Denton, another *Sun* writer, and the pair worked for a time as scriptwriters in Hollywood before returning to Vancouver to settle down and have a family.

The tip of a lifetime

Backing McConnell in his new publishing venture was fellow Liberal John W. Stewart, a Scottish lumber baron who had come to Canada as a member of the survey party charting the Canadian Pacific Railway. Such was Stewart's iron horse fervour – in 1914, he switched allegiance to Pacific Great Eastern, which was planning to run a rail line from north of Vancouver east to Toronto – that when *The Sun* backed the Liberals and took credit for the party's victory in the 1916 election, Stewart got a provincial go-ahead for the PGE, which became B.C. Rail. It was a journalistic conflict of interest that would become less tolerable as a non-partisan professionalism became standard throughout the newspaper trade.

Working for Stewart at the time was a young man named Robert James Cromie, a Quebec-born go-getter who had been to business school but decided to head west as an 18-year-old looking for work. He landed a job in 1906 as a bellhop at the Mariaggi Hotel in Winnipeg, which is where Stewart met him. The story is that Stewart tipped him generously and when Cromie gave him back some change, Stewart decided he was private secretary material and took him back to Vancouver to work for his railway company.

Robert Cromie would soon become *The Sun*'s great saviour.

A decade of firsts and a sinking ship

The premiere of another publishing kid on the block was prescient, news-wise, for it came amid a year of exciting firsts for the city and readers: the University of B.C.'s Point Grey campus was being built; the iconic Only Restaurant opened on East Hastings; the Lions Gate Bridge and Stanley Park causeway were under construction; and Hardial Singh Atwal was born at the 2nd Avenue Sikh Temple in Vancouver, the son of temple priest Balwant Singh Atwal and the country's first Canadian-born Sikh.

And the car was taking over city streets. On June 24, *The Sun* reported that roads in the city were experiencing traffic jams and "the total number of automobiles . . . in Vancouver is 1,769."

It was no less historic on the world news front. Two months after *The Sun*'s debut, the *RMS Titanic* struck an iceberg off Canada's Atlantic coast on April 14 and sank on her maiden voyage from Southampton, England to New York City. News of the disaster, which rippled around

the world via wireless telegraph, took several days to unfold for *Sun* readers, the details and death counts from news agencies, witnesses and White Star Line management changing as the days passed.

The Sun's front-page headline on Monday, April 15 reported that the steamer was afloat: "Ships Rushing to Aid Titanic, Sinking in Mid-Ocean – 1300 Aboard." The accompanying wire story out of Cape Race, Nfld. said the ship had hit an iceberg the previous night and had sent out an SOS received in Halifax harbour by *The Virginian*, which was sailing to the rescue. The last message from the *Titanic*'s wireless operator, according to the story, was that female passengers were being placed in lifeboats. Another story listed the notable passengers on board, while a short sidebar outlined the huge ship's dimensions.

The next day's seven-column headline was a shock: "TWELVE HUNDRED PERISH WITH TITANIC." The subhead: "Most Appalling and

Tragic Marine Disaster in the History of the Civilized World." Other headlines over the story – the tradition of the day had readers wading through as many as six headlines or subheads before getting to the story – included the more prosaic "Where Once Was Joy and Life, Ocean Spreads Winding Sheet Over Fathomless Sepulchres."

The April 17 *Sun* revealed that another rescue vessel, the *Carpathia*, was off the Atlantic coast "bearing the 868 lives that had been snatched from the waters." There was no estimation of Canadian fatalities, although the paper listed the names of 17 missing Canadians on the passenger list of the "ill-fated leviathan of sea," along with the names of 11 who had reportedly been rescued. Over the next few days would come news that although the luxury liner had 2,223 people on board, including industrialist John Jacob Astor IV, it was equipped with lifeboats for 1,178. Astor was among the estimated 1,517 who perished.

It took several days to obtain the information, but by April 16, 1912, *The Sun* was finally able to publish a more accurate account of the lives lost during the sinking of the *Titanic*.

Newsies Who Sold The Sun Extra

On the announcement being made one evening last week that a special edition of The Sun would be issued giving the latest and most authentic war news, there was a wholesale rush, on the part of the newsies of the city, to Seymour street. Within fifteen minutes of their arrival at the office | the extra was on the streets and within sixty minutes the entire edition was sold. The same thing was repeated on the following two evenings with the same result. The same boys awaited anxiously outside this office on Saturday evening in the hope that an extra would be put on the | streets but as the news received over the wires was not of sufficient importance, it was decided not to issue one. The photograph shows the merry bunch awaiting the extra last Sunday morning, and, by the way, every copy of the many thousands printed was sold.

Newsboys, here in front of the newspaper's offices at 711-713 Seymour Street, sold the Extra edition of the Aug. 11, 1914 *Vancouver Sun* announcing the start of the First World War. *Vancouver Sun*

Yes, we're always happy to take your money

Long before eBay and Craigslist came to dominate the virtual marketplace, a newspaper's want ads – which are now called classified ads, and are not to be confused with the pricier display ads – were not only a healthy contributor to the business's bottom line but one of the few public forums where locals could buy and sell, seek and swap, and, yes, announce that they had, unfortunately, expired.

The Sun's own entreaty to readers included a notice on Feb. 15, 1913 that the newspaper was opening a "downtown branch office" at 160 Hastings Street W. to take subscription and advertisement orders until 10 p.m. every night except Sunday, with "a guarantee of correct classification the following morning."

Want ads on April 14, 1917 included listings from private detectives, dog hospitals, junk dealers, stenographers, patent attorneys, assayers and chemists, as well as a pitch from Flack Estate Investments for "Suburban Homes" – including several acres it was offering in Burnaby, "all under cultivation with an orchard and creek, for $2,100."

If you needed a place to rent – or, as it was called in *Sun* want ads in 1917, "situations wanted" – or had lost your worldly goods or needed to unload them, you could expect to spend a penny a word to place an ad, with the minimum set at 10 cents an ad. Birth, marriage and death notices not exceeding 50 words cost a flat 50 cents, with a penny charged for each additional word. Fast forward 95 years, to 2012, and an obituary in *The Sun* costs about $12.68 a line, or roughly $1.60 a word. And a full-page, full-colour advertisement in the 21st-century weekend *Sun*? Thousands.

It wasn't a very good year

The Sun has long had an affinity for clever promotional slogans, which have changed with much regularity over the past century, but one of its earliest – "*The Sun* never stands still. It progresses all the time." – unfortunately didn't reflect the bottom line.

Among the treasures that 86-year-old Robin Denton has kept safe, 100 years after his grandfather John P. McConnell started *The Sun*, is a single-page, hand-written ledger that lists the *Vancouver Sun*'s balance sheet for March 1912 – the first full month of the paper's operations.

The editorial payroll for the first month was $2,197. Illustrations cost $372.25, while photographs were a mere $20. Telegraph and telephone costs were $500.87, press associations were $110 and correspondence was $229.40.

Under "general expense," rent and utilities tallied up at $350, insurance was $66 and taxes were $12. The advertising department had a $638.75 payroll, and paid out $50 in commissions. The payroll in the press room was $352 and the cost of paper was $2,674.39. Total expenses were $15,495.35.

On the other side of the ledger, earnings included $3,818.86 in circulation, $6,507.04 in display advertising and $860.28 in classified ads. Total earnings were $11,601.10, which meant the paper posted a net loss of $3,894.25 for the month.

The Komagata Maru served as a temporary home for 376 migrants from India in 1914, among them 340 Sikhs. Just two dozen passengers were allowed to remain in Canada before the ship was ordered out of Vancouver harbour. *Leonard Frank, Vancouver Public Library 6232*

The simmering melting pot

Vancouver in the early 1900s was home to the entrepreneurial and the opportunistic, the labourers and the homesteaders, the native Indians living and working in settlements in Kitsilano and all along the Fraser River, the Chinese who had come with the railroad and established Chinatown, the Japanese who came to work in the fishing industry and settled in Richmond and Little Tokyo in downtown, and the thousands of immigrants from the Prairies, the U.S. and Europe who flooded in looking for jobs and ended up staying to raise their families.

This increasing pluralism created much friction - especially on the part of the whites and the Vancouver-born. Racism and open hostility, usually directed toward Asians, was not uncommon and often brutal, whether it took the form of an anti-Chinese riot or children clashing in schoolyards, stories that were regularly reported in *The Sun*. Segregation was not unusual, particularly in city-run facilities. When Vancouver's Crystal Pool opened in the 1920s, it was off-limits to "negroes and Orientals" for two decades.

One of the city's – and the paper's – most notorious black eyes was the handling of the Japanese steamer *Komagata Maru*, which arrived in Vancouver harbour on the morning of May 23, 1914, with 376 migrants from India aboard, including 340 Sikhs.

"HINDU INVADERS NOW IN THE CITY HARBOR ON KOMAGATA MARU," was *The Sun*'s same-day headline, over a subhead that reported "Excited Crowd of Hindus Assemble on Waterfront – Newcomers Seem Assured of Being Admitted."

For the next two months, as the ship languished in Burrard Inlet with the immigrants still on board, *Sun* editorials, letters to the editor, cartoons and reports from government officials chronicled the growing controversy. The federal government's so-called exclusion law, an order-in-council that banned the entry to the country of immigrant labourers, was hotly debated across Canada as authorities squabbled over what to do with the ship. *The Sun* kept the story alive, a daily to-and-fro debate that would see reports of rampant hook worm disease among passengers countered by political representations to Ottawa from local Sikh leaders fighting on their behalf. The coverage, while attempting at balance, was largely negative toward the immigrants' plight. Interviews with Sikh gurus, and efforts by the paper to explain their religious practices, were peppered with incendiary language such as "Hindu buccaneers," "the Hindus are a fanatical race" and "Hindus cherish no amity for whites." But when the ship's passengers went on a hunger strike in early June, a *Sun* editorial noted "it would hardly do to let them starve."

Nor was the ethnic debate confined to what *The Sun* called the "Hindu situation." A B.C. Sugar Refining Co. advertisement, published in *The Sun* in the midst of the imbroglio, admonished those buying sugar made by "the rice-fed, half-naked, unwashed Coolies of Hongkong" and warned that "British Columbia can be Orientalized just as thoroughly by using Hongkong products as though we let down the barriers and freely admitted all Chinese."

The law that kept the *Komagata Maru* at bay was ultimately upheld and, on July 23, 1914, the ship was ordered to leave Canadian waters. About two dozen passengers who had proven "Canadian domicile" were allowed to stay behind in Vancouver, given their freedom on shore.

The Sun's front page that day included an editorial cartoon with a dove of peace and a caricature of Captain Vancouver. The dove was nesting on top of a turbanned Sikh, identified as a "Komagata Maruner," and a stern-looking officer, identified as an "Immigration Official," with the dove mollifying Captain Vancouver: "You can take off your clothes and get some rest now, Captain. I've got them both to sleep."

The next day, a cartoon on *The Sun*'s front page depicted Captain Vancouver, ear cocked toward the sea, with the caption: "They're gone!"

It was a story that would play out over the century, with the Vietnamese "boat people" in the 1970s and '80s and, more recently, the arrival in B.C.'s coastal waters of two ships carrying hundreds of Sri Lankan refugees. But it would also be tempered by less racist editorializing as the years went by and multiculturalism became an integral part of Vancouver's fabric. In August 2006, Prime Minister Stephen Harper, in a series of government *mea culpas* for historic wrongs, apologized for the *Komagata Maru* incident.

The world at war

In 1914, *The Sun*'s focus shifted from local issues to a new global conflict: the First World War was declared in July, with world powers mobilizing in Europe to fight the forces of Imperialism.

The Sun's daily coverage was expansive, with multiple stories on the front page reporting the politics and advanced firepower on the battlefront. Inside were editorials and stories focusing on the activities of home-town forces, such as the 72nd Canadian Infantry Battalion Seaforth Highlanders. Readers' appetite for news was insatiable; the numerous "extra" editions published during the conflict would sell out as soon as they hit the streets.

Through the first years of the war, as millions were dying on European soil and unease settled over the world, Vancouver was rocked by rising unemployment, labour strikes, Prohibition, shuttered businesses and a population decline. Soup kitchens and tent camps for the unemployed, along with daily newspaper photographs of striking relief workers, began to tarnish the patina of prosperity.

But *The Sun* was doing its part in the war effort, including printing coupons for free war maps so readers could follow the war's progress.

Readers were encouraged to buy Victory Bonds during the latter years of the First World War.

In August 1914, *The Sun* reported on its front page that the Vancouver War Fund had received $5,725 in donations, including $1,000 from the Board of Trade – kick-starting a campaign to raise $100,000 for "the wives and children of the men at the front." *Sun* ads urged readers to "protect those who are left behind."

In 1918, a month before the war ended, a front-page message from editors further underscored *The Sun*'s pronounced support for the war effort, applauding *Sun* employees who had bought Victory bonds and encouraging readers to follow suit in helping Vancouverites reach a goal of $15 million. "The Hun is staggering, but he is not yet finished. Hit him again," the message read. "Every bond you buy is a biff for the Kaiser. Remember the sacrifices being made by the boys at the front. Help them all you can."

The Sun was no less generous in its initiatives for the women left behind as war raged

The advent of the telegraph meant newspapers, for the first time, could publish daily accounts from the battlegrounds during the First World War. Advances in transportation meant that soldiers in the field could also receive news from home. *E.T. Sampson, Vancouver Public Library Gr War P33*

This ad appeared in the first edition of *The Sun*, offering lots in Hastings Grove for $245 – with various payment options available. Note the phone number: Seymour 5654.

overseas, offering through its contest department the biggest prize it had ever offered: a house. The 1914 promotion was simple – a woman qualified by nominating someone for a *Sun* subscription. The first prize was a Kerrisdale house and lot worth $4,000. Runner-up prizes: a four-door Russell 30 Touring car, a trip to the British Isles and a piano.

The world at peace

Armistice Day was declared on Nov. 11, 1918: the First World War was over. Four years of bloody combat had claimed 60,000 Canadian lives and drastically changed the mood of the city, its residents unwittingly inured to the new reality of personal loss and dark geo-politics.

The Vancouver Daily Sun's Armistice Day headline said, simply, "Armistice Signed Peace Declared." It accompanied a story out of Washington that began with: "The world war will end this morning at 6 o'clock Washington time, 11 o'clock Paris time. The armistice was signed by the German representatives at midnight. (This means that fighting ceased at 3 o'clock this morning Vancouver time.)"

On the bottom of the front page was a proclamation from Vancouver's acting mayor, Thos. H. Kirk: "In commemoration of the Victorious Armistice which has been Officially announced, and in order that the Citizens generally may participate in appropriate celebrations, I hereby declare Monday, Nov. 11, 1918, a Public Holiday within the City of Vancouver, and would request that the same be observed by all."

The message ended with "God Save The King."

The new journalism

The First World War changed war reporting. Until then, newspapers had been confined to publishing narratives written by correspondents after the conflicts had ended. But the advent of the telegraph allowed daily front-line reports, bringing the bloody backlash of battle into readers' homes every day. *The Sun*'s combination of harsh headlines, stark photographs and deadly skirmishes, along with heart-rending stories of local casualties, was a catalogue of human ruin unlike anything readers had seen.

Although this new journalism opened readers' eyes to the grimness of global conflict, the First World War coverage was still heavily censored, with British, French and U.S. authorities blocking the efforts of war correspondents, though the Americans did allow embedded reporters. It was a dangerous job – hundreds of journalists have died covering wars over the years, including *Calgary Herald* reporter Michelle Lang, killed in a 2009 roadside bombing in Afghanistan – but there could be no question that newspapers and evolving broadcast technology would increasingly shine

a light on the battlefield, and on the countries that entered the theatre of war. Four decades later, the blood and battle of the Vietnam War would be the first to unfold live and uncensored on television; pundits would credit the medium for giving rise to the modern-day anti-war movement.

One man's loss is another man's gain

The war years were hard on *The Vancouver Sun*. It struggled financially and John P. McConnell decided to pack it in with the paper on the verge of bankruptcy. Robert Cromie – the former bellhop plucked from a Winnipeg hotel years earlier by *Sun* investor

John Stewart – secured the paper in 1917 when *The Sun*'s nearly worthless shares were offered to him through a deal brokered by Stewart.

The financial details surrounding Cromie's acquisition of *The Sun* have always been somewhat murky, but when the dust settled the paper and its weak circulation of 10,000 were nonetheless his.

Cromie, who was 30 when he bought *The Sun,* knew little about newspapering but was an astute businessman. His focus on aggressive news coverage, along with circulation and advertising, effectively reversed the paper's faltering fortunes within a few years.

And he was quick to make a move on his competitors. On Sept. 1, 1917, Cromie purchased the rival 8,000-circulation *News-Advertiser* for $100,000 from J.S. Matson and effectively

The Vancouver Daily Sun published an extra edition on Nov. 11, 1918 to announce the end of the First World War.

Robert J. Cromie (left), with Prime Minister William Lyon Mackenzie King, was 30 when he bought *The Sun* **in 1917.** *Vancouver Public Library 30235*

shut it down. He renamed the newly amalgamated firm *The Sun Publishing Co. Ltd*, moved everything into offices and production facilities at 137 and 125 West Pender Street, and merged the two papers into a brand new title: *The Vancouver Daily Sun.*

An in-paper advertisement told readers *The Sun* had "purchased the plant and good will of the *Daily News-Advertiser"* and that subscription costs would remain about the same – 50 cents a month. Rate by mail for delivery elsewhere in Canada and in Great Britain was $4 a year.

The Sun still had rivals. *The Province,* then owned by Walter Nichol and edited by Roy Brown, and the *World,* under the management of John Nelson, were evening papers that published six days a week. The *World* was powerful enough to elect city councillors and successful enough that its owner, Louis Denison Taylor, was able to build the World Tower on Beatty Street in 1912, laying claim to it as the tallest building in the British Empire. Taylor also ruled at city hall, taking over the mayor's chair in 1910 and holding the office off and on for 11 years. In an ironic twist 25 years later, Taylor's tower would become the Sun Tower, home of Cromie's thriving newspaper.

Spreading the news, coast to coast

Yet another change was announced in that newly reconstituted Sept. 1 *Sun*, under a headline that read "CANADIAN NATIONAL NEWS SERVICE LINKS NINE PROVINCES." The co-operative news service created by like-minded publishers began operating Sept. 3, providing "to the daily newspaper readers of Canada for the first time in the history of the Dominion a truly national news service." It was the start of The Canadian Press.

THE VANCOUVER DAILY SUN, VANCOUVER, B.C., SUNDAY, SEPTEMBER 2, 1917.

PLAYS AND PLAYERS IN VANCOUVER

THE ROUND-UP

BY H. C.

Last night's show of "Britannia," which was produced by Miss Jean Mollison and Mrs. W. A. Turquand in the ballroom of the Hotel Vancouver, was a huge success, and the Red Cross societies of Wards One and Two will benefit very materially in consequence. The children were all excellent in their various parts, speaking the lines written by Alice Mary Morgan with surprising intelligence. Turns by Mrs. N. G. Hopper and her pupils, along with Mr. M. Planque and his pupils furnished a combination of ukulele and mandolin pieces which were very enjoyable. Phyllis and May Keith, Patricia Salmon, Lawrence Salmon and Connie Sibbald each did splendid turns. They are all wonderfully clever and an acquisition to Vancouver.

* * *

This Jazz business is continually haunting me. I got an invitation yesterday to a Jazz travel dance. What is this Jazz, anyway?

* * *

There are many funny little stories told of film stars. Shall always be glad to give a true one of your favorite through the medium of this column.

* * *

Bud Fisher of Mutt and Jeff fame has joined the American army and is now stationed at Plattsburg.

* * *

J. Warren Kerrigan had a nasty accident last week at Santa Barbara. His horse stepped into a gopher hole, bringing him to the ground. It was found that the tibia bone was snapped off between the knee and ankle. Mr. Kerrigan is in hospital where he will have to remain several weeks.

* * *

Rex Beach is at present in Canada on a vacation.

* * *

The Metro Film company, Inc., are offering as high as one thousand dollars for a film play of 5,000 words. Looks like easy money for someone in Vancouver to get in on.

* * *

Nelson Keys, the well known London comedian, who took such an active part in the big revue "Hello Canada," is making a hit with Bruce Bairnsfather's little poem, "My Dug-

Out," which he is working into a turn in London.

Sarah Bernhardt's tour over the Klaw and Erlanger circuit began yesterday in New York. The affectionate interest of the American people towards the great French woman borders on idolatry.

All the movie houses this week have the very best in pictures and the fans will have hard work to beat shows appearing at the Orpheum, Colonial, and Globe. Pantages have an all-star cast and the Empress, serving up their usual palatable fare, looks like a record breaker this week.

After the Slapstick
And the Pie---What?

When Mack Sennett discovered the astonishing natural phenomenon that a custard pie brought into forcible contact with the human face spreads considerably, he became the father of the slapstick movie and the soft pie picture. The slapstick he did not invent, but he made it fashionable. The pie throw was of his own invention. Neither pie nor stick were the least of his discoveries, however. There was water. Formerly people imagined that the funniest thing one could do with water was to pour it over men and women. Mr. Sennett showed us our error. He poured his men and women over water, shooting the chutes with them over lakes and ponds and watery streets and the bounding billows.

Mr. Sennett made other discoveries. One was that slapstick comedy without a comedian to do the slapstickery is not slapstick at all. He picked his comedians, all of whom are now engaged in his new Paramount-Sennett comedies, and for them he will be remembered when the slapstick turns to rotting wood. It was because of his ability to pick and train comedians that he became the most famous of comedy film producers. To his pies, his waterworks and his spectacular finales he owes but little to his reputation. Other men have followed him along the way he blazed through the wilderness, and some there are who can throw pies straighter than Mr. Sennett's first assistants, but they are not comedians. There are dare-devils who will drive motor cars over steeper cliffs than Mr. Sennett selected for his luckless actors, but they belong to the circus. So it is that he is known as the pioneer of the pie drama.

But after the slapstick and the pie—what then? Already "Fatty" Arbuckle is said to be using watermelons for the necessary squashiness of comedy pictures. And Mack Sennett is supplementing his force of comedians

On Dangerous Ground
Will Show at Colonial

"It means war," said Ritter Bloem to his young American friend, Bradford Stewart. "It means war, for I have been ordered to rejoin my regiment at once. This must be our farewell."

Stewart bowed his head in sorrow as Bloem left. Suddenly he was startled by an abrupt question. "When do you leave Germany?" This was asked by a man in the uniform of a German officer. Stewart gave the information, and the officer left, the young American having no inkling that this man was no German at all, but was in reality the head of the French secret service, Trapadoux. On leaving Stewart, Trapadoux said to the hotel proprietress, "place these in Stewart's grip," and the latter discovered to his astonishment a quantity of woman's lingerie and other feminine articles on returning to his room. Before he had recovered from his surprise, a beautiful young woman burst into the room and throwing her arms around his neck, exclaimed, "My husband, I am so glad to see you again!" Stewart nearly collapsed from amazement. "Listen," suddenly went on the girl, "I am in the French secret service. I have important papers for General Joffre. You must help me over the border by passing me off as your wife."

Stewart yielded to his fair visitor and took her safely as far as the border. There they were arrested and brought before an officer who was searching for the thief of the stolen papers. Things looked bad, but Trapadoux appeared in his German disguise and diverted suspicion from the couple. He also helped them to reach Belgium. They were entertained in a Belgian camp, when a sudden attack by the Germans separated them. The girl was taken prisoner and tried as a spy, but before sentence was passed upon her, she begged that a last message might be sent from her to Stewart. At the name of Stewart, her judge, who was no other than Ritter Bloem, sent the girl herself to rejoin the old American friend, and the two were reunited in the Belgian camp.

The foregoing is a brief summary of the story of "On Dangerous Ground," which will be shown at the Colonial theatre Monday, Tuesday and Wednesday.

CLEVER PLAYLET AT THE PANTAGES

Octavia Handworth Co. in "SALVATION SUE" PANTAGES

"Salvation Sue" is a clever, gripping sketch and is ably handled by Miss Handworth and her supporting cast.

"Environment" Strong
Lesson for Clergymen

It is easier, far easier, to preach than to practice. Everyone knows that but after viewing little Mary Miles Minter in the latest of the American-Mutual specials in which this delightful star is featured one goes away in a more neighborly spirit, a kindlier feeling for the underdog, a resolution to try just a little harder to see the good in those " who never had a chance " and an unwillingness to condemn too soon.

"Environment" is the name of the play. It is an understandable story, well pictured and artistically handled. We've all rubbed elbows with just the kind of people that move this story along to a happier conclusion than the majority of such real stories. They're all human beings, most of them, just a little too selfish, like most of us, and just a little too quick to misjudge. And those who are so ready to forget self to help others are, just as the real people we know, least able to do for others.

But with all this, "Environment" is a happy little story and one that will make friends for the Mary Miles Minter fans and recruit new followers for this little star of the big heart.

While in no way a sermon, every minister should make it a point to see "Environment." He will learn better how to handle conditions with which he comes in almost daily contact. And he may, if he be truly honest with himself, take home a lesson.

The scenes are laid in a New England village but it is not quite fair to pick on New England. The story has happened many times and in many

Empress Stock Co.
Presents "Mother"

The most beautiful theme ever created by nature for the dramatist lies in that sweet, simple word, "Mother," and the lucky author who first hit upon this great word for the title of his offering practically cornered the market for human appeal. He has given to the world a play that will be a classic for all time to come, and one which from bygone memories is bound to touch a resonant chord in every heart. In presenting this play this week, the Empress Stock company will offer a masterpiece that will be entirely different in story and play construction from any of the wonderful dramas which will ? presented during the winter season.

They will make you laugh and cry and enjoy every moment of the two hours you are with "Mother," but best of all, they will bring back to your heart some long forgotten happening of your childhood days that will make you a better man or woman for having again thought of "Mother."

But just in so delightful a dress it has not "happened" before in motion pictures.

"Environment" is a play for every member of the family. It is a family play.

"Environment" is being shown at the Globe theatre on Monday, Tuesday and Wednesday.

Mary Miles Minter
AMERICAN

MARY MILES MINTER in "Environment," at Globe theatre.

A Sept. 2, 1917 page of *The Vancouver Daily Sun* shows that even during wartime the entertainment industry remained in full swing.

The name game

While 1912 is the commonly accepted centenary of *The Vancouver Sun*, some historians still insist the paper's ink-stained roots actually date to 1886.

That's because it's a descendant of the *Advertiser*, first published in May 1886, and the *News*, which followed a month later, the two newspapers that were merged into the *Daily News-Advertiser* that was purchased by Cromie in 1917 and then merged with *The Sun* to become *The Vancouver Daily Sun*.

So it's 1886 for the historical purist, 1912 for sticklers adhering to *The Sun* nomenclature and 1917 for the undecided. And for those keeping track of the oft-changing nameplate?

Here are 100 years of *The Vancouver Sun* name game:

1912: *The Sun*
1917: *The Vancouver Daily Sun*
1918: *Vancouver Daily Sun*
1919: *The Vancouver Daily Sun*
1920: *The Vancouver Sun*
1924: *Vancouver Morning Sun*
1924: *The Vancouver Evening Sun*
1927: *The Vancouver Sun*
1959: *The Sun*
1973: *The Vancouver Sun*
1983: *The Sun*
1986 to present: *The Vancouver Sun*

Rising to the occasion

As *The Vancouver Sun* headed into the 1920s, it continued to tout not only its usefulness but its community commitment, the latter highlighted in a full-page promotional ad featuring the faces and names of 82 mostly young boys, clad in suit jackets and ties, under a headline identifying them as "The Vancouver Daily Sun's Corps of Live, Hustling Carriers in Vancouver City and Neighboring Towns." A secondary headline praised them as "Bright Boys Who Form Part of *the Sun*'s Service Organization."

Another promotion on the classified pages also urged readers to make "something from nothing" by phoning Seymour 40 and placing an ad. It used the example of Mrs. A, whose five-year-old son had outgrown his baby carriage, which she could sell for $5 to buy him a hobby horse – offering, perhaps, the first hint of the power of garage sale ads. Another ad promised readers that "If You Want Work, *The Sun* Will Insert Your Ad Without Charge."

One *Sun* advertisement offered a "bargain" price on a modern six-room Kitsilano bungalow. It was listed at $2,750, "on easy terms."

With the launch of *The Vancouver Daily Sun* came both a change in the paper's editorial stance – moving away from the Liberal-friendly editorials to a more independent voice – and a new promotional slogan: Watch The Sun Rise.

The Vancouver Millionaires hockey club won the Stanley Cup in 1915. *Courtesy of the Hockey Hall of Fame*

10   THE VANCOUVER DAILY SUN, VANCOUVER, B.C., SATURDAY, APRIL 14, 1917.

The Vancouver Daily Sun's Corps of Live, Hustling Carriers in Vancouver City and Neighboring Towns

Photo by GIBSON Co.

1. Rafer Stewart	9. Alfred Hingham	17. Norman Moore	25. Ian McInnes	33. William Mundie	41. Frank Peterson	49. Witney Marshall	56. Daniel Rae	64. Ralph White	72. Thomas Inman, Agent
2. Lionel Orr	10. Ralph Muffett	18. Ross Davidson	26. Leonard Mitchell	34. Sherwood Young	42. John McInnes	50. Roy Currie	57. Richard Twine	65. Douglas Heritage	Kamloops
3. Walter Cooper	11. Daniel Main	19. Reggie Lawrence	27. Jack Turner	35. Fenton Reeve	43. Ralph Lidgey	51. A. W. Decker, Agent	58. Elmer Harrison	66. Arthur Geddes	73. Arthur Geddes
4. Golden Darr	12. Warren Morley	20. Robert Taylor	28. Norman Toft	36. Carey Bateman	44. Morris Graham	New Westminster	59. Walter Harrison	67. Walter Harrison	74. Norman Burton
5. Fred McCall	13. Alister McInnes	21. Harold Danaher	29. John Moore	Jack Lock	45. Arthur McLaughlin	52. Kenneth Currie	60. Harden Lowes	68. Frank Bass	75. Bert Russell
6. Fergus Aird	14. Griffie Lewis	22. Glen Abbott	30. Hugh McCall	38. Homer Boyd	46. Richard Wilson	53. Harry Houston	61. Tory Palm	69. Edgar Bartrim	76. John Moore
7. Neil Lindsay	15. Charles Fredrick	23. Wesley Washer	31. Duncan McCleod	39. Harold Puder	47. Gordon Hingham	54. Add Houson	62. Spencer Houghston	70. James Hingham	77. Jack Wyard, Agent
8. Jack Allershaw	16. Milton Boyd	24. Archie Gordon	32. Frank Chester	40. H. F. Gates	48. Orra Coudfield	55. Harry Rantman	63. Harold Young	71. Thos. Lawrence	North Vancouver
				Supt. of Delivery Service					78. Nick Lavagie
									79. Keith Lyons
									80. Ralph Hayward
									81. William Marquette, Agent
									Powell River
									82. George Kerr

Bright Boys Who Form Part of the Sun's Service Organization

IF a census of the business men of the city were available, it would be found that quite a percentage in their youth were newspaper carriers, and The Vancouver Daily Sun ventures the opinion that among the more prominent of the public men of today were those who had the larger routes in their boyhood days. It has been well said that the training the lads received was of great aid in after years, and what was true twenty-five years ago is true today. The boy of today who hustles and aims to please his employers and his customers will be among the big men of tomorrow. Their little achievements in youth are often augmented ten-fold in later years; in this way character is formed and the steps-of-stairs of success made easy of access when the bigger and tougher problems are tackled.

Proud of the Carrier Boys.

The Vancouver Daily Sun is proud of its corps of carrier boys, and the bright, earnest faces that adorn this page are typical of the average Vancouver hustler of today. These lads are often about their work as early as five o'clock in the morning and in all sorts of weather perform a service that does them credit. Occasionally mistakes are made; a paper fails to reach the subscriber, but one who has been through the mill can vouch for the general demeanor and good behavior of the carriers. Many, if not all of these boys aim to give the best possible service and their reward is often found in larger routes and a greater income. This is possible under the present method of delivery. The carrier buys his paper for cash and since he receives a large share of the money he collects, every new subscriber means a larger allowance each week for the boy. If he loses a customer his income

is reduced—hence every carrier aims to maintain through careful and efficient service as large a route as his territory affords.

A Few Outside Agents.

In addition to the carrier boys in this group picture are H. F. Gates, superintendent of delivery service in the city; A. W. Decker, agent, New Westminster; John B. Wyard, agent, North Vancouver; Thomas Inman, agent, Kamloops, and William Marquette, a real live wire agent at Powell River.

Most Boys Polite and Courteous.

The boys are encouraged to be polite and courteous to their customers, and therein lies one of the corner-stones of The Sun's growth in circulation. Every manager knows that a proper delivery service is the best agency in the building up of a wide circulation.

All Working in a Good Cause.

It is safe to say there is not a father or mother in Vancouver who is wanting in a just pride in their boy. They are the future law makers and business men of the country, and in the troublous times of today, there is a double pride in the rising generation of boys. Their obligations in the future will be greater than the men of today and if one can read character in the faces of these boys, The Sun has reason to be proud of the young men now serving in the distribution of the papers every week day morning. Many of them are earning their first pocket money; others are helping their mothers at a time when the bread winner of the home is serving his country in the greatest war in history—some of them, doubtless, the heroes of Vimy Ridge. Fathers and sons

in this way are doing their bit. With a feeling of gratitude to the one and a pride in the other, The Sun makes no apology in publishing this group picture of its carrier boys.

Notable Increase in Subscribers.

A notable increase in many of the routes illustrates not only the growing popularity of the paper, but the service rendered by the carrier. Many of these lads are now delivering 60, and in some cases 70 papers, where two or three months ago they had but 35 or 40 customers. The increase in many parts of the city, especially throughout Fairview, shows one-third more subscribers than at the first of the year. Throughout Shaughnessy Heights there has been also a notable advance, the increase being 20%.

Remember the Boys on Saturday.

Now, in conclusion, the management wants to say a word in behalf of the carrier and indicate to the subscriber how it is possible to give the lads at the week end a little consideration. The boys buy their papers for cash and make their collections on the basis of 10 cents per week each Saturday. Very often a subscriber neglects to provide the dime for the boy when he calls. He is told very often to call again or to collect the 10 cents at some business address down town. This entails much additional labor which might easily be avoided. Will our subscribers kindly bear this suggestion in mind and have the 10 cents ready for the carrier when he calls on Saturday morning.

In the belief that this hint will be sufficient, the management extends its thanks to the subscribers who are served by the carrier in every part of the city, as well as New Westminster, North and South Vancouver, Powell River and Kamloops.

THE DAILY SUN, GRANVILLE STREET, VANCOUVER, B.C.
Telephone: Seymour 8534

The Vancouver Daily Sun frequently used its pages to promote its staff, including its paperboys. This page, published on April 14, 1917, thanked the paper's hard-working carriers and encouraged subscribers to make things easier for them by having their 10 cents ready for collection on Saturday mornings.

THE **1920s**

The 1920s: *The Sun*'s re-awakening

On Jan. 1, 1920, perhaps as both a reflection of the hardy stock of its settlers and a collective cleansing of the sombre memory of the First World War, hundreds of local stalwarts donned their bathing suits and plunged into the bone-chilling waters of English Bay for the city's first Polar Bear Swim.

Greeting readers of The Vancouver Daily Sun on that first day of 1920 was a banner above the nameplate that jauntily declared Happy New Year!, over a cartoon of Baby New Year riding a snorting globe-shaped steed, Father Time falling off the back haunches.

In a good-news, bad-news presentation, one front-page headline touted "Vancouver Meets New Year in Mad Monsoon of Joy" while another declared "Importation of Liquor Delayed Another 30 Days."

All that good cheer, not to mention the prospect of future good cheer, must have worked to shake off the woes, because the 1920s would prove to be a decade of unbridled growth for Vancouver, a decade when iconic commercial buildings would begin to define the skyline, when neon lights would brighten Granville Street and when the city's official boundaries would expand east and south. The Roaring Twenties ushered in a new-found North American ebullience as social, artistic, economic and cultural dynamics began shifting.

And The Sun was coming into its own.

PRECEDING PAGE: Hundreds of people flocked to *The Sun* building on West Pender on March 1, 1923 to watch Harry Houdini escape from a straitjacket while hanging upside down. *W.J. Moore, City of Vancouver Archives Port N100*

A man who loved his paper ... and his vegetables

It was no surprise that as the *The Sun* headed into a new decade under publisher Robert Cromie it seemed to have a fresh, vibrant spirit, perhaps a reflection of the boss himself. Cromie was a young publisher, in his early 30s, an enigmatic man who was both a devoted vegetarian and an energetic fitness buff who jogged, long before jogging became a fitness craze. A 1928 *Maclean's* magazine profile described him as a "physical culturist of the first order" who could "visualize in awful detail the calamitous chemical reactions of wrong food combinations. His friends describe his own meals as 'weird.'"

One Cromie story described in *Pacific Press*, a 2001 book written by former *Province* reporter Marc Edge, tells of an editor who was invited to lunch with Cromie but discovered that breaking bread with the publisher meant he had to walk several miles to Cromie's house in Point Grey, only to be served a plate of raw vegetables when he got there.

Cromie's paper was just as unpredictable, offering an exciting, if chaotic, hodgepodge of stories, photographs, briefs, cartoons, contests and puzzles. It was a dense collection of copy laid out over seven-column pages, with a mixture of serif and sans-serif typefaces and very little in the way of text-breaking art.

Aside from the top-of-page main story, the layout made no hierarchical sense when compared with modern-day newspapers, which strive through placement and headline size to let readers know which stories are the most newsworthy. The messy layout of those early *Suns* made it look as though editors had just thrown everything up in the air, section by section, and published as it landed. Bylines, aside from columnists, were relatively scarce and attribution beyond wire services seemed of little concern.

If bylines were uncommon, the columnists whose faces graced the pages were well-promoted.

Arthur Brisbane's syndicated front-page *Today* column, according to *Sun* ads, was carried by newspapers in 16 countries. His 1924 coverage of the Leopold-Loeb case, in which two teenagers charged with murder in Chicago were defended by the legendary Clarence Darrow, was just one example, *The Sun* boasted of Brisbane's "strikingly original, vividly expressive, absolutely individual" work. "His paragraphs fairly throb with life and interest."

Soft features were also important to readers of turn-of-the-century newspapers, for it was a time when entertainment was mostly confined to the radio dial or to live local venues. The daily funny pages, for instance, were a *Sun* mainstay, many of them published as part of the newspaper's efforts to attract young readers. One 1920s favourite was a full-page series called Chester Gump, a spinoff of *The Gumps* comic strip featuring the Australian adventures of young Chester.

Robert Cromie wanted to offer his readers an exciting, unpredictable paper, so funny pages were a mainstay. One of the most popular characters in the 1920s was Chester Gump, a young Australian adventurer featured in a comic strip called *The Gumps.*

Dear Dorothy

Robert Cromie's habit of breaking new ground included introducing readers to a new genre of journalism: the advice column.

Dorothy Dix, an American writer who predated another long-running syndicated *Sun* advice columnist, Ann Landers, dispensed her opinions from the women's pages, her work reflecting the social mores of the day. A 1924 Dix "bachelor's guide" suggested that a man seeking happiness should never marry a "girl who dresses beyond her means, who is a helpless little clinging vine, who is temperamental, whose hair looks as if it had been coiffed with a vacuum cleaner, who affects to despise domesticity and who chicken pecks her family." Her "maiden's guide" was no less sanguine: "Don't marry a man who is handsome, an only son who has sisters, a grouchy man, a man who isn't entertaining, a man who tells you that he never loved before, a man who wants you to reform him."

The Dix column ran alongside the pages' "fiction and feminine fashion," the former including Good Night Stories that parents could read to their children, the latter tutoring readers on how to wear demure "house dresses" that "are so very lovely they are worn for sports."

Before Ann Landers and Dear Abby, there was Dorothy Dix, a syndicated advice columnist whose work appeared in *The Sun* from the 1920s through the 1940s. At her peak she was published in 273 newspapers read by 60 million people.

John Monroe, the first distributor of *The Evening Sun*, in his delivery truck circa 1925. The truck also advertised a serial running in the paper: "Flapper Wife: The Story of a Vancouver Girl." *Courtesy of David Monroe*

A wild pioneer town, with wild pioneers

The Sun's family-oriented coverage was a sign the city was settling down, that the 1,000 or so newcomers arriving in Vancouver every month wanted to stay. But there were still remnants of the one-time wild pioneer town. In the early 1920s, as the Royal Canadian Mounted Police officially assumed duties in the province, it was estimated that 500 prostitutes were working Vancouver streets, and their numbers were on the rise. *The Sun* reported that one L. O'Neill, briskly trading in unnamed narcotics with local wanton women, was charged with trafficking. *The Sun* story appeared under the headline: "Bail in dope case will be set at $5,000." O'Neill was 87.

Meet the presses and change that dial

Along with the flourishing city came more expansion to the suburbs, and the founding of more newspapers outside the urban limits, including the *Weekly Optimist* in Delta in 1922, the *Surrey Gazette* and the *Westender* in 1923, and the *West Vancouver News* in 1926. It was a trend that would continue unabated through the century, the growth of weeklies just one of the thorns that would contribute to the deflation of *The Sun*'s circulation and advertising revenue beginning in the 1980s.

But for the time being, *The Sun* was one of the big boys in town. Seeking even more channels to espouse its editorial ethos, it joined the *Daily Province* in opening a sideline radio station in the spring of 1922. *The Sun*'s student-run station, CJCE, was the second to enter the market after *The Province* took to the airwaves. The first live music broadcast, however, came courtesy of *The Sun*, which featured local stage performer Emma Heit singing *Maytime*. As with newspapers of the day, the next few years saw stations change hands and call letters. *The Sun* was out of the radio business within a year, but, by 1926, there were six radio stations in town. It would be another 10 years before the CBC began broadcasting to Vancouverites.

Love those Liberals

When William Lyon Mackenzie King overthrew the Conservatives and became Canada's new Liberal prime minister, *The Sun*'s Dec. 7, 1921 headline trumpeted: "LIBERALS SWEEP CANADA: KING'S 122 CONTROL HOUSE."

A flowery *Sun* subhead over a portrait of the "New Premier of the Dominion of Canada" made clear the paper's Liberal leaning: "Without Funds – Opposed by Selfish Interests – Subject of Vicious Personal Attack and Misrepresentations – William Lyon Mackenzie King, Who Opened His Campaign in Vancouver, B.C., in the Autumn of 1920, Took His Fight To the People of Canada – And the People Received Him."

It was, notably, the first federal election in which women had the vote, although that milestone and its groundbreaking result were woefully underplayed.

Down page, under the King portrait, a tiny news item reported that Ontario candidate Agnes McPhail, referred to as Miss A. McPhail, was the "First Woman To Win Seat In Commons."

THE WEATHER
FAIR AND COLDER AT NIGHT

THE TIDES
Low tide 4:32 a. m. High tide 12:72 p. m.
Low tide 7:14 p. m.

The Vancouver Sun

THIRTY-SEVENTH YEAR—No. 339   VANCOUVER, B.C., WEDNESDAY, DECEMBER 7, 1921   FIVE CENTS PER COPY

LIBERALS SWEEP CANADA: KING'S 122 CONTROL HOUSE

ENDS CENTURY OLD DISPUTE WITH IRELAND

Dramatic Scene When Peace Treaty Is Signed in London

PREMIER AND SINN FEIN FOUNDER FIRST

Agreement Safeguards Ulster and Stipulates as to Army Strength

(By Associated Press)

LONDON, Dec. 6—The centuries old quarrel between England and Ireland was ended in the small hours of Tuesday morning by the signature in the Premier's cabinet room of "A treaty between Great Britain and Ireland," consisting of 18 articles, giving Ireland the title of the Irish Free State and the same constitutional status as Canada, Australia and other overseas dominions.

Without Funds—Opposed by Selfish Interests—Subject of Vicious Personal Attack and Misrepresentation—William Lyon Mackenzie King, Who Opened His Campaign in Vancouver, B.C., in the Autumn of 1920, Took His Fight To the People of Canada—And the People Received Him

New Premier of the Dominion of Canada, Mr. William Lyon Mackenzie King, M.P., C.M.G.

MEIGHEN DEFEATED WITH 8 MINISTERS IN "N.L.C." COLLAPSE

Solid Nova Scotia; Straight Quebec, With Unusual Success West of Ottawa River—Landslide Sets in to Change Nation's Political Map

Ontario Gave "William Lyon" 24; Gov't Lost all Winnipeg Seats

Crerar Leads New Opposition—Premier Goes Down in Portage la Prairie—Vancouver Ridings Return Stevens, Ladner and Gen. Clark—British Columbia Sends 7 Conservatives, 3 Progressives and 3 Grits

OTTAWA, Dec. 7—By decisive majorities, the Meighen government was yesterday defeated at the polls and a Liberal ministry will reign in its stead. It was a day of surprises. Liberals succeeded even beyond their sanguine expectations. They had expected the largest group in the next house. They will have a clear majority over all parties combined. In the three provinces of Prince Edward Island, Nova Scotia and Quebec, they sweep every seat. They made inroads into Ontario and the West. The new National Progressive party, while it stands second in the next house, did not secure the expected support east of the Great Lakes. In the Maritime Provinces, it merely retained its existing seat of Victoria and Carleton in New Brunswick. In Ontario, instead of sweeping the rural ridings, its victories totalled 19 seats. The chief strength of the Progressive movement lay in the prairie provinces, which gave it birth. In the next house, however, to judge from returns so far available, Progressives will form the official opposition.

CABINET MINISTERS DEFEATED

Rt. Hon. Arthur Meighen, premier.
Hon. I. P. Normand (Three Rivers, Que.), president of Privy Council.
Hon. R. Monty (Beauharnois, Que.), secretary of state.
Hon. C. C. Ballantyne (Montreal), minister of marine.
Hon. A. Fauteux (Montreal), solicitor general.
Hon. L. G. Belley (Chicoutimi-Montmorency, Que.), postmaster general.
Hon. E. N. Rhodes (Yarmouth, N.S.), minister without portfolio.
Hon. F. B. McCurdy (Colchester, N.S.), minister of public works.
Hon. R. Wilson (Saskatoon), minister without portfolio.

CABINET MINISTERS RETURNED

Hon. H. H. Stevens (Vancouver Centre), minister of trade and commerce.
Hon. R. B. Bennett (Calgary), minister of justice.
Hon. E. F. Pelmis (Victoria), minister of agriculture.
Hon. J. B. M. Baxter (St. John, N.B.), minister of customs and inland revenue.
Sir Henry Drayton (West York, Ont.), minister of finance.
Hon. J. A. Stewart (Lanark, Ont.), minister of railways and canals.
Hon. N. J. Maclean (Rainy River and Thunder Bay, Ont.), minister of soldiers' civil re-establishment department.
Hon. Hugh Guthrie (Wellington South, Ont.), minister of militia.
Hon. Edmund Bristol (Toronto Centre, Ont.), minister without portfolio.

RESULTS UNCERTAIN

Hon. Dr. Edwards (Frontenac, Ont.), minister of immigration.

SIDELIGHTS ON ELECTION

Hon. H. H. Stevens, Conservative leader in British Columbia, was called upon at Unionist headquarters for a speech.

General Summary at Midnight Shows King Has 122 Seats

Province	Con.	Lib.	Pro.	Lab.	Total
Prince Edward Island		4			4
Nova Scotia		16			16
New Brunswick	5	5	1		11
Quebec		65			65
Ontario	38	24	19		81
Manitoba		2	12	1	15
Saskatchewan		1	15		15
Alberta	1		10	1	12
British Columbia	7	3	3		13
Yukon		1			1
	51	122	56	2	231

It is to be noted that the Liberals have carried every seat in the provinces of Prince Edward Island, Nova Scotia and Quebec.

ANOTHER CHILD KILLED ON STREETS

Margaret Knowles, 8, Struck by Motor Car in Downtown District

First Woman To Win Seat In Commons

THE first woman to win a seat in the Dominion Parliament is Miss M. A. MacPhail, who was running on the Progressive ticket, has carried South-East Grey riding in Ontario. She was opposed by the former member, R. J. Ball, Unionist, and by Walter Hastie, Liberal.

AGREEMENT BOON TO WHOLE EMPIRE

Australian Press Is Pleased With Irish Settlement Action

HUNDRED DIE IN OIL EXPLOSION

Dynamite Works in Prussia Scene of Industrial Disaster

TWENTY-SEVEN WERE VICTIMS OF COLLISION

REFUSE AGREEMENT WITH THE SOVIET

Italy Has Turned Down Russian Trade Proposals Recently Made

At the Theatres Tonight

The Sun's front page on Dec. 7, 1921, announced William Lyon Mackenzie King's victory in the federal election.

The Sun's advertising department in the West Pender Street offices in 1923. *Dominion Photo Co., Vancouver Public Library 21685*

Holy stunt, bat man

Vancouver was increasingly a magnet for celebrities, drawn to the many theatres and venues in the downtown core. In 1923, famed illusionist Harry Houdini came to town and, in a stunt that wowed locals, escaped from his trussed-up straitjacket while hanging upside down from *The Sun* office building on West Pender.

In a front-page story oddly bylined "By J.K." in the March 1, 1923 edition, and accompanied by a stately headshot of Houdini, the writer told of taking Houdini for a test run the day before, along with Orpheum manager Bill Hart. "Well, Bill and myself slid through the hatchway like a couple of eels," the story related, while "Houdini, 'genius of escape' had a tough time making the grade." Houdini had emerged from the rehearsal so covered with dust that *Sun* staff escorted him to the "new washrooms and shower baths *The Sun* has installed."

Harry Houdini, known as the "Genius of Escape," appeared at the Orpheum Theatre in March 1923. *Vancouver Sun*

The newspaper name, and ownership game

The Sun's metamorphosis and always confusing nomenclature – it had changed from *The Sun* to *The Vancouver Daily Sun* to *The Vancouver Sun* in its first decade alone – seemed even more so in the 1920s, part and parcel of the constant swapping and merging of properties among the wheeling and dealing newspaper proprietors in town. For a time in the mid-1920s, it was almost impossible to keep track.

On March 11, 1924, Robert Cromie bought the failing *Vancouver World* for $475,000 from Charles Campbell, who had paid $250,000 for the paper in 1921; two months after off-loading the *World* to Cromie, Campbell would launch another paper, *Evening Star*.

Meantime, Cromie changed the name of the *World* to *The Vancouver Evening Sun*, a second paper to complement his *Vancouver Morning Sun* (which had previously been *The Vancouver Sun* and then *The Vancouver Daily Sun*). Together, his two papers had a circulation of 41,800.

An editorial in the new *Evening Sun* on March 12 advised readers that "The consolidation of the *World*, oldest and one of the most highly respected dailies in the West, into the *Evening Sun*, does not mean that the old is bowing its head to the new. It rather means that the old is being reborn into the new."

The newspaper swapping wasn't over yet. In 1926, Cromie sold the *Vancouver Morning Sun* to Victor Odlum, who had owned the *Evening Star* after purchasing it from Campbell. Odlum,

in turn, sold the *Evening Star* to Cromie, who in 1927 consolidated the *Vancouver Evening Sun* and *Evening Star* and once again owned one newspaper named (again) *The Vancouver Sun*, an evening paper.

The Sun was running three Hoe presses in the late 1920s; the fastest press was able to print a 32-page paper at 30,000 papers an hour, all of it produced under the watchful eye of superintendent Harry Wheatland and his 10 pressmen. Keeping up with the paper's five daily editions was a crew of 60 men working in the composing room, many of them punching in the stories on the 18 huge linotype machines.

Odlum, meantime, re-entered the market with a new paper called the *Morning Star*.

The largest circulation paper in the city, however, was still the staid broadsheet *Daily Province*. When it was announced that its owner and editor, Walter Nichol, had become the province's lieutenant-governor in December 1920, the unchallenged conflict of interest was still of little concern in a time when newspapers were active supporters of political parties.

Cromie, though, had no problem advancing the notion that his was the only real local paper. After the Southam family purchased *The Province* in August 1923, Cromie often used his editorial page to accuse the more conservative *Province* of being an eastern mouthpiece. Southam had owned *The Hamilton Spectator* since 1877 and the *Ottawa Citizen* since 1897, and was slowly moving west, gradually building a Canadian newspaper empire. The company purchased the *Calgary Herald* in 1908, the *Edmonton Journal* in 1912 and *The Winnipeg Tribune* in 1920. It would purchase *The Vancouver Sun* in 1980, adding it to an empire that by then also included

The Montreal Gazette.

If all the complicated back-room dealing was hard to digest, and it most certainly was, the good news was that Vancouver now had three daily papers – *The Vancouver Sun* and *The Province* serving the evening market, with the *Morning Star* covering the morning – all three publishing for a population of less than 200,000.

A carrier force to be reckoned with

By the mid-1920s, distribution of *The Vancouver Sun* was based out of newspaper shacks, small wooden sheds that dotted the region and served as drop sites for the trucks carrying bundles of newspapers hot off the presses. Carriers, typically young boys, would pack papers into huge canvas bags which they slung over their shoulders; the thud of the papers landing on doorsteps was a common sound on city streets. One 1924 promotional ad told readers that the paper's in-house tabloid – called *Hustler* and published monthly for carriers - included examples for newsboys on how to deposit a neatly folded newspaper near the door and out of the rain and wind. The ad urged reader cooperation in "reporting careless delivery to the Circulation Department." But to be a carrier also meant access to perks. "Boys!" read one *Sun* notice, "There's a big time on tonight for all newsboys and their friends at *The Sun* Office. Fun Starts at 6:30. Lots of Free Candy. Penny Scramble."

This billboard advertising sign was on display in Vancouver in 1926. *Stuart Thomson for Duker and Shaw Ltd., City of Vancouver Archives 99-2242*

Service Our Motto !

How to Deliver a Paper Correctly

SUN boys are trained to deliver your paper as shown in the upper left-hand picture. This picture appeared in The Vancouver Sun 'Hustler', the tabloid monthly paper published in the interests of Sun boys.

If your paper is not delivered properly, we will consider it a favor if you will co-operate with us in providing perfect service by reporting careless delivery to the Circulation Department.

Phone Seymour 40

VANCOUVER SUN
"The People's Paper"
Morning --- Evening --- Sunday

Readers were assured that young newspaper carriers had been taught how to deliver a newspaper correctly, but subscribers were urged to report any 'careless delivery' to the circulation department.

Yankee slugger Babe Ruth assumes the position at the Pantages Theatre, with Vancouver Mayor L.D. Taylor as catcher and Police Chief Henry Walter Long as umpire on Nov. 29, 1926. *City of Vancouver Archives 1477-107.*

The murder of nurse Janet Smith dominated local coverage for months, earning headlines like this one on May 1, 1925, when "houseboy" Wong Foon Sing was charged with her killing.

Murder and the Chinese houseboy

Adhering to its growing reputation as a newspaper of both surprise and enterprise, *The Sun* under the creative Cromie was finding a niche in its sensational coverage of local crime.

One of those cases, chronicled in months of breathless front-page newspaper headlines, reflected not only the readers' appetite for salacious news but also highlighted the disturbing racist underpinnings prevalent in the city's increasingly multicultural population.

The story began on July 26, 1924, when 22-year-old Scottish nursemaid Janet Smith was discovered dead in the basement of the Shaughnessy mansion of her boss, F.L. Baker. When detectives were called to the Osler Street house by Wong Foon Sing, the Chinese houseboy who found her, Smith was lying on the floor with a fatal wound on the right side of her head

and a pistol near her right hand. It was determined she died by suicide, and she was buried without an autopsy.

But the society rumour mill had the city abuzz with accusations that it was a police cover-up, that there had been an orgy in the Baker home involving prominent men and women that ended in Smith's death. Authorities dug up Smith's body, but the mortician had done such a poor embalming job that experts were unable to collect usable forensic evidence. An inquest was ordered.

The Sun covered every element of the story, but especially the inquest, which included a re-enactment of the murder, testimony of love triangles and the possibility that 27-year-old Wong was the killer. One *Sun* story was headlined "Witnesses Tell of Janet Smith's Fear of Chinese Servant" and was followed the next day by a passage from Smith's diary indicating their friendship was amicable. "Sing is awfully devoted," Smith had written several days

before her death. "He gave me sweets, and does all my washing and ironing."

When the inquest concluded that Smith was murdered, police were sure that Wong knew more than he was saying. Several officers, posing as vigilantes and dressed in Ku Klux Klan hoods, kidnapped him and held him captive in a west-side home for six weeks. He was beaten and threatened with lynching, but repeatedly professed his innocence.

The Evening Sun of May 1, 1925 featured a photo of Wong Foon Sing dressed in a suit, alongside a report that he had been found by police on Marine Drive, thrown blindfolded from a car. He was subsequently charged with Smith's murder and incarcerated in a shed on the grounds of Oakalla Prison, where his legal counsel found him delirious and covered with scratches and bruises.

It was a sordid tale reported in the shadow of a racial climate that tolerated such action, when enmity toward Chinese immigrants had prompted vicious mob attacks on local Chinese, including the 1907 rampaging of Chinatown by the Asiatic Exclusion League. The federal government had passed the Chinese Immigration Act in 1923 – known as the exclusion act in the Chinese-Canadian community – virtually ending Chinese immigration, following 38 years of a head tax instituted to accomplish the same goal. In Vancouver, Wong could not legally become a Canadian citizen, he wasn't allowed to become a doctor, architect or lawyer, and he couldn't swim in a public pool or watch a movie, except from the theatre balcony.

The Sun's coverage, unlike some of its competitors, was relatively even-handed and its editorial board joined the chorus of Chinese community groups protesting Wong's treatment, calling it "the most ghastly injustice that has ever been perpetrated in Canada." The paper's editorial board noted that if Canadians had been abused in a similar fashion by the Chinese government, "a British gunboat would have been on the job in 24 hours."

Wong stood trial, but in the absence of evidence, the case was dismissed. He went back to work for the Bakers before returning to China in 1926. The case was never solved.

Feting the first Olympic superstar

The city was beaming in 1928, when Vancouver sprinter Percy Williams won gold medals in the 100- and 200-metre sprints at the Summer Olympics in Amsterdam. The slight Williams, who had suffered from rheumatic fever as a child, was the country's first Olympic superstar, evoking a communal fever that would return to Vancouver more than eight decades later.

"City Goes Wild As Percy Comes Home" was the headline over a Sept. 14, 1928 *Sun* story that described Percy's arrival back home by railway and his hero's welcome to a ticker-tape

This 1929 promotion ad bragged about *The Sun*'s young, spendthrift readers in an attempt to attract advertisers.

Vancouver sprinter Percy Williams became the fastest man in the world, winning gold in both the 100- and 200-metre events at the 1928 Olympic Games in Amsterdam. No other Canadian has won both titles at the same Games. *Vancouver Public Library 13295*

parade. "There he stood, nervously licking his parched lips, smiling in a frightened way, fumbling with the knobby end of his black cane, while the cheers, the 'attaboys,' the whistles betokened the enthusiasm of Vancouver at his arrival. Percy Williams was home."

Williams would set numerous other sprint records throughout his racing career and receive an Order of Canada in 1979. Depressed and suffering from severe arthritis, he committed suicide in 1982.

The crush before the crash

The late 1920s found Vancouverites feeling flush. Banks were offering credit and retailers a pay-later system that had locals spending like never before, buying goods and stocks with abandon, the October 1929 Wall Street stock market crash only a shadow on the horizon.

It was good news for *The Sun*'s advertising revenues, and the paper was full of consumer enticements. The Famous store on West Hastings was a big draw with its 89-cent Saturdays, offering everything from corsets to children's wear for 89 cents. The Pierre Paris shoe store was advertising its custom-fitted footwear, while ads for "grocerterias" offered customers three-pound cans of Crisco for 69 cents, bacon at 28 cents a pound and Alberta creamery butter, $1.23 for three pounds. Layaway plans and store accounts were common: the C.M. Ladd downtown menswear shop required only a quarter of the price down, with the option to pay the balance over 10 weeks. A $35 dress suit, it noted in a *Sun* ad, required only $8.75 up front, with weekly payments to follow of $2.60.

Sun employees were well-placed to join the consumer rush. Even in the years before there were unions, the paper was paying most of its employees a basic living wage. Cliff MacKay, whose 47 years at the paper included stints as editorial page editor and associate editor, started his career as a reporter in 1928 earning $15 a week, and recalled in later years that it was "pretty standard pay."

MacKay was 19 at the time and shared a second-hand Dodge bought for $450 with two other reporters, John Dunn and Bob Bouchette, adhering to a usage contract drawn up by the paper's lawyer. Just after Dunn left town "because of some lady trouble he had had," the car died, so the two remaining shareholders returned it to the lot in the dark of night, slipping the keys through the mail slot.

THE VANCOUVER EVENING SUN, FRIDAY, APRIL 11, 1924

11

| Household Hints / New Recipes | # EDITH ADAM'S COOKERY PAGE | Cutting Living Costs / Balanced Menus | FARMS |

EASTER HAS EGGS AND EGGS--- AND EACH MEANS A GOOD DISH

By EDITH ADAMS

Eggs are symbolic of Easter and new life—but they also spell many an attractive appetizing nourishing meal to the woman who makes the physical welfare of her family a matter of daily concern. The egg shares with milk the honor of being one of the so-called "perfect foods," which means that it contains all that is needed to support life.

(body text continues in fine print)

Salads; They're With Us Again

(recipe text in fine print)

CAN YOU FEED A FAMILY OF FOUR ON $1 A DAY?

Edith Adams offers $5 for the best letter on accomplishing this difficult feat.

Do you pride yourself on your ability to "manage" the household on a small allowance? Does your husband boast of your knack of making money bring home the bacon—and the eggs, lettuce, oranges and meat—until the last penny has done its duty? If you've that kind of an efficient, 1924 homemaker, this contest is for you.

Edith Adams will give a prize of $5 for the best letter of 300 words on "Feeding a Family of Four on $1 a Day." A second prize of $2 will be offered and three $1 prizes for the next three best letters.

(contest details continue)

HOW TO MAKE DELICIOUS CAKES AND COOKIES FOR TEA

By JEANNETTE YOUNG NORTON

Cakes that keep, and cookies of various sorts, are very convenient to have in the house to use with afternoon tea, as a luncheon dessert with jam or stewed fruit, or as a dinner dessert with the fresh fruits that are now making their appearance in the spring markets at prices that make them possible even for the most careful marketer.

(recipe text continues)

Edith Adam's — the spelling and punctuation fluctuated over the years — made her first appearance in *The Sun* on April 11, 1924, asking the question: "Can you feed a family of four on $1 a day?"

Before there was Martha Stewart, there was Edith Adams

The year 1924 would mark the debut of a cherished, and fictional, *Vancouver Sun* fixture: Edith Adams. Her astonishing reign started with the introduction of The Edith Adam's Cookery Page, which appeared in the women's pages on Fridays, along with the publication of a daily prize recipe, paying the winner $1. So popular were the recipes, cooking tips and shopping advice dispensed by Edith Adams that *The Sun* started an annual cooking school, which began in 1926 and would see more than 60,000 women complete the classes by the late 1930s. Students paid a fee for the courses, which were held in large local venues. A 1937 *Sun* story noted that: "In spite of the fact that this was not a free school ... the Orpheum Theatre was filled to capacity with young girls, middle-aged women and old ladies, as well as a sprinkling of men."

To say Edith Adams was a newspaper star would be to understate her appeal. Ironically, there was no real Edith, but instead a cadre of young staffers and home economists who filled pages with copy and answered the always-ringing phone lines. Edith was, in fact, an editor's imaginary figment, as was Penny Wise, the pseudonym of *Sun* consumer columnist Evelyn Caldwell. They were simple names that fit nicely into headlines, and this confession often confused readers seeking Edith's advice on domestic topics from canning to embroidery. *Sun* columnist Paul St. Pierre tried to edify readers in a 1966 story, in which he said asking to speak to Edith Adams was "like an Arab sheikh saying 'Meet my wife.'"

But Edith would endure for 75 years, meeting and greeting readers in a Sun Tower storefront during the 1940s and '50s and perfecting thousands of recipes in *The Sun*'s test kitchen, becoming a unique newspaper institution that would leave a treasured legacy of best-selling cookbooks and untold numbers of yellowed, cake-spattered newspaper recipes glued into home-made cookbooks all over B.C.

Before False Creek became an urban residential oasis, it was an industrial area, home to sawmills, coal yards and metal workers . . . and about 5,000 people. *Vancouver Sun*

VANCOUVER SUN

'The Voice of Vancouver'

W. LAMBERT

WHOLESALE MGR.

THE 1930s

The 1930s: A decade of dark days

As the Dirty Thirties dawned, there were signs of fading optimism, both at home and around the globe.

The Black Thursday stock market crash of Oct. 29, 1929 turned the world on its ear, a calamity that Sun columnist A.J. Smith called the "chilly winds of financial adversity."

It would be a sombre time for The Vancouver Sun, as fire destroyed the newspaper offices and death claimed both its respected owner and publisher, Robert Cromie, and its beloved everyman columnist, Bob Bouchette. And while a fresh start, which included a move to the Sun Tower and the introduction of youth-friendly Sun Free Swim classes and Uncle Ben's SunRay Club, helped lighten the mood in the newsroom and in the city, The Great Depression and another world war clouded the horizon.

For many, it was about to become the worst of times.

ABOVE: While *The Sun* did its part to make life easier for readers in the 1930s – offering cash prizes with its puzzles, for example – Vancouver residents weren't spared from The Great Depression. Rates of unemployment and homelessness soared. *Vancouver Sun*

PRECEDING PAGE: As many as 70,000 copies of *The Sun* were delivered to readers each day in the 1930s, loaded on to distribution trucks which then deposited the bundles of newspapers at carrier depots all over the city. *Stuart Thomson, City of Vancouver Archives 99-4593*

Rev. Andrew Roddan (left) with men at a makeshift cookhouse at an encampment for the unemployed at the city dump in False Creek Flats in September 1931. *W.J. Moore, City of Vancouver Archives ReN7*

Soup kitchens and bread lines

The first few editions of *The Sun* in the new decade painted a somewhat rosier picture than reality might have dictated. The stock market crash was debilitating, and Vancouver did not escape the economic and social fallout.

Nevertheless, the paper of Jan. 2, 1930 featured Vancouver Mayor W. H. Malkin's optimistic address to city council, in which he predicted the city would be on a "forward march," with $50 million in building permits expected in the coming year. *The Sun*'s Jan. 3 front page, headlined "Canada's 1930 Financial Status," projected a cheery future and quoted business leaders and statistics suggesting "records to be surpassed."

Despite the felicitous headlines – and B.C.'s 340,000-plus population and per capita income of $4,339 – the city would soon be consumed by The Great Depression that was sweeping North America. All over the globe, crippled economies saw unemployment rise,

construction projects stall, crop prices fall and cities that were reliant on resource industries – such as Vancouver – especially hard hit. Thousands of locals soon found themselves frequenting bread lines and soup kitchens, and out-of-work men were living in labour camps and attending rallies.

The Vancouver Welfare Federation, employing 2,000 workers, launched a drive for donations, telling *The Sun* the $110,508 it had collected in November 1932 wasn't enough, and the city's poor families needed "action from those who can well afford it." That same month, the city's jobless, including panhandlers, were ordered to register and report to "camps for single men," where food, shelter and warmth were waiting. Dinner at camp often included bean soup, meat stew, tea and apple pudding with custard sauce. It was also reported that enrolment in the city's 80 schools was up slightly, but that several hundred of the 40,000 school children were going hungry, and the answer might best be found in PTA fundraising whist drives.

Inspiring the troops

Sun owner Robert Cromie, meantime, was doing his best to keep the paper in the black, attempting to inspire his executive team with feedback on a unsolicited report written by ad manager George Cran on how the paper might improve its fortunes. Cromie's June 1930 inter-office memo lauded Cran's initiative, but got quickly to the point: the paper needed to work harder at becoming number one.

Cromie's typewritten letter said, in part: "Vancouver and *The Vancouver Sun* have made splendid progress in the past 15 years, but we have not made anything like the progress that lies ahead of us. Our Printing Department needs expansion along many lines; our Editorial Department is sadly lacking in initiative and endeavor; there is another 20,000 circulation waiting for us from Greater Vancouver the minute we can offer a type of paper that will compel and induce those people to read it; and there is an endless volume of advertising still unborn in Vancouver."

The paper also had a new slogan, a sure sign that publishing was still a man's world: "*The Sun* is the Only Vancouver Newspaper Owned Controlled and Operated by Vancouver Men."

It was less a parochial boast – after all, Cromie had been born in Quebec – than it was another salvo in the publisher's campaign to assure readers that his newspaper was by the people and for the people in the city he had so robustly adopted and unabashedly promoted.

Musical (newspaper) chairs

Following his purchase of *The Morning Sun* from Robert Cromie in 1926, Victor Odlum immediately republished it as the *Morning Star,* but it was a short-lived rival. When his printers turned down a pay cut in 1932, Odlum closed the paper, leaving the city with only *The Vancouver Sun* and its biggest competitor, *The Province*, two broadsheets duking it out for supremacy in the evening market.

Upstart competitors, however, weren't unusual. *The Richmond Review* joined the growing community newspaper portfolio in 1932, the year that would also see two former *Morning Star* employees start *The News,* which would be replaced by *The Vancouver News-Herald* five months later. When the *News-Herald* hit the street with a four-page debut issue in April 1933, it had formidable competition: the circulation of *The Province* was 90,265, while *The Sun*'s was between 60,000 and 70,000.

The News-Herald's first city editor, notably, was Pierre Berton, who a dozen years later would find himself reporting for *The Vancouver Sun*. While *The News-Herald* never hit the circulation heights of its rivals, it did survive for 24 years.

A student uprising, *Sun*-style

Trading on its brash reputation for giving readers the unexpected, *Sun* editors turned the newsroom over to the energetic staff at UBC's student newspaper, *The Ubyssey,* on Jan. 17, 1933. The young reporters naturally focused their edition on education issues, with a page-one story that cheekily included comments from an assortment of UBC instructors, who were asked if a university education was a useful career stepping stone. All enthusiastically agreed that it was.

Among the 30 budding journalists working that day was 19-year-old Stuart Keate, who would become *The Vancouver Sun*'s publisher three decades later.

The brief internship was part of a purposeful journalistic path, as Keate would write in his 1980 memoir *Paper Boy,* because "about the only avenue to the downtown Vancouver press in the mid-1930s was *The Ubyssey* . . . The rare jobs that opened up in that bleak era were usually decided on the basis of nepotism: an editor had a son, or a nephew, or an in-law."

Thousands of Vancouverites can boast that they were once members of the paper's Sun-Ray Club, "conducted by Uncle Ben." Though the punctuation of its name changed, the Club lasted into the 1980s, providing young readers with fun facts and information, opportunities to raise money for charity, and invitations to gatherings and special events.

Beam me up: The SunRay Club

In a time of belt-tightening, with many fathers out of work and many mothers turning to the Edith Adam's Cookery Page for tips on how to stretch a meal and a budget, *The Sun* decided the kids in the family could use a new distraction: Uncle Ben's SunRay Club. Introduced June 1, 1929, it was originally written by an unidentified man whose photograph appeared with the column, but from 1958 until his retirement in 1976, the writer and the friendly, familiar face appearing with the column was that of Jack Hutchings. The former editor of the *Penticton Herald,* Hutchings was hired by *The Sun* in 1946 to help with the paper's Teen Town leadership program, which attracted hundreds of Teen Town "mayors" from around B.C. to an annual Teen Town conference in Vancouver to discuss community-based youth projects.

In its debut, the SunRay Club vowed to "enrich the minds of growing children, to give them facts which they can ultimately use and to influence without moralizing." There was a call-out for young readers to help design the SunRay button, with prizes for the winners. The column included "posers" – such as "What country is Rudyard Kipling connected with?" – as well as Bible tests, puzzles and facts. Each week, the names of new members were published. The Club, which lasted into the 1980s, grew so popular that it held spinoff events like the 1955 SunRay Revue, a week-long fundraiser at a local theatre featuring dancers and singers from the ages of two to 18. In the 1960s, the Club raised $50.25 and "adopted" Huda Younes, a five-year-old Lebanese girl living in poverty in Beirut. The money was enough to provide Huda with food, clothing and school expenses for a year. "Now let's go beyond this minimum

Changing tents for *Vancouver Sun* free swim classes, on the beach in 1933. *Stuart Thomson, City of Vancouver Archives 99-2777*

The first prize home built for the Pacific National Exhibition in 1934. *City of Vancouver Archives photo 180-597*

objective and collect enough money to care for one more overseas child," the column exhorted. Over the following years, SunRay members would adopt children in Europe and Africa.

The SunRay legacy would carry on in the work of Marilyn Stusiak, who joined *The Sun* in the Press Library in 1948 but would eventually become the youth columnist, until she retired in 1995. In her 30-plus years as a reporter, Stusiak was a strong advocate for literacy and early childhood development. She also provided games and puzzles for young readers, and was a pioneer in the school-based Newspaper in Education program. Her annual Christmas card contest attracted thousands of entries from elementary school children all over B.C., and her popular Parent Advisory column was an invaluable resource for readers.

Get your prize home here

Twenty years after a *Sun* contest awarded a Vancouver house to a loyal subscriber, the Pacific National Exhibition borrowed that unusual marketing idea and gave away its first prize home in 1934. In what was optimistically seen as a sign the economy might be improving, the PNE hosted a record opening day crowd of 51,368, attracted by the prospect of instant, mortgage-free home ownership. It was a brilliant idea: not only would the $5,000 lot and 800-square-foot bungalow in east Vancouver be a dream come true for one lucky lottery winner, it was built with B.C. products to showcase local industry.

Leonard Frewin, a 27-year-old driver for the David Spencer department store, bought the winning 10-cent ticket, number 50843, and his life changed forever. The Sept. 6, 1934 *Vancouver Sun* reported the win: "Excited and voluble, a Greek junk dealer was stopped by New Westminster police as he speeded through the city at 9:50 o'clock this morning in his rickety old truck. In great glee he waved a ticket over his head and told them he had won a bungalow, first prize in the Exhibition draw. The police let him go and away he clattered, headed for the exhibition grounds to present his claim."

Frewin and his new bride Emily – her parents endorsed their marriage after the windfall – moved into the Dundas Street house, furnished by Eaton's and outfitted with a new-fangled electric stove. The Frewins sold the home in 1936, but the house stands today and the PNE continues to give away a prize home at its annual fair, if somewhat grander and considerably pricier models than the little east-side starter home.

Changing of the guard

When *Sun* patriarch Robert Cromie died unexpectedly of heart failure on May 11, 1936 at age 48, while in Victoria on a speaking engagement, it came as a shock not only to his newspaper and the city and province it served, but to the publishing industry in which Cromie had made such an indelible mark.

His funeral, held May 14 at Christ Church Cathedral, was the biggest the city had seen. *The Sun* offices were shut down for three hours so staff could join the hundreds of local his blood, who had always exhibited journalistic promise. He was clearly the most likely of Cromie senior's progeny to carry on the family business, and before his death his father had urged him to get some experience, and some travelling, under his belt. The directive delighted Don; he was a peripatetic sort, a University of Washington journalism school dropout who briefly attended the London School of Economics, toured Russia and honed his cub reporter skills on the *Toronto Star* newsdesk before he would find his way back into the family business in the early 1940s.

When the story hits home

In the years after Cromie's death, the day-to-day business of the paper was left in the hands of P.J. Salter, who took over as president and general manager. Also running the operation were editorial director Roy Brown, managing editor Herbert Sallans and circulation manager Herbert Gates. It was a vital business, with a payroll of $600,000 and 350 full-time employees publishing four editions a day, including the so-called "home edition," which was delivered by carriers throughout B.C.

The Vancouver Sun's transition from the grip of the rigorous hands-on Cromie to its caretaker management seemed a smooth one.

Then, on March 22, 1937, after 20 years of publishing out of the editorial offices at 125 West Pender, an early morning fire swept through the four-storey building. The spunky paper published on the day of the fire, with a front-page story that told of $200,000 worth of damage and the kind but declined offers from competitors, *The Daily Province* and *The News-Herald*, of their printing facilities.

News stories included quotes from reporter Mamie Moloney, who was called in to her burning office at 3 a.m., but first checked with police, saying "This is Mamie Moloney of *The Vancouver Sun*," to which the officer replied, "Too bad, Mamie, but you're out of a job."

Social editor Helen Effinger stood outside the burning building, watching the fire from the street and lamenting that the new Easter bonnet she had bought and left at the office was likely going up in flames. Reporter Alan Morley, who was also a UBC student, lost two years worth of research on B.C.'s history, compiled for his bachelor's thesis. Morley wrote one of the few bylined fire stories that day, telling readers how *The Sun* was back in business by 6 a.m., with reporters writing longhand copy and copy boys and news editors bustling through the "floating cinders and backwash of dirty water."

With fire damage limited to only one press, the paper didn't miss a beat. An editorial the day of the fire declared that "the essence of a newspaper, the thought that gave it birth, the services that add to its stature, the traditions that lend it maturity, the principles that determine its character, are indestructible and immortal, beyond the reach of time and flame alike."

Presided over by a portrait of their late father Robert Cromie, brothers Sam (left) and Don look through a copy of *The Vancouver Sun*. Each son inherited 10 per cent of the paper upon their father's death, and would remain with *The Sun* for years. *Vancouver Sun*

dignitaries, business leaders and politicians from all levels of government who paid their respects. The mourners included several members of the Southam family, which owned the rival *Province*.

The Vancouver Sun coverage of Cromie's death spoke to his influence and community profile, and included dozens of tributes from across Canada, many of the accolades detailing Cromie's rise from bellhop to bookkeeper to successful and respected newspaperman.

"In the death of Robert Cromie," wrote B.C. Premier Duff Pattullo, "the city of Vancouver has lost a dynamic personality, a man with tremendous energy and an unswerving determination to build up the city in which he had such unbounded faith." Even *The Province* weighed in: "It was no small thing to build up a great newspaper property from nothing in less than

twenty years."

Cromie left half his ownership of the paper, and its healthy circulation of 70,000, to his widow Bernadette, with 10 per cent each to their five children: Robert Jr., Don, Samuel, Peter and Grace Ann.

Bernadette was publisher in name only, and son Robert Jr. was vice-president at age 24, a job he didn't suit. He would soon leave to take up cattle ranching. Son Peter, who was 16 when Robert died, would become internal auditor and manager of printing for Sun Publishing during the late 1940s and early 1950s, selling his holdings to his brothers in 1955. Samuel was a long-time vice-president and assistant *Sun* publisher until his death in 1957.

But it was Don, who was 20 at the time of his father's death, who had newspaper ink in

The Weather

Forecast for 36 hours, Vancouver and vicinity: Moderate, shifting winds; mostly cloudy and cool, with showers. Temperatures: High, 53 degs.; low, 42 degs. Sun rose at 6:11 a.m.; sets at 6:28 p.m.

THE VANCOUVER SUN

Only Evening Newspaper Owned, Controlled and Operated by Vancouver People

The Tides

Vancouver Harbor: High 1:55 p.m. 9.7 ft.; low 3:53 p.m., 2.5 ft. English Bay: High 1:30 p.m., 10.3 ft.; low 8:21 p.m., 3.4 ft. First Narrows: High slack, 2:10 p.m.; low slack, 9:13 p.m.

FOUNDED 1886 — VOL. XCII—NO. 1 | Trinity 4111 | VANCOUVER, BRITISH COLUMBIA, MONDAY, MARCH 22, 1937 | ***-C | Price 3 Cents | 60c per month delivered

Polic[e] Evict S[it-Down] Strikers

Detroit Mayor Defies U.A.W. Threat of General Walkout

Labor Rally In Detroit Tuesday

By Associated Press

DETROIT, March 22. — Ignoring threats of a city-wide automotive strike if raids on striker-held plants continue, police today entered the plant of the Thomas P. Henry Printing Co., and evicted strikers who have occupied the place since March 11. The strikers surrendered peacefully.

Fifty policemen entered the printing plant, apparently taking approximately 30 strikers by surprise.

The strikers were questioned at the plant but were not placed under arrest.

Thomas P. Henry, proprietor, said the plant would resume operation on an open-shop basis, and applications for re-employment will be considered.

The Henry plant has been non-union. Recognition of the International Typographical Union is the major issue in the strike.

At least one other raid on a striker-occupied plant is planned by police today.

MORE RAIDS

Mayor Frank Couzens declared the raids would continue on captive plants where the police have reason to believe that non-employees are among the occupants.

Handbills were distributed calling upon union members to "show labor's strength" in a demonstration at Cadillac Square, in the heart of Detroit, at 2 p.m. (P.S.T.) Tuesday.

The United Automobile Workers also disclosed that the organization of "Minute Men" among members, along military lines, with the avowed purpose of "protecting strikers and the right to strike.

U.A.W. THREAT

A telegram from U.A.W. officers to 29 Detroit locals states:

"Because of a grave situation created by police and the mayor in attacking the right of strikers throughout the city, the international officers have decided to take 'decisive steps'."

The telegram said "A general strike may be necessary," and instructed local officers to "appoint special strike committees," but to "take no strike action until instructed" by Homer Martin, president of the U.A.W.

The issue of sole bargaining rights continued to deadlock negotiations for a settlement of the strike in eight Chrysler Corporation plants here with nearly 80,000 workers idle.

I.L.A. Union Challenged

Aldermen Urged to Ask for Production of Records

Probability that the majority of the members of the Vancouver branch of the International Longshoremen's Association have worked very little on the local waterfront and some have never been employed here was stressed by Harry Burgess in a statement delivered today to the City Council on behalf of the Vancouver Longshoremen's Association.

He urged Aldermen to ask the I. L. A. union to produce its records for inspection so that its personnel can be determined.

"At the present time the deep-sea work is being done under agreement with properly constituted organizations, which agreement expires in 1941," Burgess told the Council, sitting as a harbors committee.

His appearance as secretary-treasurer of the V. L. A. followed recent attacks made by Ald. R. P. Pettipiece on the labor conditions under the B. C. Shipping Federation, which excludes the I. L. A. from handling ships of its members.

Although Burgess volunteered to answer any questions about his organization, the committee decided to refrain from opening a controversy. Ald. H. D. Wilson, chairman, pointed out that the city has asked the Dominion Government to conduct an impartial investigation of longshore matters.

A reply was received today from Hon. C. D. Howe, Minister of Transport, saying that he has referred the application to the National Harbors Board for consideration.

8 1-2 Inch Egg Laid by Hen In Utah Town

SALT LAKE CITY, March 22.—An egg measuring 8½ inches in circumference, laid by a White Leghorn hen, was displayed here today.

Inside it was a smaller, full developed egg, said owner Guy Throne of Coalville, Utah.

Throne said the hen died an hour later.

Justice Reveals Scriptural Lore

Mr. Justice D. A. McDonald revealed his intimate knowledge of the Scriptures in Supreme Court today, when he asked F. M. Donnenworth if he knew the origin of the name "Havilah."

Having incorporated Havilah Gold Mines Ltd., Victoria, Mr. Donnenworth agreed with His Lordship that the word appears in Genesis, where the first reference is made in the Bible to gold.

Mr. Donnenworth appeared as counsel for Arthur William Payn Lesuer, prospector, 1544 Barclay Street, who sued Havilah Gold Mines Ltd., for $6250, which he claimed was due under an agreement to purchase mining claims.

His action was dismissed without costs following a settlement. F. C. Elliott appeared for the company.

At the Height of the Blaze

The cameraman caught this shot of the front of the offices while firemen struggled to save the building. It shows the gutted editorial and business department and, at the left, the five-storey job printing and compising room building, which was not damaged. Neither was the Shelly Building, at the right, touched by the flames.

Here Are The Sun's Telephone Numbers

Until the installation of the new telephone switchboard is completed, persons having business with the various departments of The Vancouver Sun are asked to use the following telephone numbers:

Classified Advertising, Display Advertising, Circulation, Job Printing and Accounting Departments, call Trinity 4111-k, Trinity 4112-k, Trinity 4113-k, Trinity 4114-k or Trinity 4115-k.

Composing Room, Trinity 4118-k.
Editorial Department, Trinity 4116-k, Trinity 4117-k and Trinity 4119-k.

Please make calls direct to the department desired.

Alderman Hints Gov't May Take Over City

'Little Progress in Cutting Department Estimates'

The Provincial Government may be asked to take over the City of Vancouver's finances and management, Ald. J. W. Cornett glommily warned his colleagues today in an outline of budget problems.

Speaking as chairman of finance committee, he indicated that hoped-for progress has not been made in curtailing departmental estimates.

Department heads have told him flatly, he said, that they will not accept responsibility if appropriations for emergency works are deleted from their allowances.

"It may be," he continued, "that the city will have to go to Victoria, as one alderman suggested, and ask the government to take us over"

COMMISSIONERSHIP DEBATE

Ald. R. P. Pettipiece was identified as the author of the proposal.

Discussion of a commissionership for Vancouver arose when Council, in social services committee, authorized Ald. Pettipiece and Ald. Crone to go to Victoria Tuesday to seek a grant toward a $70,000 relief work project.

The point was whether the city should prejudice its claim for major contributions by asking for such a relatively small sum.

Ald Cornett said that the final draft of the budget will probably not be complete until early next fall.

He agreed, however, that Fraser Golf Course should be completed if money already invested there is not to go to waste.

The balance of the relief work scheme will be conducted in Stanley Park and other park projects.

WORK MAY CEASE

Failing assistance, men now employed on the jobs will cease work Saturday, Ald. Pettipiece said.

Relief Officer W. R. Bone was instructed to accompany the delegation to reach a basis for defining "unemployables" who are supported entirely by the city, and jobless persons who could work if they got a chance.

A strict interpretation of employability might cost the city $1,500,000 per year instead of its annual $800,000 cost now, even if the government took over the entire cost of persons who are able to work, Bone said.

Frightened Yeggs Leave Tools Behind

Disturbed before they could settle down to their work, safecrackers were forced to abandon a quantity of nitroglycerine and tools in the premises of Grant Gunn Company, 551 West Broadway, early today.

Employees coming to work at 8 a.m. today discovered that the premises had been entered. Near the safe in the office was found the quantity of explosive, hammers, punches and other tools suitable for safecracking purposes.

Cambie Bus Runs Oftener

B. C. E. R. Refuses to Bring Line Downtown

The B. C. Electric Railway Co. notified the City Council today that it cannot extend the Cambie Street 'bus line into the heart of the city as had been suggested. Such extension would be a duplication of existing services, the company reported.

On April 1, however, the company will increase frequency of the 'bus service. It has been in operation every 15 minutes during rush hours, and every half hour at other times ending daily at 10:18 p.m.

Under the new schedule it will operate every 15 minutes all day until 9 p.m. and at half-hour intervals until 12:20 midnight. On Sundays the last 'bus will leave Broadway and Cambie Street at 11:20 p.m.

King of Belgians Talks With Eden

By Associated Press

LONDON, March 22. — Youthful King Leopold III of the Belgians, seeking to identify his new "isolation policy" with Great Britain's hopes for a new treaty guaranteeing Western European security, arrived today for conferences with Foreign Secretary Eden and other British leaders.

Leopold announced in his famous Oct. 14 speech that Belgium wants her territory guaranteed as it was in the Locarno Treaty, but no longer is willing to promise military aid to any other nation.

Barbers' Union Wants $18 Wage Minimum

VICTORIA, March 22.—The Barbers' Union in Vancouver and Victoria have made an application to the Board of Industrial Relations for an increase in the minimum wage for barbers from $15 to $18 a week.

The board will probably call conferences of employers and employees shortly, Adam Bell, board chairman, said today.

Alberta to Cut Debt Principal

By Canadian Press

EDMONTON, March 22.—Plans for the introduction of new debt reduction legislation in the Alberta Legislature to replace the Debt Settlement Act declared Ultra Vires by the courts, went forward here today.

Premier Aberhart indicated that the new legislation will be introduced in the legislature shortly.

The old legislation dealt with interest. The new, it is understood, will deal with principal, forecasts placing reductions at as high as 50 per cent.

Christian Science Lecture On Page 10

The full text of a lecture on Christian Science, given in Vancouver Sunday, appears on page 10 today.

Mid Smoke and Flame

Here are the firemen fighting the blaze from fire escapes in the lane at the rear of The Sun building. Some of these men narrowly escaped serious injury when the roof of the editorial building collapsed.

Rum Prices Increased 15c

Demerara Variety Scarce Since London Dock Fire

VICTORIA, March 22.—Rum prices are due for a slight increase in British Columbia due to the world shortage of aged Demerara rum.

This week the government OK'd an increase of 15 cents a quart on one standard brand of rum. In three or four weeks after present stocks are used up, the price of the Demerara bottled by the Liquor Control Board will go up in about the same proportion, according to W. F. Kennedy, chairman.

It is all because of a London dock fire three years ago which destroyed millions of gallons of ageing rum. British Columbia has always insisted on getting Demerara at least five years old. This is almost unobtainable now.

Last fall the Board put some Trinidad rum on the shelves at a lower price but the rum drinkers have acquired a taste for Demerara. If they want it they'll have to pay a bit more and it will be four years old instead of five. In other provinces the rum drinkers are not so particular and anything from one to three years old suits them, the local board explains.

Markets at a Glance

LOCAL—Oils higher.
LOCAL SALES—Saturday, 244,288 shares; value, $77,542.
NEW YORK—Down $1 to $6.
N. Y. SALES—2,150,000 shares.
'PEG GRAIN—Gains cut.
'PEG MAY WHEAT—$1.39¼.
CHICAGO GRAIN—Strong.
CHI MAY WHEAT—$1.39½.
TORONTO—Mines lower.
MONTREAL—Easier.
SILVER—N. Y., 45.25c oz.
COPPER—N. Y., 16.75c lb.
TIN—N. Y., 62.12½c lb.
LEAD—N. Y., 7.00c lb.
ZINC—N. Y., 7.50c lb.
COTTON—N. Y., 14.38c lb.
CALL MONEY—N. Y., 1 pct.
(Full details pages 16 and 17)

Police Matron 'Gets Her Man'

Envious eyes of male members of the Vancouver Police Department are glaring green in the direction of Police Matron May Gordon today.

Miss Gordon knew there was a warrant out for a certain man.

Moreover, Miss Gordon had seen the man on Powell Street Saturday afternoon.

Dashing into police headquarters, Matron Gordon asked for a detective to accompany her to the place where the wanted man was staying.

There wasn't a detective available.

Matron Gordon went out of the office alone.

Fifteen minutes later she escorted the wanted man into the general office.

Some of the boys around headquarters are wondering just how the matron accomplished the arrest.

News Highlights From The Inside Pages

J. L. Lewis' triumph over "Steel," Page 3.

First christening of Vancouver's triplets, Page 6.

B.C. election likely June 3 or 4, Page 12.

U. B. C. again beats Dominoes, Page 18.

Texas Blast Probe

NEW LONDON, Texas, March 22.—W. C. Shaw, superintendent, told a military inquiry today he was "partly responsible" for an informal gas line connection for the heating system of the explosion-wrecked London school and that he had not known of any particular objection to the connection.

A clue to the ignition of the explosion was provided by John Dial, 15, a student.

"A flash of fire blinded me," Dial testified, "at almost that same instant a man pulled a light switch in the manual training room."

(See also Page 6.)

Brutal Gunmen Sought

Butcher Slugged Several Times by Bandits; Robbed of $80

Robbery Drama In West End

Police today continued intensive search for the two vicious bandits who beat Colin Waymark, 4055 Welwyn Street, over the head with a revolver butt and robbed him of $80 at 7:55 p.m. Saturday.

Waymark, manager of a butcher shop at 1512 Davie Street, had closed the store for the night and was on his way to the garage at the rear to get his auto when two men stepped out of the shadows.

"This is a holdup," announced one as he menaced Waymark with a gun.

Waymark lunged at the unarmed bandit and was attempting to throw him to the ground when he was struck on the head with the butt of the pistol by the other bandit.

CRUMPLED TO GROUND

The victim crumpled to the ground. Standing over him, the thugs demanded his money.

"I left it in the store," replied Waymark, and the gunman again struck him over the head with the butt of the revolver.

The unarmed thug then went through one of the pockets of the victim and removed the keys to the store and to Waymark's auto. The bandit walked around to the front of the store and boldly let himself in through the front door.

Unable to find money in the store, the thug returned.

Enraged at his failure to find money, he struck Waymark twice over the head with his weapon, then searched his pockets and removed the money.

Meanwhile, the unarmed bandit returned to the store in a further search.

FEIGNED UNCONSCIOUSNESS

Waymark pretended to be unconscious and the armed thug dragged his limp body into the garage. Standing over the bleeding victim, the gunman

Continued on Page Five

Pope Assails Nazi Policy

Vatican Letter Amazes German Catholics

By Associated Press

BERLIN, March 22. — An open fight between Nazi Germany and the Roman Catholic church appears in prospect as the result of a vigorous pastoral letter by Pope Pius XI circulated to German Catholics.

The Pope in the letter, dated March 14 which astounded even German Catholics, accuses the Nazi regime of having violated the German-Vatican Concordat of 1933 and encouraging anti-Christian movements.

Principles of the catholic faith are presented in the Holy Father's pronouncement in such sharp contrast to the philosophical teaching of Nazism that Catholic circles in Berlin fully expect the Nazi Government to cancel the Concordat.

EQUAL TO ENCYCLICAL

Read from the pulpits as a "sendschreiben," or pastoral letter, the message, said Catholic circles, because of its content and general appeal, is the equivalent of an encyclical although technically does not bear that name.

The letter arrived in Berlin late Saturday night. It was delivered to the various parishes secretely by auto messengers. At Berlin Cathedral it was read by Count Konrad von Preysing-Lichtenegg-Moors, Bishop of Berlin.

Late this afternoon the Bishop summoned all Berlin members of Catholic men's societies to a special meeting, in the course of which he

Continued on Page Five

Mona W. Johns Puzzle Winner

Once again a single participant in the Puzzleword contest wins the First Prize of $75.

When the judges made their report this morning on Contest No. 68, which closed Saturday, they revealed that a perfect solution had been entered by Mona W. Johns, 1057 Melville Street. Therefore, to Mona goes the money.

There were no solutions with one incorrect word, but there were five puzzlers whose solutions had two errors. That being so, the $25 Second Prize is divided between the five, and each receives $5, as follows:

J. Avison, 1564 Venables Street
E. E. Devlin, 1070 Haro Street
A. R. Farrell, 336 East 19th Avenue
Mrs. E. Holmes, General Delivery
A. Smith, 1081 West 16th Avenue

Following is the correct solution:

72 Rescued From Blazing Freighter

LIVERPOOL, March 22.—Lifeboats from the shore today rescued the crew of 72 from the blazing steamer "Marie Moller" off Holyhead on the northeastern coast of Wales.

The ship was abandoned when flames enveloped her after two explosions. She was bound to Liverpool from Shanghai with a cargo of peanuts.

Fire Sweeps The Sun Offices; All Editions Published as Usual

Watchman's Clock Goes Through Fire, Still Working

A watchman's clock, which was used by The Vancouver Sun watchman on duty at the time of the fire, was still going after the blaze was extinguished.

The leather covering had been burned off completely, but it was still ticking away, and the perforated sheet inside it, recording the last visits made to the various departments was singed but still readable.

* * *

H. F. Gates, circulation manager of The Vancouver Sun, was the most correctly attired member of the staff to turn out to the fire. Inability to locate a collar button caused him some trouble as he was dressing hurriedly.

"Didn't you ever go to a fire without a collar button?" queried his wife.

"No I haven't and I don't intend to start now," came the reply, as he located the missing button and continued his dressing.

* * *

Mamie Moloney of the editorial department, thought someone was playing a practical joke on her when she got a call to report to a burning office around 3 a.m., so she checked with police.

"This is Mamie Moloney of The Sun," she commenced.

"Too bad, Mamie, but you're out of a job," came back the reply.

* * *

Of course that was just a joke, and Miss Moloney's column, "A Woman Views the News," appears on the social page as usual.

* * *

One of the spectators at the fire was a woman who had thrown a coat hastily over her pyjamas. She moved up to the line of hose as she watched the firemen working. All of a sudden, the hose exploded and the curious spectator was drenched with icy water. She made a hasty retreat.

* * *

A grim reminder of the chances taken by Vancouver's firemen is a red-handled fireman's axe hanging on one of the centre posts at a point which met the roof of the building. A venturesome fireman had probably been risking his life virtually on top of an inferno and had to retreat, leaving his axe where he had been working.

* * *

Helen Effinger, social editor, watched the fire with a wistful expression.

"What's wrong, Helen?" someone called out.

"Worrying about your copy?"

"It's not that," came the reply. "I bought my new Easter hat, Saturday, and left it in the office."

* * *

One of the hardest hit of The Sun's reporters is Alan Morley, U.B.C. student, who in spare time between journalistic writing has been laboring on his bachelor's thesis. All the original research on early British Columbia history which has taken him two years to collect, was embodied in the notes on his desk. He didn't have time to watch whether firemen had rescued any on it as he was too busy writing a news story for today's issue of the paper.

* * *

Pat Slattery, sports department, and Del Finlay, copy desk, rescued their "shears" from desks in the editorial room following the fire.

* * *

Amid the debris in the building, a fireman picked up a nickel. He held it aloft as he came out to the street while the few onlookers still about called out suggestions as to what he should do with it. A bright newsboy passing at the moment called out: "Buy a paper, mister, and read about the fire."

* * *

Mae Garnett, court reporter, peered through the door from the printing department to the editorial room to discover part of the ceiling had fallen on her desk.

"There's five years' of working on my own private filing system all shot to pieces and one of the blinking market judgments coming down today. Whatta life!"

Half an hour later she was observed trying to cajole a fireman to

Continued on Page Five

$200,000 Damage in Early Morning Blaze

Main Building Escapes Flames

Fire of unknown cause breaking out shortly before 2 a.m. today roared through the editorial and business offices of The Vancouver Sun, 125 West Pender Street, resulting in damage estimated at close to $200,000 and endangering the lives of a score of employees and several firemen.

It swept completely through the four-storey structure and menaced the five-storey building next door which houses the job printing department and composing room. Neither this, nor the Shelly Building on the other side, was damaged.

Had it not been for emergency work by printers on the night shift who rigged two lines of hose and poured streams of water from the windows, this structure also might have been doomed, it is thought.

Roy Brown, editor-in-chief of The Daily Province, and J. N. "Pat" Kelly, managing editor of The News-Herald, hastened to offer all facilities of their newspapers. Happily, save for early "rush" copy, The Sun's own building furnished full facilities and publication has not been interrupted.

Printing of the newspaper will be from The Sun pressroom, only one of the presses being damaged.

$200,000 DAMAGE

P. J. Salter, president of The Sun Publishing Company, estimated the loss to the contents of the building at $100,000.

Loss on the structure, owned by the Union Assurance Company of Canton, whose local representatives are R. Kerr Houlgate and Summerfield Ltd., is approximately the same.

The loss is fully covered by insurance.

It was 10 minutes to 2 o'clock when Jack Johnson, the night janitor, who was waxing the linoleum in the business office on the ground floor, noticed sparks at the top of the switchboard at the northern end of the office.

He seized a fire extinguisher and attempted to quench the blaze, but was unsuccessful.

"Suddenly," said Johnson, "there was an explosion and flames burst out all around me."

Johnson hastily telephoned the fire department from the front of the office.

CRAWLED TO DOOR

By this time the smoke was so thick that he was almost overcome. He crawled on his hands and knees to the front door, which was locked. He managed to make his exit by removing the bolts from the top and bottom of the door.

Johnson was scorched on the back of the head.

As soon as he reached the street there was another explosion which blew out the windows of the editorial rooms on the second floor.

Johnson said that he had made a round of the building, punching his time clock, 20 minutes before he first noticed the blaze, and everything then seemed in order.

While Johnson was attempting to fight the blaze downstairs, Al Pelky, compositor, in the composing room on the fourth floor of the adjoining building, saw flames rising from the airshaft on the east side.

PRINTERS FIGHT FIRE

Pelky shouted "fire" and immediately the composing room staff sprang into action.

The compositors ran two lines of hose from the windows across to the roof of the editorial building and managed to keep the fire partly in check pending the arrival of the fire brigade.

Before the firemen arrived, however, the mysterious explosion had occurred.

"There was a dull 'boom'," said Compositor Jock McGillivray, "then sheets of flame shot up the airshaft."

The force of the explosion was so great that it blew out windows on

Continued on Page Five

After the Blaze Was Over; How the Paper Was Published

By ALAN MORLEY

She's out!

You're reading her.

"She" is this issue of The Vancouver Sun, March 22, 1937, the day of the Big Fire. It will always be the Big Fire, with "caps," to those of us who put her out this morning.

At 2 a.m. the editorial rooms were blazing.

In a short time telephones were tinkling in the homes of every editor, sub-editor and reporter, and even then a group of newsmen were clustered on the sidewalk gazing at the familiar windows belching smoke and flame.

By 6 o'clock a journalistic salvage squad was paddling through the backwash of dirty water, floating cinders and curling smoke of the second storey city room in rubber boots loaned by the fire department. They trooped out carrying a few relics—a pair of shears here, a desk drawer full of soaking notes there, a soiled sheaf of telegraphic "flimsy."

An hour later the bindery in the "job department" building next door burst into throbbing life as the entire editorial staff pounded up the stairs.

Copy boys, news editors, reporters, all stripped off their coats and got to work.

Bundles of paper, dollies loaded with hundreds of pounds of "job" and fancy printing, tables, chairs and benches, flew around as if by magic.

Somebody found a paste-pot, and with a pair of tarnished shears, a stack of flimsy," a wad of blank paper and the paste, the news-editor sat down at a hastily-cleared spot on a long table.

The Vancouver Sun was doing business again. Time: 7:20 a.m.

The space grew larger. The copy-editors clustered around.

The janitor, the managing editor and a copy boy rustled in with a load of chairs.

A couple of reporters, one standing, one sitting, wrote copy in longhand.

More shifting of great bundles of paper and cardboard, and half-a-dozen little, low tables came to light.

The big freight elevator at the rear of the room creaked and groaned to a stop, and disgorged two men with the first dozen typewriters.

There were the essentials of the news business—tables, chairs, typewriters, reporters. What more could one want?

The shouts, bustle and disorder diminished. They were succeeded by the orderly pandemonium of an editorial office.

At one end of a long table the copy-editors worked feverishly and silently, as is their wont. At the other end the "morgue" did business as usual with a pile of filing folders and the morning mail.

In the shadow of a couple of book-stitching machines Society and Finance, flanked by quartette of re-

Continued on Page Five

Off Again!

Cash

The weekly pursuit for the Puzzleword money is on . . . and anyone can win!

Turn to Page 6

Newspapers don't often publish stories about themselves, but *The Sun* made an exception on March 22, 1937, when a fire at the paper's editorial and business offices on West Pender was front-page news. The fire caused $200,000 worth of damage and forced the eventual relocation of the paper.

Wholesale department staffers Walter Herrington (right) and William Lambert (left) receive the first papers off *The Vancouver Sun's* new five-unit, 320-ton, high-speed Goss presses on March 9, 1938. *Stan Williams/Vancouver Sun*

Welcome to the Sun Tower

After the fire, there was no choice but for *Sun* management to find a new home, which turned out to be the building right across the street. On May 18, 1937, *The Sun* announced it had purchased the former World Tower on the corner of Pender and Beatty, immediately renaming the 17-storey structure the Sun Tower. The landmark terracotta Beaux-Arts building, with its faux copper dome and nine "nude maidens" decorating the cornice, came with much history. It had been built in 1912 by Louis Taylor to house his *Vancouver World* newspaper, and was later purchased by the Bekins moving company of Seattle. The new deal was a swap of sorts, with Bekins buying

the old *Sun* premises.

Several special sections were published in August 1937 as staff moved into the Sun Tower – the paper's name soon to be in lights that could be seen for miles atop the building. One four-page special featured a cover photo of the new, high-speed, three-colour Goss presses – which were being specially built and were huge at 50-feet long and 18-feet high – superimposed on a photo of the tower. Stories extolled the virtues of the new technology, which could print in 16-page units and run off a speedy 50,000 papers every hour, and told readers that a separate colour press for the comics and *The Sun* magazine section would soon be installed in the new building.

There was also a promise from editors: this

new stage in the newspaper's evolution would make the paper "to a greater degree than ever, 'Vancouver's Home Newspaper for Vancouver People.'"

The sections were jammed with dozens of congratulatory ads from local businesses, and exhortations to subscribe and advertise by dialling Trinity 4111. Promotional fodder highlighted not only the new technology, from the presses to the wire photo process, but *The Sun's* "journalistic provenance and eclectic lineup of writers," including its regular scribes and specialized columnists that included two doctors, a reverend, political experts and advice dispenser Dorothy Dix.

The Sun would stay in its new home until 1965.

The May 19, 1938 *Vancouver Sun* reported that Charlie Walker won the Sun Marathon. The race took the 200 competitors past the Sun Tower.

Sun reader Madge Marlatt, second from the left in this 1933 photo, performed in downtown Vancouver dance halls such as the White Rose and Peter Pan. *Courtesy of Madge Marlatt*

This promotion ad reminded advertisers that "women are the purchasing agents for the whole family."

Continued on Page Two

The Sun's Daily Tatler column titillated readers with the comings and goings of the city's movers and shakers.

Talk of the town

Celebrity gossip had yet to dominate the cultural landscape, but even in the 1930s, it was a reader draw. *The Sun*'s June 15, 1937 debut of *The Daily Tatler* – written by staffers such as Alan Morley, Pat Terry or, as the first column noted, "able staff writers of provocative thinking" – delighted readers with insider details of the city's movers and shakers. *The Tatler*'s featurish bent was intended to leaven the harder political and business news that consumed much of the paper's content. In one *Tatler* column, reporter Doris Milligan expounded on the influx of visitors from the Prairies during the summer months and their delight in Vancouver's "soft" water. "The young stenographer here on her first visit from Regina made me realize all over again how very green is the Vancouver grass," Milligan wrote.

The column would evolve over the years, its successors including Jack Scott's *Our Town*, Jack Wasserman's *After Dark*, Denny Boyd's self-named column and Malcolm Parry's *Town Talk*.

More than 10,000 men, women and children gathered for a "sympathy meeting" at the Powell Street Grounds (now Oppenheimer Park) in June 1938 after protesters were evicted from the federal post office by police. *Vancouver Sun*

About 2,000 women marched past Georgia and Pender in downtown Vancouver on behalf of relief camp strikers in April 1935. *Vancouver Sun*

The Great Depression goes postal

With B.C.'s relief bill topping $8 million, and continuing unrest among the jobless, an estimated 1,500 unemployed men peacefully occupied the federal post office, the Hotel Georgia and the Vancouver Art Gallery for a month in the late spring of 1938, demanding help from all levels of government. Throughout the occupation, *Sun* reporters and photographers recorded the action from the inside. The front page of *The Sun* on May 21 featured four photographs across the top of the page, taken by staff cameramen Syd Williamson and W.B. Shelly, showing occupiers sleeping underneath stamp wickets, playing cards to pass the time and critiquing the paintings in the gallery.

Sun stories throughout the sit-ins detailed Ottawa's refusal to be moved by the appeal for more financial aid, and documented the growing demand from citizens and city officials to address, and resolve, the situation. Even as the premier and city mayor vowed not to tolerate the action, Vancouver police decided not to intervene. But pressure grew to end the occupation and, at 4:30 a.m. on Sunday, June 19, the "sit-downers" were evicted in a police sweep that devolved into a bloody skirmish with officers wielding tear gas and clubs.

The eviction prompted the protesters to take their frustration to the streets of downtown Vancouver, leaving smashed windows and damaged property in their wake. The destruction was later estimated at $30,000. When it was over, at 1:30 a.m. the next day, 37 occupiers and five police constables had been hospitalized with injuries.

The Sun's June 20 front page mirrored the melee, with pictures of occupants breaking windows to get fresh air while their leader, Steve Brodie, was "hustled from the scene." In support of the protesters, a crowd of more than 10,000 Vancouverites converged later that day on the Powell Street Grounds. Inside the paper, along with dozens of stories, was a banner photograph of the thousands of hat-topped men and women mingling with hundreds of roughed-up protesters at the "Sympathy Meeting."

Brodie, recovering in hospital from head wounds, talked to *Sun* reporter James Dyer about being beaten, but thanked RCMP Chief Foster for trying to ease the tension, noting that "Chief Foster sure is a white man," the

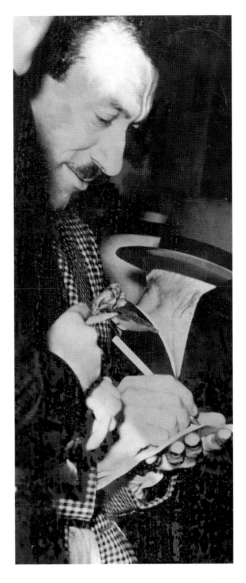

Columnist Bob Bouchette takes notes while on assignment in May 1938. *Vancouver Sun*

inference being that police understood and respected the protesters' intent even while being obliged to uphold the public peace.

An editorial noted that "This is Canada's Problem," and was sympathetic to the protesters, placing most of the blame on government: "First of all, these men must eat. Next, they must be given an opportunity to become self-supporting. If ever government had a purpose beyond the preservation of law and order, that purpose is to see that its people are given the right to food and shelter and productive work."

The riot was one of several *The Sun* would cover over the century, each a stunning contradiction of the west coast's modern image as that of a laid-back lotus land. History confirms it has been anything but, and the Depression-wracked post office occupation was just one of many shameful public brawls that would stain the city's reputation over the years. From the general strikes in 1918 and 1919 to the environmental protests and Gastown riot of the 1970s to the numerous hockey and football riots to the Occupy Vancouver protests in late 2011, Vancouver's peaceful facade has long belied a simmering undercurrent of unrest.

Saying goodbye to Bob Bouchette

In June 1938, one of *The Sun*'s favourite voices was stilled with the death of Bob Bouchette, who wrote the column *Lend Me Your Ears*. Bouchette was the conscience of the working man, and used his daily dais to urge reform in areas such as unemployment and poverty. Like many hard-driving writers of the day, Bouchette was a drinker, a rather unkempt man who was described as a "Cordova Street bum" by some of his colleagues for the bedraggled way he dressed. He always seemed to get the story, and readers loved him. Once, he was assigned to cover the Vancouver arrival of the Governor-General of Canada, Lord Bessborough, and his wife. Bouchette met them at the train station in his usual sloppy attire, but got an interview with Lady Bessborough because he was the only reporter who could speak French.

His prose married arcane parsing with empathetic first-person observations, demonstrated in the stories filed in February 1934 when *The Sun* sent Bouchette into the relief camps. In his sympathetic six-part series, he described the rampant despair and hopelessness, his work credited with changing the course of the public discussion about the men housed there. "There is no future to which these men are looking forward," wrote Bouchette. "This is why their faces are so wooden. That is why, as you drive by them on the road, they stare at you with an expression half sullen, half detached. They consider themselves outcasts from society."

In July 1934, he interviewed actor John Barrymore, whose yacht *Infanta* had stopped in Vancouver on its way to Alaska. "Barrymore, of the theatre's 'royal family,' gets so cussed tired of painting his nose for the edification of philistines that whenever the opportunity offers he goes fishin'," Bouchette wrote. "In this language, Barrymore confessed to me the faint contempt he has for his work and avowed his passion for life on the great open spaces of land and sea."

Sadly, Bouchette was widely believed to be a victim of his own depression, drowning himself June 12, 1938 in the waters off Second Beach. *The Sun*'s story of his body's recovery near the Point Atkinson lighthouse did not mention suicide, instead noting the police theory that Bouchette frequently took lone night swims and "was overcome by the chilly waters off shore."

A July 27, 1938 fire at the Canadian Steamships Pier D, at the northern foot of Granville Street, destroyed the pier, with flames reaching 60 feet.
Vancouver Sun

The world at war, again

A May 1938 headline advised readers that *The Vancouver Sun* – by now bearing the front-page slogan the "Only Evening Newspaper Owned, Controlled and Operated by Vancouver People" – would be publishing articles from a British United Press correspondent who had flown from Britain to Berlin to file "Exclusives!" from the escalating war front. The lead sentence on Webb Miller's file on May 23 noted that "Fuehrer Adolf Hitler has assured Britain that Germany has not the slightest intention of marching into Czechoslovakia."

A little over a year later came the world-shaking news: On Sept. 1, 1939, Germany invaded Poland as Hitler and the Nazis began the brutal march of fascism. Two days later, France and Britain declared war on Germany and, on Sept. 10, Canada joined the declaration.

The Vancouver Sun EXTRA edition of Sept. 3, 1939, declared in bold caps "BRITAIN AT WAR!", with a subhead "Chamberlain Tells Empire of Decision." A special report from Miller opened with: "Great Britain went to war against Germany today – 25 years and 30 days from the time she entered the conflict of 1914 against the same enemy."

One *Vancouver Sun* headline spoke to the ominous years ahead: "Two Guns to be Placed at First Narrows."

On Dec. 18, 1939, Winston Churchill announced to the world that the first wave of Canadian troops had landed on British soil. And the Canadian Daily Newspapers Association, in an advertisement published in *The Vancouver Sun*, reminded readers that newspapers are "couriers of progress providing intimate contact between the man in the street and all phases of human endeavour."

In reference to the onset of yet another deadly global conflict, its message was succinct: "The value of the service rendered by the newspaper is greater now than at any time in history."

The Vancouver Sun — EXTRA

Only Evening Newspaper Owned, Controlled and Operated by Vancouver People

FOUNDED 1886 VOL. LIII—No. 279 | OFFICIAL WEATHER FORECAST Cool, Scattered Showers | VANCOUVER, BRITISH COLUMBIA, SUNDAY, SEPTEMBER 3, 1939 | Price 5 Cents | Trinity 4111

BRITAIN AT WAR!

Ottawa Rushes Preparations

Cabinet Meets As Australia Declares War

By British United Press

CANBERRA, Sept. 4 (2:30 a.m. Monday) — Australia declared today that a state of war exists between her and Germany.

By Canadian Press

OTTAWA, Sept. 3.—Dominion cabinet ministers, aroused early by the dread but not unexpected news that Great Britain and the Empire are at war with Germany, hurried through foggy streets today to meet Prime Minister Mackenzie King in the Privy Council chamber at 10 o'clock (6 a.m. Vancouver time).

Mr. King, advised by the Canadian Press a few minutes after the flash was received that Great Britain had declared war, lost no time in communicating with his ministers, who had been warned to be ready for such an emergency.

Hon. Ian Mackenzie, minister of defense, was the first to arrive for the council. He reached the meeting at 9:45 a.m. Shortly afterwards Hon. C. D. Howe, minister of transport; Hon. Ernest Lapointe, minister of justice; Hon. J. G. Gardiner, minister of agriculture; Hon. Norman McLarty, postmaster-general, and Hon. T. A. Crerar, minister of resources, arrived.

Mr. Lapointe who, as acting Secretary of State, will have charge of any press censorship in Canada, said the cabinet has taken power to establish a censorship but could not say whether plans to put in effect have been completed.

So far, however, no censorship applies to the press and the minister declined to comment on reports of the censoring of cables and telegrams at Montreal.

It is understood, it was learned from other sources, that a subcommittee of the cabinet on censorship has been set up under the chairmanship of Mr. McLarty.

The Prime Minister appeared fresh and unworried as he entered the Council chamber after chatting for a few minutes with reporters.

He said he is not sure what procedure will be followed when Parliament meets Thursday. Whether a formal declaration of war will be made by Canada is one of the matters of detail yet to be worked out.

Only a few people watched the minister enter the East Block. A small girl with a dog on a leash played around the door as Mr. King and his colleagues began their deliberations.

As usual, Royal Canadian Mounted Policemen were on duty at the doors, but about the only other spectators were a few newspaper reporters and motion picture photographers.

All is in readiness for speedy action along whatever lines the government proposes to move now that Canada, as a partner in the British Commonwealth of Nations, stands literally if not technically at war with Germany.

It was indicated that necessary Orders-in-Council are ready for merely inking in dates and the formality of adoption to put into effect the various wartime measures which may be needed pending the meeting of Parliament Thursday.

Lord Tweedsmuir, the Governor-General, is at Government House ready to co-operate with the government in speeding orders through. No radical steps will become generally effective.

While it is accepted by all political parties and authorities that when Britain is at war Canada is at war, the actual declaration of

Please Turn to Page Two
See "Canada at War"

Churchill in Cabinet

LONDON, Sept. 3.—It was officially announced that Rt. Hon. Winston Churchill has been appointed First Lord of the Admiralty in the new war cabinet.

Today At a Glance

LONDON: Prime Minister Neville Chamberlain proclaimed by radio to the British Empire and to the world at 2:15 a.m. Vancouver time, that Britain is "at war" with Germany.

BERLIN: Germany rejected Britain's demands for withdrawal of German troops from Poland, blamed Europe's war on the British Cabinet and announced that Fuehrer Adolf Hitler today personally was taking the field of battle with Germany's eastern army. The German Army High Command announced German troops smashing deeper into Polish territory.

PARIS: France demanded a German reply to her ultimatum by 8 a.m. Vancouver time.

WASHINGTON: White House and state department officials reported that President Roosevelt and Secretary of State Hull were keeping in closest touch with European war developments. President to broadcast at 7 p.m. Vancouver time.

BUDAPEST: Hungary declared her neutrality.

WARSAW: Poland attempting to reinforce the Polish-Rumanian pact of assistance. Lithuanian troops shot down a heavy German airplane. Poland assured Lithuania that her neutrality would be respected.

MOSCOW: Soviet Russia's capital calm. Populace permitted to follow factual accounts of European events in newspapers and radio.

TOKYO. — Japan will remain neutral because of the Soviet-German non-aggression Pact, newspapers reported.

ROME: Italy, so far neutral, in accordance with Mussolini's statement that Italy will take no military initiative.

PARIS: France revealed that she considered herself at war with Germany at the moment that Prime Minister Chamberlain involved Britain in the conflict, although she was not legally at war with the Reich until the expiration of her ultimatum at 5 p.m. (8 a.m. Vancouver time).

CANBERRA, Australia. — The Australian government declares "State of War" between Australia and Germany.

EDITORIAL
Fighting For a Just Cause

You are to be proud today of your citizenship in Canada and the British Empire.

Was there ever a war so just as this one to which we are solemnly committed?

Has there ever been, in the world's history, a more noble event than for Britain and France, as they decide today, to come promptly to the relief of their ally, now in dire need of succor.

Selfish interest might have called for our two allied peoples to save their own skins, even at the sacrifice of their treaty undertakings. It is something akin to this sentiment that is relied upon by the isolationist peoples of the world today, as they seek to justify a position of aloofness.

We belong to an Empire and we belong to a breed which honors its commitments. Poland's fight, and what it stands for, is our fight today.

In Germany, the Allied Front, for what it means, will not be completely understood. The Sun has already noted that the German mistake of 1914 is being repeated 25 years later. And for the second time the lesson must be brought home to the German people. Another generation has been led away—this time by Hitler and a gang of cold-blooded adventurers who already have committed every crime of rapacity and oppression that is listed in the calendar.

In London, this noon, Mr. Chamberlain stood in his place in Britain's Parliament, as chosen head of the free people of this Empire, announced that we are at war with Germany. His was a tragic and difficult task; and we shall all of us face difficult tasks before this conflict is ended. But today we have a great satisfaction. It is that with infinite restraint and patience, we in this Empire, through our chosen leaders, have sought to intervene by every peaceful means that could be summoned to our aid. We have tried to appease and placate and advise; in every way, over a long period, we have thrown our weight and influence on the side where right is not the sole prerogative of might. We have given "last warnings" and have delayed more precious hours to allow those warnings to sink in with full effect. But Herr Hitler, holding to his record of duplicity and grab, has chosen to go unheeding the other way.

Thus, we have arrived, sadly but still firm in resolve, at today's fateful decision. We shall have no fear of the outcome. That is not the British way. It is a part of the propaganda of the Hitler-Stalin ideal that the democratic way of living is to be swept aside for that nameless shambles of ruthlessness and disorder which has reduced the peoples of Germany and Russia to practical serfdom. Don't be fooled by this nonsense! We are facing days of personal worry and national trial, but the calmness and common-sense of mankind will ultimately prevail. There shall be no other end.

Again we say we have a just cause and a clear national conscience. Last Sunday, the clergy of Vancouver and other cities in our land led the people in prayers that we might be delivered from the horror and suffering of another war. Today, we shall devoutly pray again for guidance and for victory over the evil forces which stalk through the world, seeking to ruin the liberty and decent way of life of mankind.

WAR BULLETINS

MOSCOW, Sept. 3. — The appointment of a new Soviet military attache to Berlin was announced today in line with Soviet Russia's swiftly changing foreign policy. The new appointee is M. A. Purkaieff.

BUDAPEST, Sept. 3. — Proclaiming a state of emergency, the Hungarian Government today issued decrees drastically limiting civil rights.

LONDON, Sept. 3.—The air-raid precaution animals committee attempted to call a halt today on the destruction of pet dogs and cats by owners wishing to save them from a more brutal death by bombing. The committee said it had made arrangements for the emergency care of animals.

Please Turn to Page Four
See "Bulletins"

World Radio Broadcast By The King at 9 a.m.

By British United Press

LONDON, Sept. 3.—The British Broadcasting Corporation announced that the King will address his subjects in a world-wide broadcast at 6 p.m., London summer time (9 a.m. Vancouver time).

The King and Queen heard Prime Minister Chamberlain's war declaration over the radio in their private apartments at Buckingham Palace.

NEW YORK, Sept. 3.—The American network broadcasting companies announced that they would rebroadcast a radio address of the King to the Empire at 9 a.m. Vancouver time.

Poland Invades Germany

Counter-Attack Sweeps Over Border Into East Prussia

By EDWARD BEATTIE Jr.
By British United Press
Special to The Vancouver Sun

WARSAW, Sept. 3.—Polish troops have entered Germany.

Polish troops, counter-attacking, crossed into East Prussia in the vicinity of Deutscheylau.

East Prussia is the province of Germany separated from Germany proper by the Polish Corridor.

The Poles are attempting to cut off the German army which has advanced south into the Corridor from East Prussia, has reached the Cze River, about 20 miles south of the southeast corner of East Prussia and is trying to contact the German army driving across the Corridor from West Prussia.

The Polish radio also announced the recapture of Zbaszyn, a town due west of Warsaw on the German frontier in the province of Pznania.

TOWN FALLS

The Polish spokesman confirmed that the army from West Prussia has taken the town of Sepolno, on the west side of the Corridor and that the eastern army has captured Zbaszyn and Myztniec on the southern border of East Prussia. Poles, not expecting an attack, had not been at the border to protect them, he said.

The spokesman said that the town of Wielun had been practically burned out by a "deluge" of incendiary bombs dropped from German planes.

There is heavy fighting along the border of the Polish district of Czestochowa.

(Berlin said German troops had taken that important industrial city.)

CITIES BOMBED

An official communique early today said that 12 hours after Poland had accepted a German proposal that both refrain from bombing open cities, German bombers had showered death and destruction on "not less than 24" Polish cities, killing and wounding 1500 persons.

Germany approached Poland through the Netherlands government Friday night, the communique said. Poland accepted at once. Saturday German bombers raided from dawn until dusk, it added.

"The German government Friday night contacted Poland through an intermediary, the Netherlands government, with a proposal not to bomb open cities," the communique said.

"The Polish government declared its agreement. Nevertheless, German fliers, on Sept. 2, bombed not less than 24 cities, including such a holy city as Czestochowa, which is entirely in flames, the textile centre of Lodz, the bath resort of Busco, and many others, causing not less than 1500 deaths and wounding."

HOSPITAL DESTROYED

A spokesman said that incendiary bombs dropped by German planes had destroyed the hospital at Velunje on Friday, and Saturday air raids on Lublin killed 30 persons, including five children, and injured 58. News of new bomb victims was arriving hourly.

The German Embassy staff is

Please Turn to Page Two
See "Fighting"

Chamberlain Tells Empire of Decision

France Joins in Declaration Against Germany; Prime Minister Predicts 'A Liberated Europe and Hitlerism Destroyed'

By WEBB MILLER
Special to The Vancouver Sun
Copyright, 1939, by British United Press

LONDON, Sept. 3.—Great Britain went to war against Germany today—25 years and 30 days from the time she entered the conflict of 1914 against the same enemy.

A brief announcement by Prime Minister Neville Chamberlain that went by radio to all outposts of the Empire sent Britain to war in fulfillment of her pledge to help Poland if that nation was invaded by Adolf Hitler's Nazis.

The French government set its deadline at 5 p.m. (8 a.m. Vancouver time) but announced from Paris that France considered herself automatically at war with Germany the moment Chamberlain made his pronouncement.

"This country is at war with Germany," Chamberlain said in slow, measured tones. "You can imagine what a bitter blow this is to me that all my long struggle to win peace has failed."

A radio hook-up to all places under the Union Jack was made and Chamberlain stepped to the microphone in No. 10 Downing Street to speak the fateful words.

"We have a clear conscience," declared the Prime Minister. "We have done all that any country could do to establish peace, but the situation has become intolerable, and we have resolved to finish it.

"Now may God bless you all and may He defend the right, for it is evil things that we shall be fighting against — force, bad faith, injustice, oppression and persecution. Against them, I am certain, the right will prevail."

"God Save the King" was played on the BBC's Empire hook-up as Chamberlain concluded.

Wounded Polish Airman Battles 12 Nazi Planes

WARSAW, Sept. 3. — Lieutenant Pausiniski of the Polish Air Force was hailed in Warsaw today as an early hero of the war.

Taking off in a combat plane, Pausinski attacked a squadron of 12 German bombers. He shot down one of the attacking planes after a thrilling dogfight, witnessed by thousands of residents of Warsaw.

Several bullets fired by the German planes struck Pasinski's plane, damaging its wings and wounding the Polish flier.

Despite his wounds and the dangerous condition of his plane he made a successful landing from an altitude of about 2500 feet.

'Russia Will Be Neutral'

MOSCOW, Sept. 3. — (5:30 p.m.). Foreign circles today are convinced that Soviet Russia will remain neutral in the new European war, but there was no official comment on Britain's declaration that a state of war exists between the United Kingdom and Germany.

It was unofficially reported, however, that service has been suspended on eight principal domestic airlines.

Throng in Downing Street

The curbstones of Downing Street were thronged as Chamberlain spoke. Cabinet ministers and important members of Parliament hurried to the Prime Minister's residence. Soon the entire south side of Downing Street was crowded with men and women waiting to be told that they were at war.

France, committed to the same stand as Britain in regard to the defense of Polish sovereignty, is expected to go to war, too.

An ultimatum, calling for a reply by Germany to Britain's demand that the Reich withdraw troops from Poland, was the technical step that committed the British to war. A government communique announced that unless such a reply was forthcoming by 11 a.m. (2 a.m. Vancouver time) today a state of war would exist.

The German reply did not arrive before the deadline.

Half an hour before the deadline set in the British ultimatum expired the German embassy here still was waiting word from Berlin.

"There is no news," the German embassy announced as the clock crawled toward war. "We are in constant communication with Berlin."

Apparently there was no slackening in Germany's invasion of Poland. Warsaw said there had been 1500 casualties from German air raiders. The Poles fought back and claimed that their troops had penetrated East Prussia, the isolated piece of Germany that is cut off by the Polish Corridor.

War Machine Moves

Great Britain moved quickly to set her war machine moving. The King convened the Privy Council at 11:45 a.m. (3:45 a.m. Vancouver time) to announce that a State of War exists.

The House of Commons passed the National Service Bill under which the government can conscript all men between the ages of 18 and 41 for military service.

Instructions regarding air raid warnings went out over the British Broadcasting Company system.

The formal notification that Germany must reply by 11 a.m. was delivered in Berlin by Sir Nevile Henderson, British Ambassador. He delivered that notification at 9 a.m.

Please Turn to Page Two See "Britain at War"

MR. CHAMBERLAIN: "Now may God bless you all and may He defend the right, for it is evil things that we shall be fighting against—force, bad faith, injustice, oppression and persecution. Against them, I am certain, the right will prevail."

The Vancouver Sun published an Extra edition on Sept. 3, 1939, reporting Britain's entry into the Second World War.

THE **1940s**

The 1940s: From world war to circulation war

In the spring of 1940, as Winston Churchill was installed as the new prime minister of Great Britain and hailed by the world press as "Britain's answer to Nazis," The Vancouver Sun was chronicling the efforts of the allied forces and the impact the Second World War was having around the planet and on those left at home – as it would do for much of the decade. It would be a heady time for the broadsheet. Some of its most renowned writers were dispatched to cover local news, including deadly floods and underworld crime, while the next generation of the Cromie newspaper family, Don, would take the publisher's reins and begin a campaign to woo female readers. By the end of the decade, The Sun would overtake the rival Province for circulation supremacy.

ABOVE: Newsboys hawk *The Sun*'s special Peace issue on Aug. 14, 1945. *Vancouver Sun*

PRECEDING PAGE: Reporter Pierre Berton garnered worldwide attention for *The Sun* in 1947 with the Headless Valley Expedition. Berton and his "band of intrepid explorers" – photographer Art Jones, pilot Russ Baker and mechanic Ed Hanratty – set out to investigate stories of lost miners and hidden riches in a tropical valley in B.C.'s far northwest. *The Sun* received a special award from the International News Service for the series, which INS called "the greatest real life adventure story since the end of the war." *Vancouver Sun*

With even more frequency than during the First World War, when the telegraph enabled newspapers to utilize war correspondents for the first time, members of the media reported from the front lines of the Second World War. One former *Sun* employee, Lieut. M.M. "Mickey" Dean (left, on the vehicle), joined the campaign as a cameraman with the Canadian Film and Photo Unit. He worked with driver Charlie Ross of Calgary and Lieut. G.A. Cooper of Ottawa, with Dean and Cooper shooting many pictures of Canadian troops in action in France. *Canadian Army*

Call to action

Among its many historic front pages, there are few as powerful as *The Vancouver Sun* edition of May 13, 1940, the stolid Gothic typeface of the paper's nameplate lending an appropriate air of solemnity in reporting Churchill's famous call-to-arms speech, the theatrical "blood, toil, tears and sweat" entreaty that galvanized the world and strongly declared Britain's intent toward Germany, promising "victory at all costs . . . for without victory, there is no survival."

The clarion call, reprinted under photographs of British tanks rolling into Belgium, was unremitting: "Our policy is to wage war by sea, land and air with all our might, with all the strength God can give us and wage war against tyranny never surpassed in the dark, lamentable catalogue of human crime. We have before us many long months of struggle and suffering. I have nothing to offer but blood, toil, tears and sweat."

The Sun also announced that the British army had rolled into Belgium, its 1,500 tanks "in hot battle," and that 23-year-old Royal Air Force pilot officer Barry Morgan-Dean was missing in action, believed to be Vancouver's first casualty of the war. A telegram sent to his home on West 39th Avenue stated: "Regret to inform you that your son is missing, believed to have lost his life as the result of air operations on May 12, 1940."

An editorial the following day praised Churchill's aggressive leadership, but lamented that "there are many bitter months, and maybe years, ahead."

It was an insightful observation, as the war would rage for five more years, turning *The Sun* into a heavy-hearted daily record of the devastating toll being exacted thousands of miles away, and of the country's – and the newspaper's – patriotic obligation to support the war effort.

'The Japanese problem'

When the Japanese bombed the U.S. Navy's Pacific fleet at Pearl Harbor on Dec. 7, 1941, the escalating global conflict took a new turn: war had come to the Pacific.

The toll in the Honolulu harbour was high: more than 2,400 servicemen had been killed, another 1,282 wounded. Eight battleships were lost as well as 188 aircraft. Japanese casualties were not as severe: 29 aircraft, five submarines and 65 servicemen reportedly killed or wounded.

The Sun's Dec. 8 editorial was lengthy, and gloomy: "If the Japanese sought to startle the world on Sunday, they certainly succeeded. If they attempted to intimidate the United States, Britain, Canada or any other democracy, they lamentably failed."

Another Dec. 8 story headlined "Jap Bombs Shocked U.S. Into Sudden and Bitter Discovery" – written by reporter Bruce Hutchison, who would eventually become the paper's editor and, later, editor emeritus – highlighted the politically incorrect nomenclature of the day. "Jap" and "Japs" were terms used in most *Sun* headlines throughout the war, as much a nod to discriminatory description as to the need for headline brevity.

After the bombing of Pearl Harbor, life became difficult for Japanese living and working in B.C.

Local Japanese merchants watched their business fall off, while insurance companies cancelled policies as Japanese-owned stores suffered broken windows and arson attacks. Mills, factories and even the CPR fired Japanese employees. More than 1,000 Japanese-owned fishing boats were impounded, Japanese

Before they were shipped to internment camps, Japanese-Canadian men were housed dormitory-style in May 1942 in the Forum Building at the Pacific National Exhibition. *Leonard Frank, Vancouver Public Library 14918*

newspapers were forced to close and Japanese schools were shut down by the provincial government. Vancouver's famed Asahi baseball team, founded in 1914, played its final game in September 1941.

The *Sun*'s front pages for Jan. 12 and 14, 1942 said it all: "Conservatives Demand Japs Be Moved 'East of Rockies'" and "Japs, All Enemy Aliens, to Move From Defense Zones; Whites to Run Fish Fleet."

In the spring of 1942, more than 20,000 Japanese Canadians were sent to a transit centre at the PNE grounds, part of a six-month removal campaign that forced anyone of Japanese ancestry to leave behind their homes and possessions, which were auctioned off without hope of compensation for the owners. From there, the displaced travelled by train to internment camps in B.C.'s interior, and farther east, for the duration of the war. Throughout, *The Sun*'s editorialists urged the federal government to focus its military defence on the country's west coast. A Jan. 30, 1942 front-page editorial noted that "as a result of Japanese victories, the coast of British Columbia becomes a vital defense zone which may well suffer attack in one form or another before the allies recover naval supremacy in the Far East." Hutchison, reporting from Ottawa in the same paper, wrote that "Premier King will soon reply

to British Columbia demands in a statement on the Japanese problem."

Handing the reins to a new generation

As *The Vancouver Sun* dutifully reported on battles both overseas and on the civic front, internally there were changes afoot.

In 1942, Don Cromie succeeded his late father as publisher of The Vancouver Sun, a post he would hold for the next 22 years. He was lured from Toronto by his brother Samuel, who reportedly was unhappy with the way the paper had been run since their father's death in 1936. While the family still owned the paper, and Cromie's widow Bernadette had stayed involved as a figurehead, P.J. Salter and a consortium of caretakers had been making all the decisions. Samuel, facing a stint in the air force, convinced Don the paper once again needed a Cromie at the helm.

So the 26-year-old came home, taking up the position of managing editor and then assuming the publisher's post. Circulation of *The Vancouver Sun* was somewhat stagnant at the time – at 76,000, it had only increased by 6,000 since Robert Cromie's death.

Don Cromie was an instinctive newsman, and was not only known about town for his demanding editorial standards and his roll-up-the-sleeves work ethic, but for his sartorial style. He favoured fedoras, corduroy suits, flashy ties and loud sweaters and was lauded as a hands-on boss who regularly held meetings with his editors and reporters to brainstorm on stories.

At one of those meetings, Jack Brooks, a Fleet Street veteran and one-time *Sun* city editor, was asked by Cromie about the paper's response should an atomic bomb be dropped on Vancouver. Brooks looked at his watch, cocked an ear to the floor to ensure the presses were still rolling, and said: "I think I can get a few lines in the buff," which was the nickname given to the peachy-coloured front page denoting the day's final edition.

Cromie, like his father, was also rather eccentric in his habits. He was a slender man with an odd diet, consuming hamburgers one minute and a handful of candies the next. He was a world traveller, an accomplished golfer and a devoted smoker who was always trying to quit. And while one *Sun* profile had him professing to favour the simple life, he lived in a 14-room Shaughnessy mansion and owned a yacht. *Sun* managing editor Erwin Swangard once described him as a man who "doesn't think of himself as rich. He considers himself a

The nuclear family, circa 1946: A father, mother and daughter read various sections of *The Vancouver Sun*. *Vancouver Public Library 26937*

This Dec. 9, 1941 masthead informed readers of the wartime blackout status.

poor man, with money."

The new publisher occasionally wrote stories for the paper, but mostly took pride in letting his columnists and reporters do their work without much interference. In a 1946 speech at *The Sun*'s annual staff banquet, he told his employees: "In *The Sun* I try to exercise sufficiently little authority on policy so as to encourage the greatest number of people here to seek themselves the best answers to daily problems challenging a newspaper." In that same speech, Cromie acknowledged that while his paper often supported government, it was also "vigorously criticizing its errors."

That the paper was Cromie's pride and joy is evident in a letter he wrote on March 23, 1944, typed in blue ink and addressed to The Shareholders of Sun Holdings Ltd. Tucked into an envelope scrawled with the handwritten message "Deliver to Shareholders of Sun Holdings in event of D.C. Cromie's untimely demise," the letter begins, "In case I get killed while I am away, here are a few suggestions which might be useful." It goes on to note that his brother Sam, "if he can be released from the RCAF," should be appointed president and publisher, and also details the problematic conflicting politics of the various senior managers. Cromie signs off by ensuring shareholders his estate is "in good shape" and "the company is in good condition, and should any question of sale arise, or any necessity for it, it shouldn't be because of lack of money."

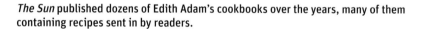

The Sun published dozens of Edith Adam's cookbooks over the years, many of them containing recipes sent in by readers.

A newspaper's war effort

The Sun's new leader had returned to a city bustling with war-time activity. Not only were local industries working non-stop for the war effort, but everyday reminders for citizens included regular air-raid and evacuation drills, commando practices on Kitsilano Beach, food and supply rationing, and the brisk sale of gas masks. Blackouts were common and often occurred without warning, prompting a run on retailers for items such as flashlights, window coverings, batteries, tar paper, wall board and black fabric.

The Sun was in war mode, too, much as it had been during the First World War. Its wire correspondents, editorials and breaking news provided readers with a daily parade of politics and sad casualties, an endless page count from the front lines supplemented with hopeful stories of government initiatives and war efforts across Canada and around the province.

The Sun was openly boosterish in its editorials, publishing advertisements urging readers to buy war bonds and promoting newspaper-sponsored grassroots programs such as the annual Sun Victory Garden contest. In a *Sun* story on Aug. 27, 1942, bylined "By The Garden Man," it was reported that the third annual contest's $25 first prize had been awarded to Mr. E. A. Percival at 242 East Fifty-Fourth for his vegetable-growing efforts to help "fill the nation's food basket."

In 1943, *The Vancouver Sun*'s Junior Victory Army club, with its specially designed winged insignia, provided weekly in-paper tutelage on the history of wartime aviation. In conjunction with the Canadian Armed Forces, the club encouraged young readers to help produce thousands of model "spotter" planes for military training purposes, providing printed templates for its members to build the paper planes. In what might have been an early iteration of the paper's successful Newspaper In Education program decades later, writers of the JVA column also reached out to the province's teachers to "assist this important movement," the result being a successful cross-Canada promotion.

The Sun Veterans' Bureau was another example of the paper's commitment to community, and to its war-time responsibilities. The bureau opened in 1945, offering free counselling, pension and rehabilitation information to soldiers and their families affected by both world wars. The "bureau" was actually room 1103 of the Sun Tower and operated under the direction of *Sun* staffer and war veteran Charles Defieux.

Leavening the weighty war coverage and lightening the city's collective mood was also an imperative. The Sun Salmon Derby, based

A strike by the International Typographical Union shut down *The Province* for six weeks in 1946, a blow from which the paper would never recover. When the paper's owner attempted to publish with non-union staff, striking workers attacked delivery trucks. *The Sun* picked up 35,000 *Province* subscribers during the strike, and kept them. *Vancouver Sun*

out of Sewell's Marina in Horseshoe Bay, continued to attract thousands to local waters every summer, most of them recreational anglers vying for an assortment of prizes. On the paper's funny pages were puzzles like *Kwiz Korner* and *Cranium Crackers*, the horoscopes and columns about babies and pets, alongside comic strips such as *Li'l Abner, Joe Palooka, Red Ryder, Little Annie Rooney, Alley Oop* and *Donald Duck*.

The Sun Walking Marathon, which found hundreds of locals ambling around Stanley Park, was a hint of the fitness craze that would grip the city decades later and lead to *The Sun*'s wildly successful 10-kilometre, family-oriented, annual Vancouver Sun Run.

Signing up The Newspaper Guild

Heading into the 1940s, a cheerless newsroom mini-revolt was afoot.

Reporters like Mamie Moloney were part of a group of employees that began meeting regularly to discuss working conditions. At that time, reporters and editors were paid different rates, with female writers the lowest on the compensatory totem pole; at one point, Moloney's $75 a week had been arbitrarily cut to $60. There was no regulation of working hours, with some shifts lasting twice as long as the now-standard eight hours, and there was certainly no such

thing as overtime pay. Moloney would recall in later interviews that those meetings ultimately led to talk of a union and the formation of The Newspaper Guild, which signed its first contract with *The Sun* in 1941. Some employees welcomed the move, while others groused about its interference with journalistic professionalism. There was no question, however, that the union's incursion into *The Vancouver Sun* newsroom would ultimately shape the paper's future, a good-news, bad-news reality that saw employee salaries and benefits rise to among the most generous in the profession while also leading to crippling labour disputes that many would blame for the newspaper's future financial misfortunes.

Darkness on the world front

On D-Day, the allied forces moved into Normandy and began pushing across Europe.

The Sun's June 6, 1944 front page, in red ink, screamed INVASION!, and a subhead provided the stark details: "11,000 Planes, 4000 Ships Strike, Allies Win Beachhead in France."

The announcement brought a surge in sales of government Victory bonds, but the Vancouver Stock Exchange suffered, bottoming out at 11 million shares. Sun headlines over the next months would serve up a daily cauldron of stark statistics, blitzkrieg battle cries and military machinations.

A couple of characters

In a newsroom famous for its characters, Himie Koshevoy was a standout of the era, hired in 1942 by managing editor Hal Straight from his sports editor job at the News-Herald. The gnomish, garrulous new assistant city editor – who would work his way up to managing editor, twice – was renowned as the newsroom's king of puns, coming up with headline bon mots like Eire Today and Guam Tomorrow, and even wrote a book showcasing his talent, A Treasure Jest of Best Puns, in 1969.

On Nov. 1, 1944, Straight hired a new recruit, by telegram, to be Koshevoy's $22-a-week assistant. Simma Holt, however, had other ambitions and would soon become a news reporter, one of only three women in the Sun editorial department covering hard news at the time (along with Doris Milligan and court reporter Mae Garnett). But it was a slow start, and Holt spent the first few years tracking down stories of local war casualties, checking with emergency services and occasionally taking dictation from other reporters in the field. In a 1994 piece for a Sun reunion publication, Holt recounted that one of the first journalistic lessons she learned came courtesy of Koshevoy, who read a story she had written and then showed it to Straight, who walked over to Holt and said: "Great story. Good work. Now get the hell out and find the other side." When she did, the story evaporated.

Holt's colourful Sun career included the time she stomped over to city desker Jack Scott to loudly complain that her story had been altered by the deletion of three essential words: By Simma Holt. When Scott fled to the men's washroom, Holt followed him, stood on the toilet in the next stall and smacked him on the head.

Straight had his own mini-dynasty at The Sun. He had come to the paper, via UBC, as a sports editor in 1933, and would do two terms as Sun managing editor, from 1942 to 1948 and 1951 to 1957, spending the interim as publisher of the Edmonton Bulletin. In the mid-1940s, he hired his brother Lee as The Sun's outdoor columnist. At a time when hunting and fishing were favoured recreational pursuits, Lee's tales of hunting pheasant on the Prairies and tuna fishing in Cuba, his coverage of the Sun

The A1 headline on the extra edition published June 6, 1944 delivered the historic news: The allies had successfully invaded Normandy.

Salmon Derby, and his dedication to preserving the province's natural environment attracted a loyal readership for many years – so loyal that to keep his stories afloat The Sun provided him with two boats, a 20-foot runabout called the Sunfisher and an aluminum skiff called the Tinfisher.

Also working alongside Straight and Koshevoy was Pierre Berton, who in January 1946 had been toiling at the News-Herald when he was conscripted to The Sun as a $45-a-week assistant city editor.

Berton's greatest legacy in his brief time at The Sun was his expedition to the so-called Headless Valley in northern B.C. in 1947, continuing a long Sun tradition of regaling readers with the stories told by prospectors of

mysterious gold rush legends. The series filed by Berton and Sun photographer Art Jones made headlines around the world, even though Berton reported it was just "another lonely valley." But the story continued to intrigue: In 1971, Sun reporter Moira Farrow was assigned to cover the British military expedition to the Headless Valley – led by a real noble, Sir Ranulph Twistleton Wykeham-Fiennes – and also had to report to readers that the explorers were surprised to discover that the Nahanni valley was neither as mysterious, dangerous nor as remote as they had been led to believe by previous Sun stories.

It was, as Berton would describe in a first-person recollection a year later, an era when newspaper writing was not only breathless, but

While life in the newsroom could be complicated, there were also fun times. On May 26, 1948, *The Sun*'s editorial department was joined by four-year-old Shirley, a baby circus elephant. *Vancouver Sun*

cliche-ridden.

"People never fell out of windows or off cliffs. They hurtled or plummeted. They didn't jump; they plunged. Fires were mystery blazes . . . thugs and yeggs never hit people; they slugged or bludgeoned."

When Berton left the paper later in 1947, jumping ship to *Maclean's* magazine and a stellar career as the pre-eminent author of historical Canadiana books, the newsroom threw a wild party and sent Berton and his wife off in style, strapped into straitjackets in the back of an ambulance.

The end of war; the beginning of peace

As publisher, Don Cromie was trying to boost *The Sun*'s profile and its support of the war with regular speaking engagements, continuing a practice that had begun with his gregarious father, Robert. In an address to the Vancouver Board of Trade in June 1944, following a visit to Britain where he had spoken with Lord Beaverbrook, Cromie suggested the war would "strengthen Canada's international position" and, even though the conflict was untenable and citizens were growing weary, "they will never stop until they get what they are fighting for."

There had been hints, however, that the war might soon be ending. *The Sun*'s final edition on April 30, 1945, had a two-line, above-the-nameplate headline that read: "Nazi Surrender Expected Shortly." It was published in red ink, on pink newsprint. The next day's front page brought the news: "ADOLF HITLER DEAD."

And then, on May 7, 1945, early morning air raid sirens signalled VE Day: Victory in Europe. *The Sun*'s front page, under the boldface headline "GERMANY SURRENDERS," featured a whimsical photo illustration of a mother dreaming of reuniting her young son with his father, a returning soldier. The main story, datelined out of London, told readers: "It was announced officially today that Germany has surrendered unconditionally to Britain, the United States and Russia."

The allied campaign moved its focus to the Japanese front and, on Aug. 14, 1945, VJ Day, the Japanese surrendered.

The Second World War was truly over, and *Vancouver Sun* newsboys hit the streets hawking copies of the PEACE edition, with banner headlines and details of the allied victories.

One of those carriers was Dorothy Cassels Wiebe, who as a young girl delivered *The Sun* with her brother in White Rock, and who as an adult recalled the excitement of VE Day: "The presses had been running through the night, and our driver arrived with papers around 6 a.m. when we were still fast asleep. We were up, dressed and running in short order. Imagine — a hundred papers and the town still asleep. As we ran along the streets shouting, "VE Day! Read all about it!" doors were opened as pajama-clad citizens rushed out to buy papers."

A new victor in the circulation wars

After decades as the perennial bridesmaid in a market where *The Province* had always been the bride, *The Vancouver Sun* suddenly found itself winning the Vancouver daily circulation war.

In what has long been considered the turning point in the relationship between the two broadsheets, a typographer union's strike shut down *The Province* for six weeks in 1946. *The Sun*, taking advantage of its foe's absence, continued to publish through the dispute, and *The Sun*'s advertising manager hired extra telephone salespeople to capture *The Province*'s classified business – the want ads at the time being the lucrative backbone of a newspaper's revenue. Even an attempt by owner Southam to publish the paper with non-union staff backfired, prompting an uncivilized push back from striking workers, as delivery trucks were vandalized and the paper was branded anti-union. *The Sun* converted 35,000 *Province* subscribers and would keep them.

When the strike was declared illegal by the B.C. Supreme Court, *The Province*'s rocky return to publication, hampered by continued internal labour unrest and advertising boycotts, included an extensive editorial and advertising campaign to restore its dominance. But the strike was a blow from which *The Province* would never recover. In March 1946, *Province* circulation was 124,000 compared with 98,000 for *The Sun*; by September 1947, the numbers were reversed. *The Province* had fallen to 92,000, while *The Sun* was at 124,000, a telling and lasting reversal of fortunes between the rivals.

The strike, and its debilitating denouement for *The Province,* would pave the way for the merging of the two evening broadsheets into a cost-effective shared operating agreement the following decade.

Through it all, *The Sun* continued to add to its stable of writers, every new hire sending a message to readers – and competitors – that the once second-place broadsheet was now the dominant paper in the market.

In a July 1948 *Maclean's* magazine article titled *Vancouver's Rising Sun*, Pierre Berton wrote of *The Sun*'s brand of journalism as "racy, hard-hitting, ruggedly independent and highly irreverent," lauding the Cromie family for three decades of leadership that had transformed the once-scrappy little paper into the fifth largest daily in the country (behind the *Toronto Star, Montreal La Presse,* the Toronto-based *Globe and Mail* and the *Toronto Telegram*). *The Sun* was doing so well, Berton noted, that it "had to throw away a page and a half of want ads three times a week."

Cromie's hands-off relationship with his three left-wing columnists was one reason for *The Sun*'s success, even when the opinions of Elmore Philpott, Mamie Moloney and Jack Scott differed from the paper's. Scott's column, in fact, had a "built-in editorial denial," according to

The Sun's Extra edition on Aug. 14, 1945 announced the surrender of Japan and the end of the Second World War.

Berton, who also related several stories of legendary newsroom shenanigans, like the time a *Sun* photographer was given a cash bonus for hiring a steamroller to block a road and thus prevent a rival *Province* photographer from getting the same news shot.

The Jacks of the trade

Among the newsroom recruits in the 1940s were two of the three Jacks (Scott, Webster and Wasserman) who would come to personify *The Sun*'s renown for attracting journalistic talent.

The Fleet Street-trained Jack Webster was a blustery young reporter from Glasgow when he joined *The Sun* newsroom. "When I walked into

The Sun in my bare feet as an immigrant from Britain in 1947," Webster wrote in a *Sun* reunion special in 1994, "it was like walking into a set from *The Front Page*. It was a great place. We would go to any extent to beat *The Province*."

His beat was Vancouver *noir*, where bootleggers and brothels and ne'er-do-wells ruled the night, the kind of Vancouver most readers could only imagine. In the fall of 1948, editors put Webster on a special assignment; he lived in a seedy downtown hotel for two weeks, "cutting himself off from normal associations and pursuits," and emerged to write a series of four articles on what he called the city's "underworld." Under the Sept. 8, 1948 front-page headline "Gambling Rise in City Sun Probe Discloses," Webster wrote that "Vancouver, city of police

Jack Scott endeared himself to readers with his popular Our Town column, which took him on varied assignments that included flying the new light aircraft Ercoupe in December 1946. *Vancouver Sun*

purges, is still wide open for gamblers, book-makers and bootleggers . . . Bookmakers, their employees, touts and runners, operate in beer parlors, cigar stores, hotel lounges, taxi offices and what amounts to open betting halls."

Webster sat in on poker games and inter-viewed players in gambling dens all over the city, describing desperate people, from sailors to doctors, losing thousands while the lucky ones were making a princely living – as much as $1,000 a week. In another story in the se-ries, he reported that in the dozens of illegal "booze lounges" around the city, "bootleg liquor is almost as easy to buy in 'dry' Vancouver as a package of cigarettes."

Webster's gritty reporting and larger-than-life personality were the hallmarks of the tough-newsie reputation that would follow him from *The Sun* to open-line radio in 1953 and then on to a celebrated television news career trade-marked by his heavily accented signature line: "9 a.m., precisely!"

Another *Sun* star of the era was Jack Scott, a *News-Herald* transplant and master storyteller whose tenure would also include his elevation to various editor positions. But it was Scott's

five-day-a-week column, *Our Town*, that would be his legacy, endearing him to readers for a dozen years with its quixotic mix of institution-bashing and stylish profiles of average folks. A Feb. 27, 1947 *Our Town* offering unravelled the fascinating narrative of a local inventor named Arthur Brooks, who designed skis on wheels, built a "gyrochute" out of biscuit tins and who, wrote Scott, "had a brooding look about him which may be explained by his feeling that peo-ple steal his ideas."

Scott was also left largely unbothered by his bosses, who encouraged his occasional swipes at his own paper (he hated all the *Sun* contests, for one thing), and rewarded his carefree in-subordination by sending him off to file stories from around the world. Scott's witty reportorial take on life ended when Cromie appointed him editorial director of the paper in the 1950s, lur-ing him with the promise that he could spend $2,000 a month however he liked. Scott used the money to pursue his journalistic bugbears, assigning other writers to the most interesting stories he could conjure up – like sending the fashion editor Marie Moreau to Cuba to inter-view Fidel Castro.

Calling all women

Nowhere was *The Sun*'s effort to woo female readers throughout the 1940s more apparent than in the newly opened Edith Adams Cottage, a demonstration kitchen staffed by home econ-omists that began operating in March 1947 out of the Sun Tower at 510 Beatty, trading on the popularity of the well-read Edith Adams column in the women's pages.

The storefront, with its inviting colonial door-way, included a suite of rooms decorated in turquoise and coral with bleached mahogany furniture. The cooking lessons and free domes-tic advice attracted thousands of local house-wives wanting to brush up on their kitchen skills and learn new ways to stretch a dollar. One popular macaroni and cheese dish was called the Oriental, and taught dozens of eager home cooks how to dress up basic comfort food by simply adding broccoli.

The newspaper's weekly food sections were also jammed with pages of sweet and savory recipes, along with food advertisements and household tips. Readers couldn't seem to get enough. A 1947 *Sun* recipe contest attracted more than 1,000 entries for the $500 prize, with contenders such as salal jelly, clam foo foo and squab casserole, while another "Vacation From Marriage" contest was the talk of the town, sending one lucky local housewife to Hollywood for a week-long hobnob with the stars.

The Sun's food coverage, with its constant culinary offerings and weekly words of encouragement for busy housewives, created a useful yet homey interaction with female readers that was not only a sign of the times, but would prove a cherished *Sun* legacy.

Or, as one promotional ad, featuring a beaming housewife tackling *The Sun*'s food ads with a sharpened pencil, touted: "*The Sun*'s Cookery Pages save me money and effort and benefit my family."

Springing into action

If *The Sun* newsroom was a rowdy riot of roguish personalities, it was also a case study in how a seasoned team of journalists could adroitly respond to a breaking news story.

The disastrous May 1948 Fraser Valley floods, which saw the Fraser River overflow its banks for the second time in 50 years, was a primer on newspaper disaster coverage. The floods claimed 10 lives, thousands of homes, and caused more than $20 million in damage, wiping out roads, bridges and railways, and cutting the city off from the rest of the country for days. The state of emergency marshalled 3,000 troops and thousands of locals, working around the clock to fill sandbags and hold back the rising waters.

It was the type of event that would dominate the paper for days. Editors scrambled night and day to coordinate coverage and provide readers with all the details of the floods and the ruinous fallout. "Women Ordered To Leave Flood-Invaded Agassiz" was the May 27 headline, explaining that amid the loss of electrical power and the flooding of schools and homes, local men were losing their battle to hold back the swollen river.

The paper published hundreds of stories and photographs filed by a rotation of *Sun* staffers who trudged to the ravaged sites to witness breaking dykes, flooding acreage and residents fleeing their homes in boats. Stories were filed from the field and copy was taken over the phone, although the severity of the situation made it unlikely that the reporters calling in greeted the clerk answering the city desk phone with the traditional and playful, "Hello, Sweetheart, Get Me Rewrite."

Edith Adams' Cottage (note the ever-changing spelling and punctuation) opened its storefront in the Sun Tower in 1947.
Vancouver Public Library 82863

The devastating Fraser Valley floods of 1948 didn't stop *Sun* carriers like John Follett, who waded through water with his stack of papers in the Milner-Fort Langley area on June 5. *The Sun* used private airlines, navy rescue boats, trucks, railways and Red Cross services to ensure the papers made their way to subscribers. *Vancouver Sun*

The Fraser Valley floods of 1948, including this June 3 photo of the Hatzic Lake dyke break, killed 10 people and caused more than $20 million in damage. *Dave Buchan/Vancouver Sun*

THIS IS AN
EMERGENCY

Disaster Has Struck British Columbia

THOUSANDS ARE HOMELESS...
DWELLINGS WRECKED...
FARMLANDS RUINED...

...The Fruits of Years of Toil
Swept Away by Swirling Floods

You may not be able to work on the dykes, but you can help succour the stricken!

$1,000,000

IS NEEDED URGENTLY
for vital emergency relief!

DIG DEEP, BRITISH COLUMBIA
— YOU KNOW THE NEED!

Send your Cheque, Money Order or Cash
TODAY...NOW!

To Your Local FLOOD EMERGENCY COMMITTEE
Your Newspaper, Bank or Direct to
THE ROYAL TRUST CO.
626 West Pender Street, Vancouver

This advertisement donated by The Vancouver Sun

The Vancouver Sun tried to help flood victims by donating advertising space for this notice, encouraging readers to help raise $1 million in emergency relief.

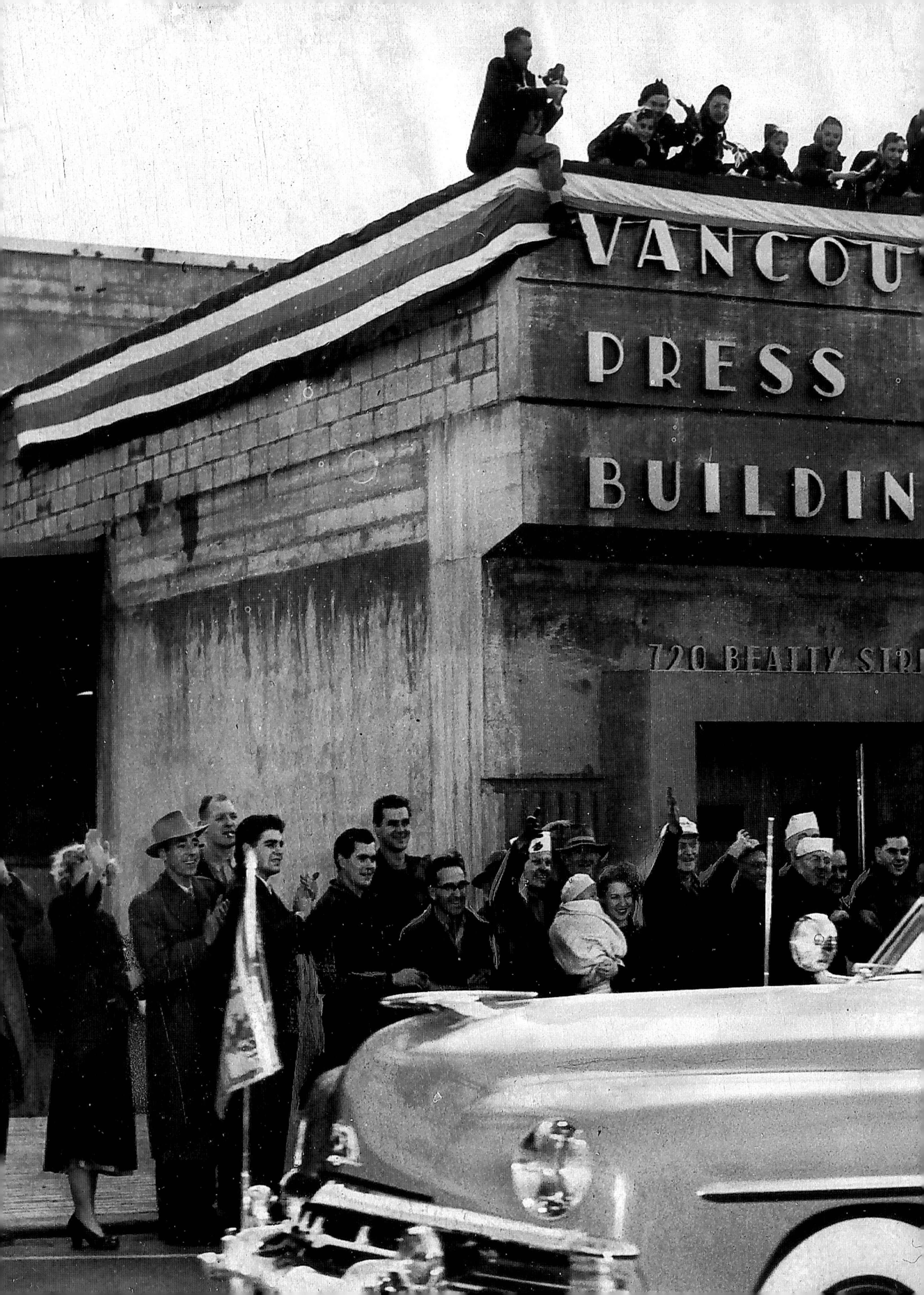
VANCOU
PRESS
BUILDIN
720 BEATTY ST

THE 1950s

The 1950s: Boom time for a city and its newspaper

Propelled by a robust post-war economy, Vancouver and its residents headed into the 1950s on a wave of optimism. New stucco bungalows began lining city streets, television took over the living rooms of readers and icons like Elvis Presley were defining a bold pop culture. The exodus of the exploding population into the suburbs saw the creation of instant bedroom communities and a rush to build infrastructure and services, especially south of the Fraser in Surrey and Richmond, and east into Burnaby and Coquitlam.

The post-war baby boom was on its way to becoming one of the world's most profound demographic phenomena, and with the unprecedented growth in the region, The Vancouver Sun set about extending its reach, appealing to readers with more and more coverage related to the home front.

ABOVE: *The Vancouver Sun* published a special supplement on television on May 27, 1953, providing advice on reception and offering tips on viewership, including how far away one should sit from the new-fangled set.

PRECEDING PAGE: The motorcade of Princess Elizabeth and Prince Philip travels past *The Vancouver Sun* printing plant at 720 Beatty Street on Oct. 22, 1951. Note the retouching grease pencil marks on the photo. *Harry Filion/Vancouver Sun*

Tickling the funny bone

Among the mid-century changes at *The Vancouver Sun*, in what would prove to be a decade of much change, was the introduction to the paper's daily funny pages of the comic strip *Pogo*, cartoonist Walt Kelly's sardonic and sophisticated take on politics and the vagaries of human nature.

While Kelly was busy skewering sacred cows with his sharp-tongued swamp menagerie, fellow cartoonist Charles Schulz was starting to craft his softer societal take with his pint-size bumbler, Charlie Brown, a beagle named Snoopy and the charming cast of characters that populated *Peanuts*, the strip that over the years would become *Sun* readers' all-time favourite.

Also leavening *The Sun*'s more serious content were the new artistic musings of local cartoonist Len Norris, whose whimsical observations of Vancouver life – especially in tony British-tinged West Vancouver, which he called Tiddlycove – strayed from the overt political symbolism common to satirists.

Norris's wry humour depicted the average citizen's reaction to the news of the day and would become a mainstay of *The Sun*'s editorial page until his retirement in 1988. He won many awards over his 38-year reign, including a coveted National Newspaper Award in 1951. Norris would be joined a dozen years later by the venerated Roy Peterson, whose sharp-edged brilliance would win a record seven NNAs for *The Sun*, earn him an Order of Canada and cement the paper's reputation as the home of two of the country's greatest editorial cartoonists.

The Vancouver Sun: A woman's place

The 1950s was the era of the housewife, and for many of *The Sun*'s 150,000-plus subscribers, columnist Penny Wise – who was actually reporter Evelyn Caldwell – was a must-read, dispensing homey tips and introducing amateur cooks to such gastronomic exotica as the Caesar salad.

Caldwell's aspirations were initially not of the domestic goddess variety, but her newspaper career - which began in 1928 at the *Vancouver Morning Star* and would last from 1945 to 1974 with *The Sun* - reflected how difficult it was for women like herself, Mamie Moloney and Doris Milligan to be respected as hard news reporters in the early days, to escape editor-imposed "ghettoization" in the society pages.

When managing editor Hal Straight hired Caldwell, he immediately wanted her to take over the Penny Wise column, but she resisted and managed to cover a few murders before he noticed and exiled her to the consumer beat. She initially wrote six Penny Wise columns a week, reducing the number to five after discovering Jack Wasserman only wrote five a week.

"Mostly, I wrote about vegetables," she said in a 1989 *Sun* interview commemorating her 80th birthday, nine years before her death.

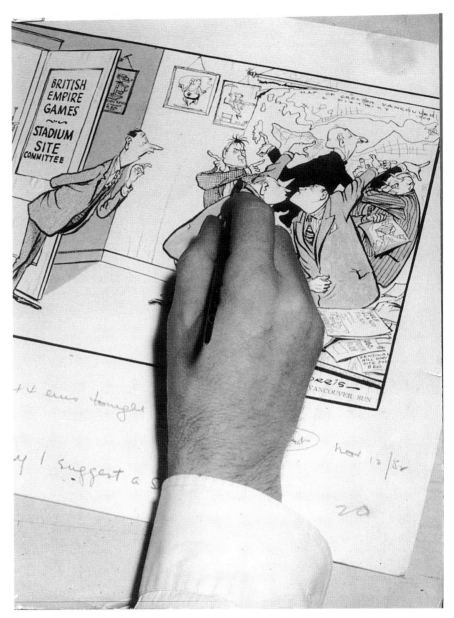

Cartoonist Len Norris works on an editorial cartoon in November 1952 about the British Empire Games stadium site committee. *Vancouver Sun*

"That's what the man who did the column before me wrote about so that's what I did, too. Then one day my editor called me in and asked me what on earth I was doing and told me just to write whatever I wanted."

And so she did.

Readers loved her and the paper began sending her all over the world. She called her fans the FFFers, for Feminine Fighting Force, and frequently engaged them in letter-writing campaigns to change consumer laws, such as the ban on margarine in B.C. When it was decided that Penny Wise would go to Moscow and file dispatches from behind the Red Curtain, *The Sun* published a photograph of Caldwell packing her red nightie for the trip.

A July 1951 *Time* magazine article – headlined "The Press: Girls Meet Boys" – noted another Caldwell assignment: "Pert, brunette Evelyn Caldwell, 42, who writes the Penny Wise shopping column for *The Vancouver Sun* (circ. 161,603), got a chance two months ago at a free air trip to Australia. When she asked *Sun* publisher Don Cromie for permission to go, Cromie, thinking of the local soldiers fighting overseas in the Korean War, meditatively twirled the globe on his desk. 'You know,' he said, 'Korea is only about four inches from Australia. You'd better drop in there and see how our boys are making out.'"

And so she did.

"Evelyn had a tremendous following," Moloney recalled in the same 1989 interview. "Nothing fazed her. I remember her washing her hair in a soldier's helmet in Korea. The soldiers loved her. And they'd visit her when they came back."

The Penny Wise column was truly the forerunner for modern-day consumer reporting, and her popularity paved the way for future *Sun* columnists like Nicole Parton. The paper's so-called women's pages were also the first to really engage readers, to employ the news-you-can-use ethic, something that would become

Vancouver Sun lifestyles editor Marie Moreau made flipping pancakes look easy in October 1957, but if you look closely, you'll notice she had a little help: the pancake is tied to a string. *Henry Tregillas/Vancouver Sun*

standard practice for newspapers decades later. When *The Sun* brought Hollywood gossip columnist Hedda Hopper to town to speak at a *Sun* fashion and beauty clinic, hundreds showed up to absorb her wisdom. A 1952 *Sun* feature series by "cover girl, model, actress, film star and business executive" Anita Colby, entitled Beauty You, was advertised for "feminine readers" as a "four-weeks' course in self-improvement."

Despite their contribution to circulation numbers, it wasn't unusual for newspapers to pay women less than men, especially men with families, and to limit their duties – although things

were slowly changing through the 1950s, following *The Sun*'s signing of a Newspaper Guild contract.

Reporter and future Canadian senator Pat Carney, who joined *The Sun*'s business section in the mid-1950s after a stint at *The Province*, recalled in a 1994 *Sun* reunion publication called *The Fabulous '50s* that a city editor once told her she couldn't work the graveyard shift because she was married, and a mother. To discourage her, he sent her out to fetch a photograph of a four-year-old victim of a traffic accident from the child's grieving parents. It didn't work. Another editor was furious she

hadn't told him she was pregnant when the paper hired her. She told him she hadn't known, but he didn't believe her and she would be given just five weeks maternity leave.

If equality had yet to hit the newsroom, it was no less so in the real world. A 1950 *Sun* front page, noting the three recipients of UBC law school scholarships were women, headlined its story "3 Girls Top Law Exams" and opened with this quote from one of the women: "It should do us a bit of good after what the men students said about us." On the same page: a story about the awarding of four *Sun* carrier scholarships, all to young men.

Penny Wise – who in real life was reporter Evelyn Caldwell – visits the B.C. Lions training camp in Courtenay in July 1961. *Brian Kent/Vancouver Sun*

Before she entered politics, Pat Carney – shown here in 1958 – worked as a reporter at *The Sun*. *Vancouver Sun*

Entertaining the masses

While *The Sun* was earnestly engaged in keeping readers in the know on the Korean War, it was also reporting on less-serious slices of life. On the big screen, movies like *Harvey, Oklahoma* and *Hamlet* were attracting record audiences, while youngsters were heading to local movie houses like the Fraser Theatre to take in the Saturday matinee of Disney's *Cinderella*.

The 1950s saw a shift in the Vancouver entertainment scene when impresario Hugh Pickett took over Famous Artists and became responsible for booking the big touring acts: Louis Armstrong played Exhibition Garden and Kitsilano high school, while Duke Ellington appeared at the Palomar. A downtown nightclub, the Smilin' Buddha Cabaret, opened with a dazzling neon sign.

To keep on top of the arts action, *The Sun* launched *Week-End* in September 1951. The 48-page, features-heavy, entertainment magazine was published in conjunction with *The Toronto Telegram, The Montreal Star* and *The Montreal Standard*. It effectively boosted circulation of the section to 800,000, quadrupling regular Saturday sales.

There was much to fill *Week-End*. Dick Clark and *American Bandstand* were rocking Saturday mornings and Vancouver deejay Red Robinson was rocking radio around the clock with the likes of Bill Haley and the Comets, who would star in the city's first rock concert, in 1956 at Kerrisdale Arena, attended by 6,000 and described by *Sun* reviewer Stanley Bligh as "the ultimate in musical depravity."

Long live her majesty

British Columbians were feeling the love for royalty when, on Oct. 20, 1951, Princess Elizabeth and Prince Philip visited Vancouver. *The Sun*, under the headline "Hail to Their Royal Highnesses," featured a full-page photograph

World weightlifting champion Doug Hepburn showed off his skills in 1954 by lifting members of the Vancouver Canucks.
Roy LeBlanc/Vancouver Sun

This house ad, published Sept. 9, 1952, extolled the many virtues of *The Vancouver Sun*.

A *Sun* memento, requested by Prince Philip, had already been sent to Buckingham Palace: the original version of a Len Norris cartoon cheekily implying that if the Duke of Edinburgh wanted to get a decent seat at the upcoming British Empire Games in Vancouver, he should sign up for the high hurdles.

On May 28, *The Sun* reproduced the letter to the paper from Buckingham Palace and the Duke's private secretary on its front page: "His Royal Highness has asked me to enquire whether it would be possible for him to purchase the original. I should be most grateful if you could let me know about this."

It's all about us

From day one, *The Vancouver Sun* had never been shy about reminding readers they were getting their money's worth – seven cents for 48-plus pages in the '50s – and publisher Don Cromie ensured the regular publication of promotional ads about the paper's high-profile writers and their gripping stories. One 1950s series included numerous full-page promos that boasted the paper was "read and enjoyed by two out of every three Greater Vancouver families" and that its content, with sports reporters like Erwin Swangard, Pat Slattery and Hal Straight, was the best in town. Its three "globe-girdling services" – British United Press, Associated Press and Canadian Press – along with world wire photos and local coverage was "daily proof that a newspaper, like people, does not have to be dull to be good." Editors lived up to the promise. *The Sun*'s average front page held at least a dozen stories, ranging from world news and weather predictions to court trials and light-hearted features about girls and their puppies.

The paper also regularly published photographs of staffers and editors out in the community, doing their jobs or interacting with readers in contests and presentations.

As if to drive home the point, a 1954 editorial page noted *The Sun* "owned and operated by Vancouver People, Is a Newspaper Devoted to Progress and Democracy, Tolerance and Freedom of Thought."

The unsolved case of the Babes in the Woods

Crime stories have always sold newspapers, and if tabloids were becoming notorious for larding their pages with societal dysfunction, broadsheets like *The Vancouver Sun* were just as quick to satisfy the seemingly insatiable public appetite for lurid details. In January 1953, a mysterious murder case hit *The Sun*'s front page, a sign that the newspaper's genetic predisposition for crime reporting was as entrenched as ever.

The Jan. 15, page-one headline read: "Two Mystery Skeletons Found By Workmen in

of the royal motorcade taken from the fourth floor of the Marine Building, 15 minutes after a 21-gun salute.

Inside the *Sunday Sun* were dozens of pictures of the couple attending various events on the tour. One colourful story noted: "A thunderous, heartfelt cry of welcome welled up from 300,000 throats today and echoed across the city as a beautiful, smiling Princess, the most beloved in all the world, took Vancouver by storm."

Local businesses such as Eaton's and Birks bought newspaper ads expressing their affection for her highness and, in keeping with the princess theme, *The Sun*'s Women Today section reported on local debutante "princesses"

making their society debut at the Trafalgar Ball. Penny Wise wrote of the travails of press photographers, who required the "stamina of a wrestler to get close to the Royal Couple."

Two years later, on June 2, 1953, the world was transfixed on Britain for Elizabeth's coronation.

"Millions in London For Coronation Day," headlined the May 30th *Sun*, which told readers that "every feature of the greatest spectacle of our age will be reported by *The Sun*'s special staff of famous writers," including wire writers such as Churchill's son, Randolph, and *The Sun*'s Harold Weir, an authority on the Commonwealth and the "only Vancouver newspaperman with a seat in the Abbey."

A photo of the courtroom during the Royal Commission inquiry into the Vancouver Police Department before commissioner Reginald H. Tupper in 1955. Disgraced police chief Walter Mulligan is seated on the lower left. *Bill Dennett/Vancouver Sun.*

Stanley Park." The story reported that the remains of two children had been found lying feet to feet, covered with a woman's coat. Nearby was a small rusty hatchet, a lunch bucket and, on top of the skull of one of the skeletons, a boy's aviator-style helmet. Readers were both horrified and transfixed as the tale unfolded, as the news came from the coroner that the victims were a boy and a girl. It was widely believed the unknown mother had committed the murders, but the case was never solved, and the story would fade and reappear over the years. The Babes were back in the news in 1998, when DNA tests indicated the victims were both boys. On its 50th anniversary, retired police sergeant Brian Honeybourn told *The Sun* the case still haunted him, so much so that when he found the children's bones on display at the Vancouver Police Museum in the 1990s, he had them cremated and gave the children a burial at sea off Kitsilano Point, presided over by a police chaplain. Vancouver author Timothy Taylor resurrected the mystery in his 2001 bestseller, *Stanley Park.*

The corruption of a police chief

When tough-fisted Walter Mulligan took over the VPD in 1947, the new chief vowed to rid the city of bookies and bootleggers and tackle the twin evils of crime and drug use. Gambling dens and graft abounded, and the big confident cop

vowed to sweep the town clean.

In 1955, Mulligan was hit by his own tawdry scandal, as he and members of his force were accused of accepting bribes from bootleggers. *The Sun*, along with *The Province*, had been doing its own long-time investigation but had held back on breaking the story, nervous about libel laws and the involvement of various community leaders in alleged illegal activity.

Hints at the widespread corruption had been published, however, including a May 7, 1952 Jack Wasserman column in *The Sun* that noted: "Loud howls of 'foul' are echoing up from the depths of lower Pender Street lately. Seems that a pair of uniformed beat constables, not unaffectionately dubbed 'Hawkeye' and 'Gorgeous' by the Hootch Who, have taken a hand in the after-dark liquor trade."

Editors determined the whole story was simply too hot to handle, until *Province* reporter Ray Munro, who had uncovered much of the incriminating evidence, quit the paper and published his expose in a Toronto tabloid called *Flash.*

The media frenzy was under way.

Mulligan immediately filed a lawsuit against Munro and the paper and, the day after the *Flash* story appeared, VPD detective Sgt. Len Cuthbert, who had been implicated in the news reports, tried unsuccessfully to kill himself. That afternoon's *Vancouver Sun* ran the headline "Detective Shoots Self, Mulligan Reported Out in Police Crisis" above *Sun* photographer Bill Dennett's graphic photo of Cuthbert being rushed to hospital.

The scandal prompted the Tupper Inquiry, a sweeping probe of the VPD that exposed details of widespread police corruption, including Mulligan's involvement. In the middle of the imbroglio, which lasted nearly a year and seldom fell off the front page, police superintendent Harry Whelan committed suicide rather than take the witness stand. Mulligan was eventually fired, his downfall immortalized in a book, *The Mulligan Affair*, written by *The Sun*'s Ian Macdonald and Betty O'Keefe of *The Province.*

The race of the century

For a city that had been captivated by crime, the British Empire Games provided a timely distraction. The Games opened July 30, 1954 in the new, purpose-built, Empire Stadium at Hastings Park, the $2-million pet project of mayor Fred Hume and the biggest sporting stadium in the country. Lord Alexander of Tunis was on hand for the opening ceremony, as was U.S. politician Adlai Stevenson, as 29,350 spectators and 652 athletes from 24 countries were treated to celebratory cannon fire.

It was a two-week sporting spectacle unlike anything Vancouver had ever seen, especially on Aug. 7 when the eyes of the world were focused on the much-anticipated foot race between Britain's Roger Bannister and Australia's John Landy. The 'Miracle Mile' saw both men break the four-minute mark – the first time two men had done so in the same race – with Bannister edging Landy in a thrilling finish.

The Vancouver Sun

TAtlow 7141   36 PAGES   BRITISH COLUMBIA, MONDAY, AUGUST 9, 1954   FINAL ★★★C

TODAY'S TIDES: Low 9:35 p.m., 11.6 feet. Sun sets, 8:38 p.m. TUESDAY'S TIDES: High 1:27 a.m., 12.7 feet; low 9:27 a.m., 3.7 feet; high 5:25 p.m., 13.5 feet; low 10:26 p.m., 11.4 feet.

BANNISTER'S, LA___S OWN STORIES

EXCLUSIVE—'How I Beat Landy'

FIGHTING ON HEART ALONE... A STORY OF SHEER COURAGE

Agonizing steps of England's heroic marathoner Jim Peters as he lurched to entrance of BEG stadium Saturday shocked crowd of 35,000. He was in coma and running on heart alone.—Don LeBlanc photo.

Painful struggle down the stretch in front of 35,000 horrified spectators went on for 15 minutes as Peters battled pain and exhaustion to reach the finish line.—Hux Lovely photo.

Pleading with his team-mate to get up and finish is shot-put champion John Savidge. Also urging on the tragic Peters is English team manager Leslie Truelove (left).—Don LeBlanc photo.

Act of disqualification came when Nicky Mayse, English team masseur, grabbed Peters as he crossed regular finish line. Marathon finish was further around track. (Story page 15.)—Brian Kent photo.

Landy Had Stitched Foot

Accident to Australian in Village Hut Revealed Today

John Landy ran the Miracle Mile Saturday with four stitches in the sole of his right foot, it was reported today.

He suffered the gash on Thursday night in an Empire Village hut by stepping on a photographer's flash bulb "while engaging in a bit of horseplay," according to Andy O'Brien, sports editor of The Vancouver Sun Weekend Magazine.

O'Brien learned of the accident Friday but held it back on Landy's request. He didn't want it used as an alibi. Today O'Brien released the news with apologies to Landy but said, "I believe the sports fans of the world agree it should be told."

At Empire Village today, Landy said there was "nothing to the report."

★ ★ ★

English marathoner Jim Peters, whose race thrilled and horrified the Games' crowd Saturday, is in fair shape today, but reports from London said he received such a setback from Saturday's strain that he has withdrawn from this month's European championships.

★ ★ ★

Awesome spectacle of Peters' heart-breaking marathon finish drew tears from a hard-bitten Life photographer. Calgary newsman Gordon Hunter was sick at his stomach. Women wept.

★ ★ ★

Dr. Roger Bannister himself said Peters should have been taken off the track sooner. "It's like throwing Christians to the lions," he said.

★ ★ ★

British newspapers were in an uproar today over the "ridiculous" marathon. Some registered horror that Peters hadn't been stopped sooner. Others, recalling a similar marathon finish in the 1908 Olympics in London, scored running of this gruelling race over tough course at the hottest part of the day.

Bannister and Les Truelove, Peters' coach, both visited the exhausted marathoner, Jim Peters, today in Shaughnessy Hospital.

When Peters staggered into the stadium Life photographer Ralph Morse, leaving with a load of film for special BEG Life edition, dropped everything to shoot the dramatic finish.

The Duke of Edinburgh was shocked by the Englishman's straining attempts. He turned away several times with a grim expression on his face.

★ ★ ★

What does a man do the day after winning the Miracle Mile? Bannister was reported mountain climbing, believe it or not. Landy, though the fresher at the race's finish, slept late Sunday.

★ ★ ★

Miracle milers won't meet again, despite attempts by U.S. and European promoters to stage such an event. Landy says he's going to concentrate on two and three-mile races, and Bannister, soon to start training for the European Games 1500 metres, says it would take too much effort.

FULL GAMES RECORD FOUND IN TODAY'S SUN

The record-breaking British Empire Games are recorded in full in eight pages of today's Sun.

Pictures of the historic fifth Games may be found on Pages 10, 11, 12 and 13. Stories of the historic events are on Pages 14, 15, 16 and 17.

Last person in the stadium to realize that England's Roger Bannister had taken the lead 90 yards from the tape was Australia's John Landy who at that moment glanced over left shoulder to see where Bannister was. Bannister is making his famed "kick" which took him on to five-yard victory.—Charlie Warner photo.

VANCOUVER'S Only HOME-OWNED NEWSPAPER

'Landy Ran Too Fast'

All According to Plan, Says Winner Bannister

Exclusive stories by England's Dr. Roger Bannister and Australia's John Landy were recorded verbatim on tape at the finish of the world's greatest mile race by Jack Webster of Station 600. Webster presented the milers' stories to The Vancouver Sun for publication. Here for the first time Dr. Bannister reveals the strategy he devised to win the Miracle Mile.

As Told by DR. ROGER BANNISTER

I had breakfast at 7:15. I tried to bring my day forward by an hour. That's an hour earlier than I usually run.

So I got up at 7, had breakfast at 7.15, went for three-quarters of an hour's walk and then I just rested, then I had a little bit of lunch at 10:30. For lunch I had a few slices of bread, tomato and a bit of honey. I think, that was all, except a glass of orange juice.

You only need glucose if you are attempting to recover rapidly from a race you've just run. Other forms of carbohydrates are rapidly converted into glucose and as I hadn't had a race for a few days, since the heats, I knew that I would have plenty of sugar.

Dangerous Backstretch

I felt I had the race by the last corner. I felt that Landy was tiring. I knew that he would expect me when I got into the straight and so I deliberately did my trick a few yards earlier while I was on the bend.

I noticed that he looked on the inside hoping to see me behind him and at that moment I was going around on the outside.

Q: (It all went according to plan?)

A: Yes. I thought he would run a bit too fast for the first two laps and so I was a little bit anxious to have to let him go by 15 to 20 yards.

It's a terrifying experience to let a man get so far ahead, but I let him go.

I thought that the overall time wouldn't be faster than 3:59 and so I reckoned that a 1:57.8 half was too fast for me. That was why I allowed that gap to open up, then closed it when I thought he was slowing. And I think that my race was more evenly run than his.

I know what the times of my laps where. They were 1:59.5, 2:58, I think, and then a last lap. I'm not sure about the three-quarter time.

I know that there was a

Please Turn to Page Two
See "He Let"

Chadwick Fails But Wants to Try Again

Cold water and racing tides in the Strait of Juan de Fuca today defeated Florence Chadwick five hours after she had started her 18-mile swim from Victoria to Port Angeles, Wash.

The famed swimmer announced she is considering a further attempt on the formidable channel August 11, when she will start the dangerous feat at about 3 p.m. instead of the chillier 4:45 a.m. when she stepped into the icy water today.

Miss Chadwick's sponsors said she will get the full $10,000 prize.

BARRY MATHER ON PAGE 2

One of sport history's most iconic photographs was snapped by *The Sun*'s Charlie Warner on the last lap of the showdown, showing Bannister on Landy's right, passing him as Landy glanced to his left. The photo would be the inspiration for a bronze sculpture by Vancouver artist Jack Harman, who more than a decade later would be working on a controversial piece for *The Sun*'s new home.

In Warner's oft-repeated accounting of the photograph, for which he used a "battered" 4x5-inch Speed Graphic camera with a standard 50mm lens, he recalled his decision to take the shot away from the finish-line crowd of "hundreds of sweating, shoving, champing-at-the-bit photographers, mostly from the east coast, U.S. and overseas.

"I had no desire to merge with the herd, so I sauntered off, heading track-side some distance from the finish line. An eerie silence settled over Empire Stadium as the classic confrontation began. John Landy, considered the faster runner but known to lack a finishing burst, easily held the lead for almost three laps. He hoped to increase the gap between him and Roger Bannister and minimize his opponent's well-known finishing kick. My limited equipment and single-negative format meant I had time to fire off only one shot each time the sprinters passed by. As perspiration beaded on my forehead, my face remained almost frozen to the camera viewfinder while watching every move the combatants made. Each time they hurtled past, I tripped a single exposure.

"Bannister persisted and tightened the gap in the fourth lap. Approaching my location, he caught up and began passing Landy. At that moment Landy inexplicably glanced over his shoulder looking for his opponent. He didn't spot him, because at that instant Bannister strode past on his right side. I had seen Landy making his controversial head movement and luck was on my side. I had captured the climactic image on film."

It was *the* photograph of the Games, reproduced countless times. But it would also become a bone of contention between Warner and *Sun* management, as Warner claimed he took the photo on his own time, with his own equipment, and therefore owned the copyright – and thus the right to all future income from its re-publication. It ignited an internecine dispute that simmers to this day, highlighting the thorny issue of newspaper copyright, which in the age of the Internet has become even more blurred in the rush to re-purpose original work online, often without benefit of attribution or recompense.

Who gets to cover what and why

Sun reporter Stu McNeill, a Canadian Army 100-yard sprint champion in Europe during the war, was originally assigned to cover the Bannister/Landy matchup at the Empire

Games. McNeill was known for enjoying a taste of the grape and, a week before the event, he was spotted leaving a lacrosse game he'd been covering at Kerrisdale Arena, madly waving around $20 bills while trying to hail a taxi, or anyone, to give him a ride. Sports editor Erwin Swangard was not amused with his behaviour, and demoted him to covering archery and badminton, while giving the marquee track assignment to cub reporter Allan Fotheringham. The decision prompted McNeill to trash a number of newsroom typewriters by throwing them against the columns that held up the Sun Tower, thus ensuring he would be the least likely candidate to cover the B.C. Lions when the new Canadian Football League franchise kicked off its history at Empire Stadium a month after the Games, on Aug. 28, 1954, with By Bailey scoring the team's first touchdown in an 8-6 loss to Winnipeg.

Get your freebies here

Vancouver was not only getting bigger but was becoming an increasingly expensive place to live, especially given the price of housing, a topic that would become a perennial *Sun* story. The rising costs of land, labour and lumber in the 1950s meant the average Vancouver-area resident was hard-pressed to buy a lot and build a house for less than $15,000, considerably more than even a decade previously.

But if you were a *Sun* subscriber, you were in luck, as the paper tried to soften the economic blow for families by offering dozens of free

programs and services.

The Sun Free Salmon Derby, the Sun Soccer Rose Bowl and the Sun Free Ski School were only a few of the paper's community outreach offerings, many of them sports-focused. The Ski School, for instance, ran for eight years and saw 8,000 *Sun*-sponsored youngsters hit the slopes of Grouse Mountain (which was owned by the Cromie family in the 1950s). The Sun Free Swim Classes, launched in 1932, and lasting 42 years, taught 274,000 swimmers aged four to 16 to tread water and do the breaststroke in pools all over the Lower Mainland, from North Vancouver to Ladner, from Trout Lake to Lumbermen's Arch.

The annual Salmon Derby, which was launched in 1937 and taken over by *The Sun* in 1941, was a fisherman's dream, with upwards of 4,000 boats and 10,000 anglers hitting waters off Horseshoe Bay and vying for the top prize of an Evinrude-powered Sangstercraft boat.

Sun sports writer Eaton Howitt wrote of being a fishing newbie when, in the 1953 Sun Salmon Derby, he was sent to cover the action. His light-hearted story told of fellow scribes Lee Straight and Pat Slattery entertaining the crowds, and of the tired hopefuls pulling into the dock at day's end, many of them empty-handed. The average winning fish in those days, when the fishing industry was robust and salmon were still plentiful in coastal waters, was in the 30-pound range.

The hugely popular derby was quietly shelved when salmon stocks began to decline in the 1980s.

A crowd of journalists watched the results of the 1952 election posted on a chalk board in *The Sun*'s newsroom. *Garnet Fletcher/Vancouver Sun*

The Vancouver Sun has offered numerous free programs over the years, including swimming classes at the Lumbermen's Arch swimming pool in Stanley Park. *Vancouver Sun*

Sam Cromie (left) presents a boat to Tom Hawes, winner of the Sun Salmon Derby at Horseshoe Bay in 1951. *Vancouver Sun*

Circulation wars and strange bedfellows

As more and more people settled into new housing subdivisions in places like Richmond – now linked by the modern, four-lane, Oak Street Bridge – the daily newspaper became ever more important for spreading the news, including telling readers that in a single month it had advertised 11,012 jobs.

The once-upstart *Sun* – which had steam-rolled its underdog origins with a resolute combination of aggressive reporting and celebrated writers – was also winning the daily circulation wars, posting circulation figures in 1957 at close to 200,000, while the *Province* numbers were about 120,000.

In May 1957, the two rivals decided to follow the lead of other major two-newspaper cities on the continent and merge their mechanical and financial departments, which then saw both papers being printed off the presses at

720 Beatty while the record books were managed in *The Province*'s Victory Square offices. The new operation was called Pacific Press.

An article in *Time* magazine on June 10, 1957 noted that the merger signalled a "newspaper truce" in B.C., but despite the strange bedfellows arrangement, both publishers told *Time* the circulation war was still on. "We shall continue to scoop them," Cromie said, while *Province* publisher Arthur Moscarella countered: "On practically every major news story, *The Province* has been out in front."

A subsequent Combines Investigation Act concluded the merger was illegal but, citing economic imperatives, allowed its continuation. With the change, *The Province* took over the morning market and *The Sun* maintained its strong hold on the evening. Working fathers, it seemed, still wanted their *Sun* delivered with the supper being served by stay-at-home moms, whose kitchens were fitted with the latest modern conveniences, including electric stoves and ice boxes.

The beginning of a beautiful friendship

One night in July 1957, two eager young men reported for work in the Sun Tower, sharing an elevator up to the fourth floor newsroom and, it would turn out, a lasting friendship as fellow sports reporters and columnists. Denny Boyd was 27 and had taken a 35-cent bus ride in from Burnaby to start his new job. He'd been hired away from the *Victoria Times*, where he was the sports editor, lured by *The Sun*'s princely offering of $100 a week. Archie McDonald had worked for a month as a junior cityside reporter after his second year at UBC before being transferred to the sports department. He continued to work part-time while attending university and joined *The Sun* as a full-timer when he graduated in 1959.

Boyd would later describe that first day as "going to the big time . . . What we had actually done, we had run off and joined the circus, show only his third performance outside the U.S. Emcee Red Robinson stated on the radio that, "This was the first time there was ever a performer in front of 26,000 people in a rented stadium. Sinatra, Crosby, no one ever rented stadiums before him." According to promoter Hugh Pickett, there were close to 26,000 paid admissions, with tickets going for up to $3.50.

But the superstar with the swivelling hips and smouldering eyes would manage to belt out only five songs before thousands of screaming, out-of-control fans forced him off the stage at Empire Stadium.

"They knocked the fence over and chased him, and that's when he got away," *Sun* photographer Ralph Bower reported. "They came like a herd of cattle. I was standing there and they ran right over the top of me."

Bower got the shot, of course, which commanded *The Sun*'s Sept. 3 front page, along with reviewer John Kirkwood's damning critique: "A hard, bitter core of teenage troublemakers turned Elvis Presley's one-night stand at Empire Stadium into the most disgusting exhibition of mass hysteria and lunacy this city has ever witnessed."

It's a bird. It's a plane. It's Sputnik.

In October 1957, the world witnessed the start of the space race, as the data-gathering satellite *Sputnik* was launched by the Russians, spurring a new nervousness in the Cold War era, along with an exciting new frontier of exploration.

As *Sun* columnist Allan Fotheringham would often relate the story, Cromie ordered *Sun* photographers to the top of Grouse Mountain, thinking they would be that much closer when the Russian satellite went overhead. An enterprising photographer took a photo, scratched his fingernail over the negative and presented his snapshot of *Sputnik* for publication. That story would become *Sun* legend – except it wasn't true.

The front page of the Oct. 9 *Sun* actually featured two photographs: one was taken by *Sun* shooter Ken Oakes of *Sun* photographers Dan Scott and Dennis Rowe, who, along with other spotters, were aboard a Canadian Pacific Airlines DC-3 chartered by the paper to take photos of the satellite. Reporter Tom Ardies' story noted Capt. Bob Kerr, piloting the "Satellite Special," saw "a strange object hurtle out behind a streak of cloud" at 5:28 a.m. and that it looked "just like a star." The third *Sun* photographer in the plane, Deni Eagland, also reported seeing something. The other front-page photograph, the actual *"Sputnik"* shot, was taken by Scott and showed a dark morning sky punctuated by a thin white line running across the top of the frame. In the cutline, Scott admitted he didn't know if it was *Sputnik*, while a UBC physics professor who examined the photograph expressed doubt.

Vancouver disc jockey Red Robinson spent some time with Elvis Presley before his concert at Empire Stadium on Aug. 31, 1957. *Courtesy of Red Robinson*

Commander Cromie's Flying Circus." He would later write that "Don Cromie was a quirky, impulsive, up-yours operator and his personality radiated out of every page of his sassy broadsheet." When two of Boyd's daughters met sports editor Erwin Swangard, the four-year-old looked up at her dad and said: 'Was that your master?'

Writing about his early days at the paper (he would go on to have a long and illustrious *Sun* career as a sports columnist), McDonald recalled 2 a.m. gatherings at Leonard's Cafe on Pender and Granville with Dick Beddoes – "our dapper poet laureate" – who would wax eloquent about the niceties of writing while his acolytes ate $1.55 steaks. In the newsroom, McDonald would often be dispatched to pick up burgers at the nearby White Spot for the "rim

pigs," the editors working on the newsdesk. He told of poker games that would go on until the wee hours, staff surrounded by cigarette butts and empty liquor bottles, and of the unreliable single elevator in the Sun Tower that was "like waiting for a bus. Sometimes you thought you had missed the last one."

When the King came to town

Celebrity fever struck Vancouver on Aug. 31, 1957 when singing royalty came to town. Elvis Presley arrived by train from Spokane, the second stop of a northwest concert tour shortly before the release of *Jailhouse Rock*. Presley had performed earlier in the year in Toronto and Ottawa, reportedly making the Vancouver

The collapse of the Second Narrows Bridge on June 17, 1958 was one of the worst workplace disasters in Vancouver history, killing 18 workers and a diver involved in the recovery of bodies. *Bill Dennett/Vancouver Sun*

Classified telephone operators at *The Vancouver Sun* offices in the Sun Tower in 1955. *Vic Spooner, Vancouver Public Library 82888*

Disaster on the Second Narrows

When *Sun* night editor Alex MacGillivray walked into the newsroom at 4 p.m. for the start of his shift on June 17, 1958, the place was a madhouse. The under-construction Second Narrows Bridge had collapsed as a crane was attempting to connect the north and south ends, plunging 79 men along with the twisted wreckage into the water 100 feet below.

The 26-year-old MacGillivray was assigned to coordinate the coverage and, over the next 12 hours, he dispatched reporters and photographers, edited copy and fielded calls from off-duty reporters looking to pitch in. He hired a tugboat for Jack Wasserman to get to the disaster site and made sure to keep his crew fed, ordering fish and chips for them to eat on the run.

Sun photographer Ralph Bower was on the grounds of the Pacific National Exhibition when the bridge collapsed and was the first journalist on the scene. "It was disastrous," he recalled. "Tugs going everywhere, throwing bodies on the back. It was the loudest crunch you could ever hear, that bridge coming down. Just a big crrrrraaaasshhhhh! Like a bomb going off, a bomb exploding steel. Someone yelled to me, 'Get over to that bridge!', so I zoomed over."

Eighteen workers, likely weighed down by their tool belts, drowned, as did a diver involved in the recovery of the bodies. The collapse was later blamed on a miscalculation by engineers. The bridge eventually opened in 1960 and, 34 years later, would be renamed the Ironworkers Memorial Second Narrows Bridge in honour of the 23 workers who died during its construction.

MacGillivray, with *The Sun* from 1952 through 1993, recalled it being the "jump" that got him noticed by management. He would soon work his way up the newsroom ladder, taking on responsibilities such as editorship of the Friday *Leisure* magazine before becoming assistant managing editor in 1974. In 1989, he moved to the editorial pages as associate editor. An erudite, sharply-dressed man, MacGillivray was perhaps best-known to *Sun* readers as the daily's long-time restaurant critic.

Legendary actor and comedian Bob Hope joined *The Sun* for a day as editor in May 1954. *The Sun* has brought in many guest editors over the years, including recent stints by environmentalist David Suzuki and the Dalai Lama. *Bill Dennett/Vancouver Sun*

In which Hunter S. Thompson doesn't get the story

The Sun's growing repute as a haven for great writers did not go unnoticed by Hunter S. Thompson, who would one day become a successful U.S. journalist and author but who, on Oct. 1, 1958, wrote a letter from New York to *Sun* editorial director and former columnist Jack Scott asking for a job. Admitting to Scott that he was in a "frenzy of drink," Thompson said he had read about *The Sun* in a *Time* magazine article and wanted to offer his services.

It's no surprise that both the newspaper and Scott had caught Thompson's attention, for Scott was renowned for both his talent with the

language and his love of journalistic stunts – like assigning fashion editor Marie Moreau to interview Fidel Castro in the aftermath of the Cuban revolution (she won a Canadian Press Club award for her work) and sending football writer (and former CFLer) Annis Stukus to Formosa (now Taiwan) to interview Chiang Kai-shek.

Thompson's letter included clippings and a confession that he hadn't seen *The Sun* lately and that every other editor he'd worked for had despised him, and that even though journalism was overrun with "dullards, bums and hacks, hag-ridden with myopia, apathy and complacence" he'd still like to work for *The Sun* and "unless it looks totally worthless, I'll let my offer stand."

He wasn't hired.

Swan's song

In 1959, Erwin Swangard was named managing editor of *The Sun*, presiding over stories that included the opening of Oakridge shopping centre and the Vancouver Maritime Museum, and the ribbon-cutting of Queen Elizabeth Theatre. Swangard also co-managed the opening of the first western news bureau in China, a joint undertaking by *The Sun* and the Toronto-based *Globe and Mail*. Swangard was a no-nonsense editor and when the respected Tom Ardies, a first-rate reporter who would go on to write suspense thrillers, marched into his office one day and demanded a raise "or else," Swangard told him he'd take the "or else." Ardies went back to work, *sans* raise.

Jack Wasserman died in 1977, but remains one of *The Sun*'s best-known writers. A portion of Hornby Street was named Wasserman's Beat in his honour. *Vancouver Sun*

Jack Wasserman: Man About Town

In a newsroom known for its writers, Jack Wasserman was a standout, the kind of columnist talked about with reverence long after his time at *The Sun* had ended. His beat was the night, lit by neon and thick with cigarette smoke, and his subjects were the characters who filled the downtown clubs and cafes after dark. Wasserman hit the streets at 4 p.m. and kept going until dawn, uncovering the gossipy items that were his hallmark. His office was the Hotel Georgia bar and his inside stories, as he once described, immortalized "the lifter, the grifter, the chiseler, the hoister, the gonnif, the thief, the taxi driver reading a comic strip by street lamp light, the tired waitress, the hat check girl."

Wasserman dropped out of law school to report for *The Ubyssey* and, after UBC, he began covering the cop beat for *The Sun*. His writing talent caught editors' attention when he phoned in his notes while reporting on the 1951 royal visit of Princess Elizabeth: they were published verbatim. On May 12, 1954, the bespectacled storyteller officially became *The Sun*'s man-about-town, a must-read for the next 23 years (with a brief break as a radio host) until his death from a heart attack on April 6, 1977 at the age of 50 while speaking at a roast for Gordon Gibson at the Hotel Vancouver. Wasserman was eulogized not only as a legendary "saloon reporter," but as the tough, sometimes sentimental, chronicler of Vancouver's transition from milltown to metropolis. In commemoration, a Wasserman's Beat plaque was installed on Hornby Street. His ground-breaking style would later inform the work of *Sun* columnists like Denny Boyd and Malcolm Parry.

The star and the starlet

One of Wasserman's biggest scoops was his coverage of the demise of actor Errol Flynn, who was in Vancouver on business when he collapsed and died on Oct. 14, 1959 in the West End apartment of a local doctor, and in the company of 17-year-old actress Beverly Aadland.

Wasserman's front-page accounting in the next day's *Sun* employed the characteristically embellished prose of the era: "Movie swashbuckler Errol Flynn died on the bedroom floor of a West End penthouse Wednesday while his young blonde protege desperately tried to to breathe life through his pain-twisted lips. The 50-year-old actor succumbed to a heart attack after undergoing treatment for a slipped disc in surgeon Grant Gould's apartment at 1310 Burnaby."

The headline, inexplicably, was: "Starlet Fails To Save Errol Flynn."

This photograph of the Vancouver Mounties baseball team was published on April 28, 1958, on the front page of *The Sun*'s sports section, under the headline "Vancouver's Pride and Joy." *Charlie Warner/Vancouver Sun*

No good deed ...

By decade's end, *The Sun* was thriving, with circulation topping the 200,000 mark. It was a prosperous and convivial time. Reporters and photographers worked long hours, and competition with *The Province* fostered a fierce pride in getting the story, and the photo, first. The camaraderie and success were well-rewarded; staff travelled regularly on assignment, received bonuses and attended more than a few parties, some of them even planned.

Allan Fotheringham, writing in a 1994 reunion publication titled *The Fabulous '50s*, was nostalgic about the annual Commodore Ballroom office party where fist fights were frequent and where, one year, publisher Don Cromie unveiled a huge neon sign celebrating circulation of 200,000 – and then presented circulation manager Herb Gates with a white Cadillac convertible.

There were perks, too, for the paper boys, as newspaper carriers were then considered the front line of the business and were often feted at candy-larded parties in the Sun Tower and with trips to Camp Gates on Bowen Island, a vacation spot named after their circulation boss.

THE 1960s

The 1960s: A decade of change

As the city, indeed the country, continued to revel in prosperity, The Vancouver Sun was about to face some of the most significant changes in its history. The nameplate was altered again in 1959, from The Vancouver Sun to The Sun, and the Saturday paper was dubbed The Sunday Sun for the next few years, to create the impression it was a weekend-long read. And after nearly five decades of local ownership by the respected Cromie family, the paper was sold in 1963. Two years later, it would move out of the legendary Sun Tower and into shiny new quarters on south Granville, along with a roommate, The Province. But new publisher Stuart Keate would prove a stabilizing force, and The Sun would continue to thrive, esteemed for both its writing talent and its journalistic enterprise.

ABOVE: A 1967 *Sun* fashion shoot in front of the United Kingdom building at Burrard and Georgia. *Charlie Warner/Vancouver Sun*

PRECEDING PAGE: The new home of *The Sun* and *The Province*, under the banner Pacific Press, at 2250 Granville Street, shown here in February 1966. *Vancouver Public Library 42625*

EXTRA

The Sun

EXTRA

VOL... No. 44 ... MUtual 4-7141 74 PAGES   VANCOUVER, BRITISH COLUMBIA, FRIDAY, NOV. 22, 1963   PRICE 10 CENTS

KENNEDY SHOT DEAD

Separatism Threat Clear

Canada Now Facing Its Biggest Crisis

By BRUCE HUTCHISON
First of a Series

QUEBEC CITY — No English-speaking Canadian can guess the depth, the nature or the threat of so-called Quebec separatism until he sees it here at first hand.

Separatism is not, of course, a single or coherent thing. It is many different and incoherent things, most of them misjudged outside Quebec.

But the meaning of all these things, as they fuse in practical politics, is perfectly clear—Canada now faces the largest crisis of its history.

Deaf Mutes' Dialogue

BRUCE HUTCHISON
...studies Quebec

If the crisis is to be resolved short of national disruption, each side in the present racial dialogue between deaf mutes must quickly grasp the intentions—and more than that, the emotions—of the other.

The time left to us is short. We have wasted years already in evading, denying and totally misconstruing the central problems and the interdependent interests of the two Canadian races. Now we must come to grips with these issues at the worst imaginable moment when all our energies are required to solve our non-racial economic problems.

Nov. 25 will be a decisive milestone on the long, joint march of two peoples that began on the Plains of Abraham in 1759.

Awful Truth of Duality

Next week's federal provincial conference cannot settle anything finally but it will begin to show whether any settlement is within our reach.

Meanwhile the English speaking visitor to Quebec feels, like a physical blow the awful truth of Canada's duality. Then he slowly senses the opposite forces warring within the French Canadian spirit its and threatening to split the nation.

Dimly, and very late, we fail to compromise these two Anglo-Saxons have started to opposites, as the Anglo-Saxon surmise the mixture of genius mind meets, or fails to meet, and folly, of selfishness and the mind of French Canada, idealism, of good will and ma-the nation will achieve a new

that makes contemporary its certain death, slow or fast.

Bridge Between Solitudes

Our supreme need today is easy to state, hard to fulfill. The moderate, sensible elements of the two races must join to subdue the extremists, who are minorities but make noise and trouble out of all proportion to their numbers.

This is Prime Minister Lester Pearson's task, undoubtedly the most difficult and dubious ever undertaken by a prime minister since Sir John A. Macdonald built the nation.

Pearson has to mobilize the moderates and build a bridge between the two solitudes. His success or failure will make or break him and his government but their fate is a small incident in history. Will he, or his successor, make or break Confederation? That alone matters.

Since Quebec Premier Jean Lesage came to office and launched a quiet French Canadian revolution.

Please Turn to Page Two
See: "Canada's"

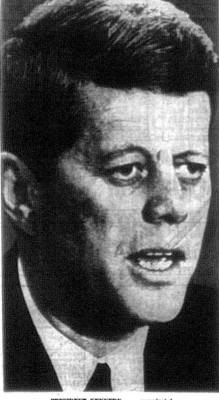

PRESIDENT KENNEDY . . . assassinated

Phil Would Padlock Pubs Rather Than Test Vehicles

Sun Victoria Bureau

VICTORIA—If safety experts want to cut the B.C. traffic accident toll they should padlock the pubs, according to Highways Minister Phil Gaglardi.

This, claims the outspoken minister, would be a lot more effective than establishing a province-wide automobile inspection system.

Motor vehicles superintendent George Lindsay said recently that study is being given to a mobile auto inspection program that might be introduced next year.

Minus Signs In Early Trade

Minus signs predominated in quiet early trading on Vancouver stock market today.

Endako took a 10-cent loss at $4.10 and Granduc was off five cents at $4. Cowichan dropped one cent to $1.01. Western Mines was unchanged at $3.80.

On Thursday, the B.C. Parent-Teacher Federation asked the provincial cabinet to order establishment of vehicle testing stations and legislation requiring annual inspection of all vehicles.

"I'm opposed to that," said Gaglardi.

"We know that only around one per cent of accidents are caused by faulty vehicles, compared with 79 or 80 per cent where it is the driver and drinking," he said.

"Before we spend hundreds of thousands of dollars on inspection to eliminate one per cent of the accidents, I'd sooner close down all the beer parlors and bars to solve the 80 per cent."

'SPIES' SEE NATO GAMES

HALIFAX, N.S. (UPI)—Commodore Robert P. Welland, the senior Canadian naval officer afloat, says Russian trawlers spied on recent NATO exercises between Scotland and Iceland.

Welland said the trawlers were there solely to acquire information and not to admire the anti-submarine exercises being conducted in poor weather to test equipment.

Slaying Confessed, Say Police

NEW WESTMINSTER (Staff) — A statement in which a man admitted he murdered a young Mission City girl was read Thursday to an Assize Court Jury.

The statement was read by Staff Sgt. E. D. Anderson, in charge of Kimberley RCMP detachment, at the trial of Kimberley farm hand Kenneth Lloyd Meeker, 30.

Meeker is charged with capital murder in the death of Alice Mathers, 12, who disappeared while walking home on June 9. Her body was found in a gravel pit 14 miles east of Mission City on June 24.

Anderson said he took the statement from Meeker at Kimberley police office on July 3.

Admission of the statement as evidence was the subject of two days of legal argument in the absence of the jury. The judge ruled it admissible.

IN BATHING SUIT

In the statement, Meeker said he had travelled in his small European car through the interior of the province last spring.

On June 9, the statement said, Meeker left Vancouver and at Mission stopped to pick up a little girl dressed in a bathing suit and green sweater.

She refused to get in the car and he grabbed her and drove about 20 miles to a gravel pit, the statement said. Meeker said in the statement that at the gravel pit, he took the girl's clothes off and molested her.

STARTED TO SCREAM

statement said, and he strangled her, with his hands "at first."

Fearing she was not dead, he took a rope from the car and put it around her neck until her face turned blue, Meeker's statement continued.

He said he took her body to the bush nearby, put her bathing suit back on and threw her sweater over her.

The statement said he then drove 200 miles to a park site, the name of which he did not know, and stayed two days.

Questioned by Staff Sgt.

Please Turn to Page Two
See: "Trial"

DALLAS (AP)—Two priests stepped out of Parkland Hospital's emergency ward today and said President John Kennedy died of his bullet wounds. This was confirmed by government sources in Washington.

A secret service agent was also killed.

Police arrested a 25-year-old man near the scene of the assassination.

DALLAS (UPI) — President Kennedy was cut down by an assassin's bullets as he toured downtown Dallas in an open automobile today.

Texas Gov. John B. Connally, riding with him, was also struck.

Reporters about five car-lengths behind the president heard what sounded like three burst of gunfire.

Secret service agents in a follow-up car quickly unlimbered their automatic rifles.

The president, his limp body cradled in the arms of his wife, was rushed to Parkland Hospital.

The governor also was taken to Parkland.

Representative Albert Thomas of Texas said he was informed both men were alive but that Kennedy was in very critical condition.

He was rushed to an emergency room in the hospital.

The corridors of the hospital erupted in pandemonium.

The incident occurred just east of a triple underpass facing a park in downtown Dallas.

The bubble top of the president's car was down.

The agents drew their pistols, but the damage was done.

The president was slumped over in the back seat of the car face down, Connally lay on the floor of the rear seat.

It was impossible to tell at once where Kennedy was hit, but bullet wounds in Connally's chest were plainly visible, indicating the gunfire might possibly have come from an automatic weapon.

There were three loud bursts.

If Kennedy is dead or dies, Vice-President Lyndon B. Johnson would take over as president. Ironically, Johnson is from Texas.

Dallas motorcycle officers escorting the president quickly leaped from their bikes and raced up a grassy hill.

At the top of the hill, a man and woman appeared huddled on the ground.

In the turmoil, it was impossible to determine at once whether the secret service and Dallas police returned the gunfire that struck down Kennedy.

New President of the United States is Lyndon Johnson.

It was also difficult to determine immediately whether Mrs. Kennedy and Mrs. Connally were injured.

Both women were in the car.

Both women were crouched down over the inert forms of their husbands as the big car raced toward the hospital. Mrs. Kennedy was on her knees on the floor of the rear seat with her head toward the president.

Vice-president Johnson was in a car behind Kennedy's.

The president had flown down to Dallas and was on his way to deliver a luncheon speech.

Two Escape Blazing Rig

LYTTON (Staff)—Two men escaped when fire broke out in their tractor-trailer rig on the Trans-Canada Highway nine miles south of here Thursday night.

Simon Allen, 44, of Wash., said he was driving the heavy rig up a hill when a sheet of flame broke out in the front part of the cab.

He stopped the truck and woke Ward Allen, of Seattle, who was sleeping in a compartment behind him, then leaped to the ground.

Allen followed but broke a bone in his left foot when he hit the ground.

Index

The headline on the first extra edition on Nov. 22, 1963, following the shooting of U.S. President John F. Kennedy, was "KENNEDY SHOT DOWN." The headline changed to "KENNEDY SHOT DEAD" after the news of his death.

Sun reporter Paul St. Pierre spent the early part of 1960 discovering B.C., but would eventually take up a second career as an author. *Dave Buchan/Vancouver Sun*

Penny-pinching money writer Mike Grenby, here in 1977, offered readers useful and entertaining advice on personal finance, and often included his wife Mandy and son Matt in his columns. *Tony Cousins/Vancouver Sun*

Tales from the back country

To jump start the new decade, *The Vancouver Sun* decided it was time for readers to learn more about their province, so editors dispatched reporter and master story-teller Paul St. Pierre on a "voyage of rediscovery around B.C."

In a Jan. 2, 1960 file from Nakusp, St. Pierre regaled readers with the strange tale of Bertie Herridge – a log cabin hermit known as the "socialist of the Kootenays" – whose father told the reporter "don't pay any attention to my boy Bertie. He's my son and I love him dearly, but Bertie was shot in the head in the first war and he's never had any sense since."

St. Pierre was one of those *Sun* scribes whose lush prose belied his significant reportorial skills. The future member of Parliament was an inveterate wanderer, and favoured filing his stories from the rolling hills of the Cariboo. His character development and scene-setting were almost novel-like, no surprise given he would later abandon his newspaper career to write books about home-on-the-range cowboys.

The medium expands its message

The 1960s was the era in which television laid claim to leisure time, the small screen becoming the most ubiquitous technological advance ever to capture the hearts – and the living rooms – of the people. From its early broadcasting forays and tiny black and white sets of the 1950s, television burst out of the gates in the 1960s in full colour, an era dominated by popular westerns and sitcoms such as *Bonanza* and *Bewitched*. The average North American household had at least one television and it was an irresistible magnet, its influence and reach not only altering the

cultural landscape but the reading habits of North Americans.

Vancouver was certainly not immune to television's charms, and when CHAN-TV signed on as the city's first independent station, on Oct. 31, 1960, the irony was that its founder was a former disgruntled *Sun* photographer. Art Jones, and one-time *Sun* shooter Ray Munro, had been unhappy with the dictates of managing editor Hal Straight in the late 1940s and left the paper to start their own freelance company. When Jones's Artray Productions won the station bid in 1960, it joined CBUT (the future CBC) and Bellingham's KVOS-TV in serving the Vancouver market. CHAN would eventually evolve into Global BC.

The Sun responded immediately to readers' interest in the new medium, publishing daily TV listings and a weekly TV magazine that continue to be circulation draws. But the tube's pervasive popularity signalled a fracturing of the news market that would continue unabated for the next half century, growing even more crowded with the advent of the Internet, the 500-channel universe, downloadable movies and in-home theatres, a pop culture polyglot that would contribute to the gradual decline in daily newspaper circulation.

The Friendly Miser

For baby boomers and their aging parents, personal finance – and retirement planning – were the new hot topics. And for readers with money questions, Mike Grenby had the answers. When Grenby began writing about financial issues in *The Vancouver Sun* in 1961, his parsimonious ways and chatty writing style delighted subscribers, and his money column and "money makeovers" using *Sun* readers were firsts for a Canadian newspaper.

The lanky Grenby – who often wrote about his wife, Mandy, and who admitted to serving his guests watered-down orange juice to make it last longer – was soon one of the paper's favourite personalities. One *Sun* billboard showed him sitting in a bathtub ("Grenby reveals the facts on personal finance"). Another showed him, all legs, aboard his moped, promoting a series of columns on why the friendly miser had ditched his car to save energy costs. Grenby's columns were eventually syndicated and his no-nonsense advice often saw him appearing on radio and television, and even hosting cruises. Grenby's annual RRSP sections were circulation boosters, and he wrote eight books during his time at the paper, Canadian best-sellers that included 10 editions of *Mike Grenby's Tax Tips*. One memorable column even hit page one, when he admitted he'd made an error calculating his own tax return. Grenby's self-deprecating and often amusing take on personal finance continued until he left the paper in 1986 in a dispute over freelancing.

Holt and Bramham: Tale of two city reporters

Sun headlines in the early 1960s were dominated by the saga of the Sons of Freedom, the Doukhobor sect that was setting the West Kootenays on fire. The Freedomites, a social and religious group with roots in Russia, had settled in enclaves across Canada, including eastern B.C., and openly rejected materialism and secularism and often marched in the nude to protest capitalism. Their long and violent campaign against the dictates of the B.C. government had seen sect members set fire to schools to protest compulsory education, bomb a transmission tower and courthouse and, in 1961, blow up a railway bridge near Nelson. The government had responded, in part, by seizing Freedomite children and keeping them in a detention centre. Dozens of jailed Doukhobor leaders, later acquitted, were charged with plotting against law and order, including conspiracy to bomb and arson.

Much of *The Sun*'s coverage was the work of reporter Simma Holt, whose smoking typewriter and dogged pursuit of crime stories made her not only a hard-news female pioneer in *Sun* editorial – she started in 1944 covering skid row and chasing fires – but a natural to report the ongoing conflagration. Her story on the final Doukhobor chapter, the RCMP pre-dawn raid on March 24, 1962, called it the "greatest-ever drive" by the force. Filing from Nelson, she wrote that most of the Freedomites were asleep when the Mounties "swooped on sleeping Doukhobor villages early today in the biggest peacetime roundup of Canadian history."

The front-page headline declared "59 Top Freedomites Seized in Mass Raid," but it was in the sidebar with the overline "Threaten to Strip Girl Reporter" where Holt's doggedness became apparent. The Freedomites blamed her previous coverage for the crackdown, and when a group of irate Doukhobor women approached her during the raid, threatening to strip her of her clothes, Holt stood her ground until police arrived. After years of extensive research, hundreds of interviews and her ongoing coverage of the Sons of Freedom, Holt wrote a book titled *Terror in the Name of God*. She would leave *The Sun* to successfully run for Parliament, receiving an Order of Canada in 1996. Her 2008 autobiography was titled *Memoirs of a Loose Cannon*.

Fifty years later, after Holt's heyday, another determined *Vancouver Sun* newswoman would be at the centre of yet another controversial story involving an eastern B.C. religious sect:

Many *Sun* reporters have turned assignments into books, including Simma Holt, whose *Terror in the Name of God* was based on her coverage of B.C.'s fiery Doukhobor community. It was published by Jack McClelland (centre) in 1964. *Dan Scott/Vancouver Sun*

the polygamists of Bountiful.

When Daphne Bramham joined *The Sun* in 1989, she covered city hall and wrote business stories before moving into management as associate editor overseeing the editorial pages. In 2000, she became a full-time columnist, and four years later found herself heading to Bountiful, a community of polygamists living in B.C.'s Creston Valley. The reception was chilly – leader Winston Blackmore snuck out a back door rather than talk to her, while the women of Bountiful challenged her to "write the truth." She did just that and, that fall, the B.C. attorney-general asked the RCMP to investigate the Mormon fundamentalist group's practice of plural marriages involving underage girls.

It was a story that would captivate readers across the country, and wind in and out of the courts for the next decade, Bramham leading

the charge with her unbending coverage – including stories about sister wives who had left Bountiful, the "lost" boys who were kicked out, the complicated house of cards that were Blackmore's finances and the Utah trial of FLDS president Warren Jeffs, who would be jailed in 2011 for child sexual assault.

When charges of polygamy against Blackmore were stayed, the B.C. government, along with the Canadian government, referred the anti-polygamy law to the B.C. Supreme Court in a constitutional reference to determine whether the law was contrary to sections in the Charter of Rights and Freedoms that guarantee religious freedom and freedom of association. In November 2011, Chief Justice Robert Bauman upheld the law. In 2012, Blackmore was back in court appealing a reassessment of his personal income tax.

Considered a sect tradition, Doukhobors often stripped naked for protests and violent actions, including the burning of this house in June 1962. *George Diack/ Vancouver Sun*

In 2011, *Sun* columnist Daphne Bramham interviewed Truman Oler, one of the "lost boys" who left the polygamous compound at Bountiful. *Brian Clarkson/Vancouver Sun*

Death of an icon

The entertainment world was rocked by the Aug. 5, 1962 death of actress Marilyn Monroe, reportedly of a drug-overdose suicide. The 36-year-old blonde bombshell instantly became one of the world's most famous and enduring dead celebrities, her untimely departure eerily similar to the circumstances of future global superstars such as Michael Jackson and Diana, Princess of Wales. *The Sun*'s front page wire story on Monroe's funeral – headlined "MM Beautiful in Death" – described the throng of 100 journalists and hundreds of mourners and "curiosity seekers" gathered outside the Los Angeles mortuary. Inside, the star was on display in an open bronze casket. According to the story, Monroe's "famed blonde tresses were done in a page boy style, neck-length" and "she was clad in an Irish green sheath dress with a green silk scarf around her neck."

Hollywood icon Marilyn Monroe made a quick stop in Vancouver during the height of her career in 1953, taking time to vamp for the cameras beneath the tail of a DC-6. Monroe had just finished filming *River of No Return* with Robert Mitchum in Banff. *Bill Cunningham, Vancouver Public Library 62485*

Bramham's book, *The Secret Lives of Saints: Child Brides and Lost Boys in Canada's Polygamist Mormon Sect*, was released in early 2008 on the day that Texas child protection authorities and armed police raided Jeffs's Texas compound and took nearly 500 women and children into protective custody.

Bountiful has been the story of Bramham's career because, she says, "it actually seems to have made a difference for the women and children in Bountiful. When I first went there, they were all wearing pioneer clothes, were terrified of strangers and few were allowed to finish high school. Kids dove into the ditches and hid behind bushes. Now, at least those who follow Winston Blackmore dress like everyone else and many more are finishing school and even going on to college.

"It's made me a much better journalist because I have better research skills now – not that I could have done much of this without the help of *The Sun*'s fabulous librarians. But more importantly, it's reinforced my long-held belief that journalists – backed by their editors and newspaper owners – can make a difference. We can help make people's lives better."

Calling Jack Webster

Ten years after leaving the paper for a broadcast career, former *Sun* reporter Jack Webster was back in its pages following the April 19, 1963 prison riot at the B.C. Penitentiary, during which three inmates took hostages and demanded that authorities bring in the radio host as a mediator. Webster met with the prisoners in a tense standoff and agreed to air their grievances, which included abolition of solitary confinement. A guard, held hostage and tied to a chair for 14 hours, was released after convicts made a deal: three of them were loaded on a plane and transferred at their request to eastern prisons.

"At least 200 of the 670 prisoners in the jail were in full riot," reported *The Sun*. "They tore down doors, broke windows, shouted and screamed at the guards before being subdued by charging steel-helmeted police and tear gas." Subsequent stories, under the front-page headline "Night of Terror," included interviews with the warden and 53-year-old hostage Patrick Dennis.

Webster, in a special report for the newspaper where he once worked, also related the dramatic details in a first-person piece. He wrote of being with the guard during the hostage-taking and reported that one of the convicts, "mad ringleader Gerry Casey," held a knife against Dennis's throat and yelled at the gritty Scot: "Tell Warden Tom Hall if the bulls break in here, the guard dies first. You'll die, too, Webster. We'll all die. Get on that telephone."

Selling *The Sun*: The end of a family legacy

After decades of vaunted leadership and fiscal acumen, after taking *The Vancouver Sun* from second place in the market to the top, after establishing a much-admired newsroom filled with respected journalists, owner/publisher Don Cromie and family sold the paper in July 1963 to Max Bell and his Alberta-based FP Publications newspaper syndicate.

Bell had formed FP with Victor Sifton in 1958, joining his four western dailies, including *The Victoria Times* and *Colonist*, with Sifton's *Winnipeg Free Press*. The business partners would embark on a buying spree that included not only *The Sun*, but the *Ottawa Journal*, the *Globe and Mail* and the *Montreal Star*, effectively creating a nation-wide chain of dailies and a new term: concentrated ownership.

The surprising sale of *The Sun* was precipitated by numerous factors, including family pressure on Cromie to divest their collective assets, which included the family's controlling interest in *The Sun*. Dispirited by the 1957 drowning death of his younger brother Samuel, who at 39 was an assistant publisher and in charge of the paper's lucrative printing division, and facing the reality that more and more North American dailies were owned by fewer and fewer men, Cromie relented. When the insistent Bell finally

Sun scribe-turned-broadcaster Jack Webster was called in to act as a go-between following a prison riot at the B.C. Penitentiary in 1963. *Ken Oakes/Vancouver Sun*

Jack Webster's account of the riot and hostage-taking at the B.C. Penitentiary made the front page of *The Sun* on April 22, 1963.

tempted Cromie with an offer of $30 a share, $10 over the market value, he caved.

Pacific Press had a new 50/50 deal: FP owned *The Sun*, while Southam owned *The Province*. And the city, for the first time, was without a locally-owned daily.

Bruce Hutchison, a revered *Sun* writer who had started his journalism career in 1914 as a sports reporter for the *Victoria Times*, was named *The Sun*'s editor and, a rudderless year after the sale, Stuart Keate was appointed publisher. Keate, a UBC grad, had been a *Province* sports writer and a 14-year publisher of the *Victoria Times* before moving to *The Sun*'s masthead. It was a position he would hold for

14 years, until his retirement in 1978.

Detailing the ownership changes in his 1980 memoir *Paper Boy*, Keate wrote that Cromie would ultimately regret his decision to sell the paper, calling it a "great mistake, a virtual forfeit of his patrimony and millions of dollars." After the sale, Cromie stayed on as publisher for six months, his pay cut almost in half to $45,000.

"Street talk in the trade," wrote Keate, "was that Cromie had actually made an offer to buy back the paper but it was academic on at least two grounds: Cromie by this time did not have the money to buy and Max Bell was not inclined to sell."

Stuart Keate, pictured here in his office in 1966, joined *The Sun* as publisher in 1964 – almost 30 years after he worked on a special edition of the paper while a student at the University of B.C. *Deni Eagland/Vancouver Sun*

Enter Stuart Keate

New ownership meant something of a transition for *Sun* staff, who had enjoyed decades of steady steerage under the Cromies. *Sun* columnist Jack Scott wrote on May 1, 1964, in a welcome to new publisher Keate and a farewell to the retiring Don Cromie, that after 20 years "it is not an easy switch to do without him. Don is a restless man, all bone, sinew and nerve ends ... I never worked for a more difficult man, or as fair and decent a one or, for that matter, a better newspaperman."

Keate, he noted, would find *The Sun* to be an "unorthodox, unpredictable" newspaper with "a flavor, a character, a personality."

In *Paper Boy*, Keate recalled his first days as publisher: "When I arrived at *The Sun* in 1964, the impelling challenge, it seemed to me, was nothing less than a complete change in its character and personality. From its inception, it had been an erratic and unpredictable

newspaper – vibrant, sassy and aggressive, but nonetheless erratic, sensational and strongly partisan."

One of its problems, he determined, was that it had failed to keep pace with the growth of its community, seemingly content to battle *The Province* and stick to its parochial coverage.

"By the spring of 1964," he wrote, "*The Vancouver Sun* was in a restive and demoralized state. The Big Apple of western Canadian journalism, it was shiny on the outside (circulation, 240,000; pre-tax February profit of $480,000) but bitter at the core."

Keate recalled that he was paid $36,000 a year to reinvigorate *The Vancouver Sun*, and when he accepted the job, he was given a four-page typewritten manifesto by Dick Malone, publisher of FP's *Winnipeg Free Press*, titled "How to Be Publisher of The Vancouver Sun and Find Misery." Its salient points, which Keate referred to as "Thou-Shalt-Nots," included the FP credo that "we cannot have the big shot, bon

vivant type of publisher."

Further instructions ranged from "the new publisher should strongly avoid the social swing and cocktail circuit of Vancouver" to "the publisher must demonstrate that he knows his business and show that he can apply himself directly to each problem ... the advertising and circulation departments must be given drive and enthusiasm."

Keate was 50 years old, a 30-year newspaper veteran, and disagreed with much of it. But he took the job anyway, and focused his considerable journalistic chops on the task at hand.

"My aim was to reduce the strident tones of its columns; to take the paper out beyond the bounds of British Columbia to concern itself with national and international affairs; and in the process to make it as independent and responsible as humanly possible. I reckoned this change, introduced quietly and subtly, would take about five years. In the end, it took ten."

The Beatles, protected by police, at Empire Stadium on Aug. 22, 1964. *George Diack/Vancouver Sun*

The charitable heart of a newspaper

One of the things that didn't change with *The Sun*'s new ownership was its long-held corporate commitment to community philanthropy. Since its 1912 debut, *The Sun* has initiated and sponsored dozens of charitable undertakings, most with a special emphasis on helping children.

One of the first Christmas campaigns was the 1920 Empty Stocking Fund (the name co-opted decades later by *The Province*), followed by the 1921 Santa Claus Fund. In 1963, the paper launched its Cup of Milk campaign, a decade-long fundraising enterprise in conjunction with the Ottawa-based Unitarian Service. A year later, it contributed $100,000 on behalf of its 750 employees to the three Capital Funds for UBC, Simon Fraser and the University of Victoria and, in 1969, announced *The Sun*'s House of Hope Appeal to help build a farm house in Ladner for

"retarded boys."

Such was the paper's charitable focus that Sun Publishing Company annual reports from the 1970s showed a "social audit" of the newspaper's grassroots benevolence.

In 1981, then *Sun* publisher Clark Davey would start The Vancouver Sun Children's Fund, vowing to tell stories of B.C.'s needy children and ask readers to open their hearts and wallets. To date, generous readers have donated $11 million to the fund. A portion remains in an untouchable endowment, while $7 million has been dispersed to 900 children's charities throughout B.C. The fund's latest campaign, kicked off in the fall of 2011, is Adopt-a-School, which aids inner-city school children.

The Sun's Raise-a-Reader campaign, which began in Vancouver in 1997 with local celebrities hawking newspapers, appropriately mirrored the paper's emphasis on literacy and would eventually go national, spreading to 28 Canadian cities and raising close to $20 million since its inception.

Beatlemania comes to town

It was Aug. 22, 1964, and *The Sun*'s front-page was filled with stories of a British invasion. The arrival in Vancouver of The Beatles caused traffic jams and forced increased police security when a crowd of 200,000 turned up for the PNE parade hoping to catch a glimpse of the Fab Four. *The Sun* also reported that hundreds of fans "kept up a vigil outside the Hotel Georgia where the four tousle-haired Liverpudlians were expected to check in later in the day for an Empire Stadium performance tonight."

Jackie DeShannon and The Righteous Brothers were opening acts for the concert, but when The Beatles bounded on the stage at 9:23 p.m., it was Elvis Presley-style mania all over again. Their performance lasted only 29 minutes. Emcee Red Robinson and the group's manager, Brian Epstein, interrupted the show in an effort to calm the screaming crowd, but fans rushed the stage, crushing those in front

Bill Munsey relaxes at home with his wife Rosemary, the day after the B.C. Lions won the 1964 Grey Cup. The defensive halfback was the game's outstanding player, returning a fumble 71 yards for a touchdown – then adding another touchdown on offence. *Ralph Bower/Vancouver Sun*

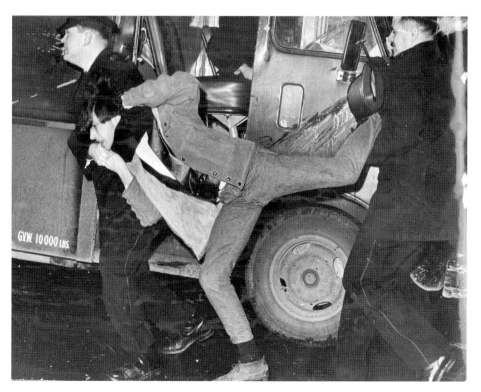

Two years after the Lions' 1964 Grey Cup win, the city welcomed Saskatchewan and Ottawa for the CFL's championship game. The event was preceded by a riot after the Grey Cup parade. More than 300 people were arrested. *Deni Eagland/Vancouver Sun*

and forcing John, George, Paul and Ringo to sprint for their limousines and a police escort away from the fray.

Perhaps more memorable than the show – attended by 20,261 fans who paid as much as $5.25 a ticket – was the pre-concert press conference held at the airport, where The Beatles' famous cheeky repartee was recorded by 89 newsies, including reporters from the U.S., Eastern Canada and Britain. The Victoria press corps alone numbered five journalists. When asked why the group was delayed in customs, John Lennon quipped: "We had to be deloused."

Reviews in *The Sun* were dismissive, although the Monday paper devoted pages of coverage and photographs. "Seldom in Vancouver's entertainment history have so many paid so much for so little," wrote classical music critic William Littler, who had been sent to cover a band he knew nothing about.

Football fever and a coveted Cup

It had taken 10 years, but on Nov. 28, 1964, the B.C. Lions won their first Grey Cup, defeating the Hamilton Tiger-Cats 34-24 in Toronto with an all-star team that included Joe Kapp, Willie Fleming and Norm Fieldgate. The Lions' victory was, of course, front-page news. "Never a Doubt," declared *The Sun* headline, under a kicker that read "Love Those Lions." In the sports-centric industry that is newspapering, it was just part of *The Sun*'s extensive game coverage celebrating the big day.

Fans were not so sporting two years later, when they inexplicably took to Vancouver streets to riot on the night of Nov. 25, 1966, following a peaceful evening Grey Cup parade attended by 150,000 fans. In what *The Sunday Sun* dubbed "The Battle of Georgia Street," more than 300 people were arrested in a downtown melee in which "billy-swinging police fought three pitched battles with screaming, bottle-throwing mobs who turned Grey Cup Eve celebrations into a riot."

Jack Wasserman, who watched the riot from the seventh floor of the Hotel Georgia, wrote: "From where I sat, it was Watts all over again, without the guns, without the fire and without the racial overtones. But it had the same uncontrolled, frenzied, destructive drive, with the crowd lashing out at the police for lack of any other specific target."

The following day, the Saskatchewan Roughriders won their first Grey Cup, beating the Rough Riders from Ottawa 29-14 at Empire Stadium. Notably, some of the many game shots featured in *The Sun* were taken from a helicopter, hired by *The Sun* to ensure the film made the trip from Empire Stadium to the paper's darkroom in a timely fashion.

When disaster strikes

As it did with the 1948 Fraser Valley floods and the 1958 Second Narrows Bridge collapse, *The Sun* would throw all its resources at the big breaking story of the day, instantly dispatching reporters and photographers to the scene to interview witnesses and survivors. Such was the case on Jan. 9, 1965, when a deadly landslide covered the Trans Canada Highway near Hope, killing four and leading to years of speculation that others were buried under tons of rock and dirt.

Just six months later, on July 8, *Sun* reporters were back in full disaster-coverage mode when a Canadian Pacific Airlines jet crashed near 100 Mile House, killing the 52 passengers on board.

From the plane crash site, *Sun* reporter Jes Odam filed this lede (the newspaper term for the all-important first sentence of a story) from Kamloops: "When first light came there was something queer about the countryside." Odam's gripping interview with logging mechanic Bill Wolfgramm, who witnessed the crash aftermath, told of the strewn wreckage and scattered bodies. "The tail of the plane was half a mile away from the fuselage," the weeping man said, "and there was a constant trail of broken and bent bodies between them. I saw the body of a young child but I could not tell if it was that of a boy or a girl. All we could do before it got dark was to pick up a few bodies."

Setting up a new shop

By late 1965, *The Sun* was turning its attention to 2250 Granville Street, where a new four-storey, purpose-built, $14-million building was about to make newspaper history on the corner of 6th Avenue.

The Sun and editorial rival *Province* had previously combined several of its departments under the collective banner of Pacific Press, but *The Province* was still operating out of a building at Cambie and Hastings, and *The Vancouver Sun* was still publishing from its now outgrown space in the Sun Tower at 500 Beatty St.

With the new building, they were about to become bona fide roommates.

Their corporate co-habitation began on Dec. 11, 1965, sharing not only their spiffy new quarters but the spanking new, $1-million Goss printing presses in the building's cavernous basement. The editorial departments, while occupying the third floor, remained separate, divided by a shared newspaper library; long referred to by staffers as "the morgue" it acted as a demilitarized zone between the two newspapers. Both papers were visible from the corridor, but staff were only permitted to meet in the middle at the library counter, and could never set foot on enemy turf.

Sun reporter Wayne McDonald weighed in with a story on the new building, a low-slung modern structure that had been some time in the planning stages, with "eight acres of floor

In a special section, *The Vancouver Sun* commemorated its 1965 move from the Sun Tower to 2250 Granville Street with a series of photos from both buildings.

space, 360,000 square feet" designed by project engineer Duncan McEwen and architect Adrian Lozano. Although utilitarian – "news must move quickly and efficiently from the editorial department to the composing room; page casts must move smoothly and speedily from the stereo department to the press room; the printed newspapers must be rushed from the presses to the mailing room and truck bays" – the design did not exclude "warmth and beauty." McDonald gave a special nod to the subdued lighting, the bold colours throughout the building, including orange, yellow, red and blue, and the building's sculptured white panel cladding that played with "light and shadow."

More than 500 pieces of furniture had been designed specifically for the building, including *Sun* editorial's new horseshoe-shaped news-desk "where the bank of editors sit, polishing copy and checking facts and style." The reporters' desks were metal (the senior editors', though, were wood) and were outfitted with manual typewriters, desktop wire baskets and metal spikes – the latter to save the carbon copies of filed stories that had been sent by pneumatic "zip" tubes to the composing room – along with rotary-dial telephones and more than a few ashtrays.

But the newsroom, with its spectacular northern panoramic view, was functional: sports, deserted until early evening most nights, was off in the northeast corner, its liquor-filled drawers and racy pinup calendars out of sight. The arts and features staff were clustered on the west side of the room; city reporters and editors' offices were in the middle. The publisher's office and the editorial pages were tucked into the northwest corner, defining a boundary based

Wearing a traditional pressman's hat, Vancouver mayor William Rathie pushed the button to start the printing of the March 14, 1966 edition of *The Vancouver Sun* at its new plant.
George Diack/Vancouver Sun

that the cafeteria "is prepared to service your boss with any brands he wishes."

In a Christmas Eve message to readers, Keate wrote: "The move to the new premises marks the end of an era, but more importantly, the opening up of a new one. We enter on this stage of our history at new peaks of circulation (245,000 copies daily) and advertising support (30,500,000 lines last year) with new plans, dreams, hopes and aspirations for our country and our community."

The first *Vancouver Sun* published out of the new plant hit the doorsteps of those nearly quarter million subscribers on Tuesday, Dec. 28, 1965, featuring photographs of staff leaving the old building for the new, and headlines that ranged from "Sadness marks Sun's departure from its home in tower" to "Nostalgia soon fades with excitement of fabulous new home."

The move did not go unfeted. There was an open house for employees and their families, followed several months later by an invitation-only opening ceremony at the plant and an evening reception at the Hotel Vancouver.

Invitees included newspaper publishers from around the region, as well as dignitaries from politicians and police chiefs to the premier. Among those unable to enjoy the buffet of prime rib, rainbow trout, fried oysters and Pouilly Fouisse served at the March 14, 1966 event, which was hosted by Keate and *Province* publisher Fred Auger, was Prime Minister Lester Pearson. He sent his regrets in a letter addressed "Dear Stu" and signed "Mike," and followed up on the day of the party with a telegram of congratulations that said: "May I wish you and everyone connected with *The Sun* many years of good journalism and good health. With kind regards. L B Pearson Prime Minister."

Several pieces of tower history quietly made the move to the paper's new home, including the "chapel slipboard" from the composing room – a slatted wooden wall-hanging record of who was working and who was not and how many subs had been hired for the day. The board, which was later donated to a local museum, had round numbered tags hanging from little hooks, one for each employee.

Although it wouldn't be rediscovered until the paper moved again 32 years later, someone had also packed up the beautiful cast metal *Sun* sign that had graced the front door of the tower, which the boys working in the basement of Pacific Press would use as a mini table for their coffee cups.

The Family affair

When publishers Stu Keate and Fred Auger decided to commission Jack Harman to sculpt a bronze statue to grace the entrance of the new Pacific Press building, they couldn't have known the furore that would ensue.

Harman had been recommended by a local gallery owner and was one of several local artists who submitted proposals.

on the unwritten code of church and state, which dictated that the opinion of the newspaper remain separate from non-partisan news gathering.

The library was completely modernized in the move. Gone were the index wheels and 26 filing cabinets, as a new, semi-automatic, records retrieval system – called a Lektriever and taking up 50-per-cent less storage space – was installed to instantly dispense thousands of newspaper clippings in the new digs. Also new to the library was a microfilm reader-printer.

Serving both papers was a snazzy new B.C. Tel phone system, called Centrex, which a *Sun* promotional ad claimed would provide "faster, streamlined service for incoming calls, and calls within Pacific Press . . . three times as fast as when they go through a central switchboard.

Centrex virtually makes private lines out of the 425 telephones that will be in service at *The Sun* and *The Province*."

The top floor housed the cafeteria, with two huge patios and a spectacular wall-of-glass offering 180-degree views of downtown, the ocean and the mountains to the north. And, as a special treat, every department had something new: piped-in Muzak.

Staff were also advised by memo that "smoking will be permitted for both males and females in all departments, except where, as a matter of good manners, it would be inadvisable when dealing with the public." To make things easier, the company that managed the new cafeteria sold a variety of cigars, cigarettes and pipe tobacco. Publisher Stuart Keate's assistant was also advised, by separate memo,

His presentation, in February 1965, included a model of *The Family*: a cast bronze of a mother holding a baby, a father and a naked juvenile boy. The figures were elongated, with the father reaching 12 feet in height. The panel ultimately chose Harman, but on one condition: that the boy's naughty bits be clothed or covered in some manner. Harman agreed and quoted $11,700 for the piece, promising completion by December that year.

By year's end, however, Harman had advised the publishers that he had run out of money, and assistants. Keate and Auger also discovered that Harman had ignored the condition and had already cast the boy with an exposed penis. A series of missives among the parties followed, as did a visit by Keate in February 1966 to Harman's studio. In a memo to his worried peers the next day, Keate told them he didn't find the "statue of the boy, as cast, offensive" but "if strong protests arose from the public, consideration could be given to donating the work to the University of B.C. or the Art Gallery." He also noted that "Harman says that the symbolism in it is 'the new generation before the old' – the new vitality of young Canada, new trends in education, etc. I think we should go ahead and let the chips fall where they may."

It was agreed. Harman was given an extension and another $2,500 and *The Family* was finally installed on July 6, 1966 in front of the plant's main entrance on Granville Street.

And the chips fell. The phone lines lit up in the publishers' office as hundreds of citizens complained about indecency. Over the years, pranksters painted over the penis, put clothes on it and, in one attack, cut it off with a hacksaw, necessitating a repair the next day by a welder who was so embarrassed he insisted on working under a protective sheet.

Read all about us (our men, anyway)

Firmly ensconced in its new South Granville digs, *The Sun* produced a special supplement on March 14, 1966, the plant's official opening, explaining the move and the technological changes to the paper and the industry. In it, *Sun* editorial director Bruce Hutchison spoke to the importance of a newspaper's content, especially the editorial pages.

"The editorial itself," wrote Hutchison, "is different from any other article in the paper because it is rarely the work of one person. While one typewriter turns it out, in provisional form, hours or days of conference, argument and research have usually gone into it." His column was illustrated with a photograph of the current editorial board: eight men, including editorial page chief Cliff McKay, Trevor Lautens, Mac Reynolds and Allan Fotheringham.

The photographs in the picture-heavy special edition reflected the historical patriarchy of the business, page after page showing men at work: managing editor Erwin Swangard,

Artist Jack Harman's controversial sculpture, *The Family*, is lifted by crane into its location in front of the Pacific Press building at 2250 Granville Street in 1966. *Ken Oakes/Vancouver Sun*

assistant managing editor Bill Galt, picture editor Earl Smith, telegraph editor Lionel Salt, news editor Dave Driver, city editor Bruce Larsen, sports editor Dunc Stewart, sports columnists Denny Boyd and Jim Kearney, business editor Bill Fletcher, advertising director John Toogood, pressmen George Daris and Ernie Demer (wearing a trademark, hand-folded, newspaper hat) and compositor Irv Kleiman.

It was still a time when men ruled the business, with women mostly relegated to the "potted plants" sections, like Fashion and Food, sections that brought in much of the lucrative advertising but where the journalism produced wasn't considered as worthy as hard news or sports, the latter of which has traditionally attracted very little paid advertising.

One page in the 24-page extra was devoted to the "women's department" – which in those days was often referred to, derisively, as the

"ovary tower" – with a story that referred to the "women's pages" as "gay, feminine and full of news." No longer a home just for "pink teas and bridge parties," the pages were starting to feature news on the arts, education, politics and children's welfare. An accompanying picture featuring six women's pages staffers included editor Thelma Hartin ("a newswoman since she wore pigtails"), as well as fashion editor Diana Ricardo, columnist Penny Wise (Evelyn Caldwell), and reporters Ann Barling, Kathy Hassard and Helen Abbott.

"The girls form a fast, efficient organization," noted the cutline.

Notably, shirts and ties were the order of the day for the men while women were in dresses and skirts, a strict dress code that would slacken over the years as modern business attire embraced a more casual wardrobe for white collar workers.

In that same supplement, Jack Wasserman wrote of the new offices for himself and other *Sun* columnists, deliberately separated from the rest of the newsroom so that nobody could watch the masters at work. "What would happen," Wasserman mused, "if they saw worldwide gourmet Penny Wise munching on a hot dog and sipping a Coke, or business columnist Pat Carney working barefoot."

From whales to wars, we protest

By the late 1960s, the North American protest movement was in full bloom and had galvanized the nation's disgruntled youth, especially in Vancouver. The spring of 1967 saw *The Sun* reporting on several anti-Vietnam War protest marches in the city and, on March 26, the Super Human Be-In in Stanley Park, which attracted 1,500 flower children, bedecked in bell-bottoms and shaggy locks, burning incense and serving notice of a growing generational gap.

Elsewhere in the city, another movement was finding its legs, a fledgling group of like-minded rag-tag environmentalists and eco-revolutionaries who, enraged by U.S. plans to detonate a one-megaton nuclear bomb on Amchitka Island in Alaska in the late 1960s, began organizing protests in Vancouver. Among their numbers were Paul Watson, Paul and Linda Spong, Irving Stowe, Ben Metcalfe, Bob Cummings and *Sun* columnist Bob Hunter. It was the beginning of Greenpeace, a grass-roots organization that would not only shape provincial politics in the years to come but shine a light on global environmental issues while earning its Vancouver base the universal distinction as a friendly, photogenic, "left coast" haven for misfits, malcontents and social activists.

A *Sun* photograph taken a few years earlier provided ammunition for the fledgling protest movement, and for the mandate Greenpeace was formulating on the road to public enlightenment on environmental and animal rights issues. The snapshot, taken by *Sun* photographer Brian Kent in July 1964, was of Vancouver Aquarium director Murray Newman hand-feeding the facility's newly captured killer whale, Moby Doll. The accompanying story noted that $2 had been donated by a 10-year-old local girl to begin the fundraising for a $500,000 whale pool. She'd sent the money to the aquarium with a note that said: "We read in the paper that our mayor wants to sell the whale that was caught last week. We would like to donate this money to whoever is in charge of the whale in the hopes that it may help keep it in Vancouver. We also would like to suggest the name of Bo-Peep for our whale." When Moby Doll died within the year, animal rights activists began a long bitter battle that would end in 2001 when the aquarium shipped its last orca, Bjossa, to San Diego's Sea World.

Vancouver Aquarium director Murray Newman feeds killer whale Moby Doll at a pen near Jericho Beach, a photographic moment that would help launch Greenpeace. *Brian Kent/ Vancouver Sun*

Greenpeace was born, and Save the Whales had become a worldwide rallying cry.

Introducing the fuddle-duddle man

The indisputable power of telegenic politics – which had been mesmerizing television viewers with real-time snapshots of popular leaders such as U.S. president John Kennedy and civil rights crusader Martin Luther King, and disturbing images from the Vietnam War – was once again evident in April 1968 with the arrival of a dashing new world leader: Pierre Elliott Trudeau.

The mercurial Montrealer, whose energy seemed to fill television screens and who was an irresistible subject for newspaper writers, was a polarizing force, an intellectual who danced the pirouette, immortalized the phrase "fuddle duddle" and implemented official Canadian bilingualism, all of it playing out in the living rooms of the nation. *The Sun* was no less captivated by the new Liberal prime minister, introducing him to readers in its April 20, 1968 edition by juxtaposing a photograph of the young, energetic Trudeau on page one beside a shot of the older, retiring Lester Pearson leaving Parliament Hill with his granddaughter. "Trudeau Picks Caretaker Gov't" headlined the page, with inside stories devoted to speculation on the makeup of his new cabinet. When Trudeau later made an official visit to *The Sun* – it was then, and is now, common practice for political, social and business leaders to meet with the paper's editorial board – it was as if a jolt of electricity had hit the newsroom, as dozens of hard-bitten

The Sun's Denny Boyd engages in some one-on-one flight time with Prime Minister Pierre Trudeau in 1968. *Ralph Bower/Vancouver Sun*

reporters stopped in their tracks to size up the enigmatic leader.

We are the champions

Throughout the 1960s, *The Vancouver Sun* was doing its best to uphold the paper's enviable and well-earned reputation as an industry breeding ground for clever but mischievous editors, reporters and photographers, a cabal of men and women who were mostly young, mostly driven and who partied as hard as they worked to break news and tell stories.

For every story that made the paper, however, there was one that didn't.

In 1967, reporter Scott Honeyman was hired by *The Sun* and relegated to the paper's New Westminster bureau, working with colleagues like Bruce Smillie and Jack Ramsay, all of whom filed their stories to the downtown office by teletype machine. One of their daily tasks was to "memo off" assignments, which was done by writing a long note on folio paper letting editors know why the assignment couldn't be completed. Ramsay was the undisputed champ of the "memo off," once composing a memo more than eight feet long detailing the non-delivery of an assignment about a chinchilla ranch in the Fraser Valley. The crew was eventually

patriated to 2250 Granville, where the hijinks continued with even more accomplices getting up to no journalistic good. Honeyman soon found himself covering the environment beat. One day, back at the office from an assignment in Coal Harbour, where a small oil spill had killed a few ducks, Honeyman was filing on deadline – which amounted to typing the story on two sheets of folio paper, ripping it out of the manual typewriter, removing the carbon between the sheets and, clutching a copy in the air, shouting "copy" to summon a copy runner – when he was asked by an editor, in the middle of furious typing, what kind of ducks they were. "Dead ducks," Honeyman fired back.

The Sun was full of characters in the 1960s, including photographers (clockwise from left) Dan Scott, Ralph Bower, George Diack, Ray Allan, Dave Buchan, Ken Orr and Charlie Warner. *Ralph Bower/Vancouver Sun*

Calling Car 8

If anything spoke to the free-wheeling newsroom spending of the day, it was Car 8, at the time a cheaper and faster alternative to taxis or photographer/reporter car-pooling. The car, part of the company's fleet, was on standby virtually around the clock, available at a moment's notice to pick up and deliver packages and drive reporters to assignments and managers to engagements, provided that newsroom copy runners, who were the designated drivers, were not only available and had drivers' licences but were sober. One copy boy, who hailed from Colombia, was a rather popular driver, especially for those reporters who liked to speed to assignments not just high on life.

By hook or by crook

South of the border, youth unrest continued to roil in the wake of the 1963 assassination of

U.S. President John Kennedy and the mounting opposition to the unpopular Vietnam War. Calls for political and social change were further exacerbated by the April 1968 assassination of revered civil rights leader Martin Luther King.

The Sun's Denny Boyd, who openly battled the bottle and his bosses over his drinking problem (he once quit the paper and was then hired back, and would write often about his assorted demons), wanted to cover the historic event but the editors refused to send him. Abetted by well-oiled buddies, Boyd hopped a plane to Atlanta, writing in his 1995 autobiography, *In My Own Words*, that "the guys took up a cash collection. I called my travel agent and booked a flight and a room. I tore home, packed a bag, picked up my portable typewriter, told my roommate to cover for me for as long as possible and, quite drunk, was on the midnight plane to Georgia."

Needless to say, *The Sun* ran every inch of his copy.

A 1960 *Sun* ad promoting the advertising department.

The Sun's Erwin Swangard had a lasting impact on the local sports community as sports editor, and managing editor, and today has a Burnaby stadium named after him. Here, Swangard presents the Sun Match Play Open Trophy to golfer Johnny Russell in May 1966. *Deni Eagland/Vancouver Sun*

The name game is over the moon

The Sun's notoriously playful sense of humour was evident again on July 21, 1969 when editors embraced yet another opportunity to tinker with the nameplate. When U.S. astronaut Neil Armstrong took his giant leap for mankind with his first step on the moon, The Sun marked the historical achievement by changing its name to The Moon! over its banner headline "MAN WALKS ON MOON." Coverage included a special supplement commemorating the space walk. One of The Sun's in-house ads used the feat to applaud its hard-working newspaper carriers. "Meanwhile . . . back on earth," it read, "we admire young people who reach for the moon."

One editor's swan song

The hard work of a venerable Sun editor was recognized in the spring of 1969, as Swangard Stadium debuted on the corner of Boundary and Kingsway. It was a fitting tribute to Erwin Swangard, who had held many jobs at The Sun since 1951, including city editor, assistant managing editor and, lastly, managing editor from 1959 to 1968. But it was Swangard's earlier stint as Sun sports editor that had raised the bar for sports coverage in the city, and it would be no surprise that he was at a table for the Second Annual Sportsmen's Dinner – a fundraiser held at the Hotel Vancouver on Sept. 26, 1967 – tucking into Crab Rockefeller, charcoal broiled streak and broccoli mornay alongside his boss, Stu Keate, and table of luminaries that

included Roger Bannister, John Landy and Bob Hope. Hope's keynote speech was four pages of typed notes written by Keate, kicking off with: "Vancouver, a city of 900,000 population, once described as the city of wampum and whoopee." A month later, Hope's secretary sent a letter to Keate on the comedian's behalf thanking him for his scrapbook from the dinner and a book of Norris cartoons.

Swangard's devoted promotion of amateur and professional athletes and local sporting events ultimately primed the paper's talented sports columnists and reporters for the October 1969 announcement that the city had been awarded an NHL franchise. Sun columnist Allan Fotheringham, weighing in regularly on the subject, had documented the negotiating process and suggested the city's overt eagerness and

FACING PAGE: *The Moon* just seemed a little more significant than *The Sun* on July 21, 1969, when the paper published a special supplement about the lunar landing.

The Moon !

THE SUN, VANCOUVER, BRITISH COLUMBIA, MONDAY, JULY 21, 1969   58 PAGES   ★★★★

MAN WALKS ON MOON

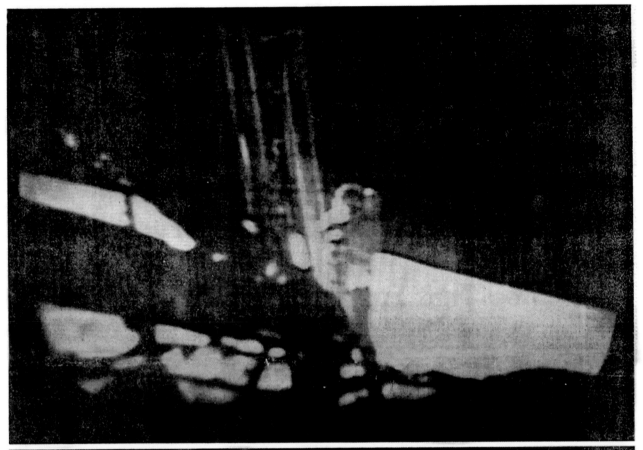

'That's one small step for man, one giant leap for mankind'

The Supremes perform at the Cave in 1967. *Ken Oakes/Vancouver Sun*

the backroom dealing by then Canucks president Cy McLean to acquire the expansion team was all "deliciously ludicrous."

But the city, and *The Sun*, were delirious: "It's official," screamed the second-coming front-page headline on Dec. 2, 1969. "VANCOUVER IN NHL. Effective Next Fall." The report out of the NHL governors' meeting in New York outlined the long negotiation, and quoted new owner Tom Scallen: "We're delighted. We're going to do our best to give Vancouver a top-flight major league hockey team."

The NHL was coming to town.

A purple haze at the stadium

In preparations to welcome the city's new hockey team, the Pacific Coliseum opened on Jan. 8, 1968. Its then-cavernous 15,713-seat indoor space was filled regularly with trade shows and touring acts in advance of the Canucks' debut in October 1970. Among the first superstars to rock the Coliseum stage was Jimi Hendrix, who reminded fans that his grandmother, who was in the audience, had grown up in Vancouver. Lloyd Dykk, the brilliantly acerbic *Sun* entertainment critic, suggested the Hendrix concert, which also featured the band Vanilla Fudge, would "give impetus to the realization that future historians are going to document and dissect the sociology of 20th century rock, the enfant terrible of music."

LEFT: The 1967 stage production of *The Ecstasy of Rita Joe* at the Queen Elizabeth Theatre, with Chief Dan George and Frances Hyland. *Vancouver Sun*

RIGHT: Granville Street was aglow with lights in the 1960s, neon calling cards for establishments like the Vogue Theatre, the Orpheum and the Crown Dining Room. *Ken Oakes/Vancouver Sun*

Standing by your men, women and readers

The Vancouver Sun was thriving under Stuart Keate's leadership, just as he'd promised, its circulation nearing 260,000 by decade's end, easily eclipsing the once-stronger Province. It often ran to 152 pages, a 20-cent compendium of everything editors felt local readers needed. Staff was being hired, reporters and photographers were travelling, and it appeared that the languid paper Keate had inherited had shaken itself out of the doldrums.

Keate was the kind of publisher, like Cromie, who hired good people and let them do their jobs, supporting and defending editorial decisions, even when it landed him in hot water.

When reporter Moira Farrow wrote a hard-hitting expose about car dealerships bugging their showrooms so they could covertly listen to customers' conversations, local car dealers were furious and started a boycott against the paper, withholding the considerable sum of $25,000 in monthly advertising. But Keate held fast, standing behind his reporter and her story, and the dealers eventually returned to the fold.

Keate's judgment wasn't as great, however, when it came to the so-called soft side of the paper. When he told The Sun comics committee – a group of staffers who debated the acquisition of new comic strips – that it was time to replace the long-running reader favourite Rex Morgan MD, his decision produced such outrage that even the CBC morning show called him at home demanding an explanation. Dr. Morgan was soon restored to his spot on the daily funny pages.

Readers had spoken.

ABOVE: Five Siamese kittens drink milk from champagne glasses in this 1968 photo, one of the most reprinted photographs in the newspaper's history. *Ken Oakes/Vancouver Sun*

NEAR RIGHT: A March 7, 1968 parade through Vancouver celebrated Olympic gold medalist Nancy Greene. *Ralph Bower/Vancouver Sun*

FAR RIGHT: Bathing beauties catch some rays at English Bay in 1964. *Ralph Bower/Vancouver Sun*

THE **1970**s

The 1970s: Hippies, hosannas and hostilities

If the 1960s had spawned both a sexual revolution and a hippie-inspired counterculture, the 1970s was the era of the environmentalist. Nowhere was the anti-establishment protest movement stronger than in Vancouver, where the fledgling Greenpeace movement was working to change the ecological conscience of the world. While the city and its suburbs continued to be swamped with a migrating and growing population from both inside and outside the country, and eco-warriors were taking to the high seas, The Vancouver Sun and its healthy mid-decade circulation of nearly 250,000 was celebrating national recognition for journalistic excellence in photography and investigative reporting while grappling with two labour disputes that would inexorably alter its future fortunes.

ABOVE: *Vancouver Sun* photographer Glenn Baglo won a National Newspaper Award in 1971 for this photograph of a nude family at Wreck Beach.
Glenn Baglo/Vancouver Sun

PRECEDING PAGE: *Vancouver Sun* carriers, with their wagons, meet pre-delivery in May 1974. *Bob Dibble/Vancouver Sun*

Sun reporter Bob Hunter was a passionate environmentalist who would become one of the co-founders of Greenpeace in 1972. In this February 1971 photograph, Hunter addresses a crowd at **Peace Arch Park** *Ray Allan/Vancouver Sun*

Pacific Press employees were on strike for three months in early 1970, meaning neither *The Sun* nor *The Province* was published. In this November 1972 photo, the presses were idle during a labour dispute. *Vancouver Sun*

Strike one

The Pacific Press plant producing *The Sun* and *The Province* comprised eight unions, the Newspaper Guild representing editorial employees among them. The so-called "hard hat" unions, which covered plant maintenance and newspaper production, included the pressmen, mailers, stereotypers and typographers.

In Febuary 1970, ongoing contract negotiations between the company and the unions broke down over "manning" clauses, or staffing numbers, in the pressroom, as well as over economic issues such as wages and benefits.

There had been slowdowns in the pressroom, prompting editors to print apologies to readers for the late delivery of papers, including a Feb. 14, 1970 in-house *Sun* notice advising readers that the 1,100 employees of Pacific Press were "among the highest paid in the North American newspaper industry." It asked: "Would you turn down a $1,600 pay increase? Of course you wouldn't." The mailers' union, the message said, did just that, rejecting a raise that would have bumped their annual salary to $10,556.91 for working the night shift. "This is good money by anyone's standards."

The paper went on strike the next day.

The three-month dispute shut down both dailies and provided a daily newspaper vacuum that was soon filled by the *Vancouver Express*, produced by staffers from both idled newspapers.

The plant would stay shuttered until May 15 – the settlement saw a five-year senior reporter's minimum rate increase to $225.87 a week, up from $177.50 – and *The Sun* re-emerged with a George Dobie story headlined: "Can newspapering survive if labor strife continues?"

In the same edition, columnist Allan Fotheringham noted that no one wins when a company is surrounded by picket lines, that Pacific Press employees lost one-quarter of their annual salary, the company lost untold millions in advertising revenue and "even more serious was the gradual unbinding of the seams that hold a city together."

In a message to readers, publisher Stuart Keate noted "our 4,000 carrier boys may have a little trouble getting their route books up to date . . . our newsprint may be a bit brittle and susceptible to cracks after 90 days on the floor. The presses and conveyers will need a manicure and some baby oil. Full color comics will not be available for three weeks."

But: "We have learned some useful lessons. We hope, by dint of our hard work and your good will, to produce a strong and vigorous *Sun* which will continue to merit the confidence of this community and country."

Labour peace at Pacific Press, however, would be short-lived.

Too big for our britches

A news feature by *Sun* reporter Neale Adams in October 1970 reflected the newspaper's take on the ever-changing physical and social landscape of the region, suggesting that Greater Vancouver's population of one million was having a deleterious effect on the city.

Many newcomers, especially immigrants, were settling their families into new Vancouver Specials, the boxy utilitarian houses designed to maximize square footage on the average 33x100-foot city lot.

Although the architectural design would long suffer critical indignation for its ungraceful exterior, it was an affordable option for growing families – and hundreds of the controversial houses began to fill the far reaches of the city. In Vancouver's southeast corner, council was working on plans for the development of Champlain Heights, a residential neighbourhood that would consume the last large undeveloped tract of land in the city.

"Growth will make life unbearable here," was the headline over Adams's story, which lamented "mass migration, swamped suburbs."

Paul Watson of Greenpeace (left) and Bob Hunter in 1976. *George Diack/Vancouver Sun*

The Greenpeace connection

After months of anti-nuclear protests, a rusty fishing boat named *Phyllis McCormack* set out from Vancouver for Amchitka in Alaska's Aleutian Islands on Sept. 15, 1971, in what would be considered the founding voyage of the Greenpeace movement. Among the motley crew was a long-haired hippie named Bob Hunter, a wildly passionate environmentalist and former *Winnipeg Tribune* reporter who had been distinguishing himself since the late 1960s as a *Vancouver Sun* columnist writing on ecological issues and local counterculture.

The boat didn't make it in time to stop the U.S. Atomic Energy Commission's planned atomic bomb test, but the worldwide publicity generated by the renegade eco-warriors – and by Hunter's reports, published in *The Sun* throughout the 45-day trip – worked, and the AEC cancelled further tests.

But Hunter's ambitions were bigger than *The Sun*. A founder of Vancouver's anti-nuclear Don't Make A Wave Committee, his mission was to save the planet and, in 1972, he joined a like-minded group of locals, including Paul Watson, Ben Metcalfe, Patrick Moore, Jim Bohlen and Irving Stowe in officially establishing Greenpeace, the global organization that today boasts three million members in 40 countries. Hunter, who was Greenpeace president from 1973 to 1977, was soon knee deep in grassroots campaigns against whaling, old-growth logging, the seal hunt, nuclear testing, toxic waste dumping and, in later years, climate change.

He spent much of the 1970s aboard inflatable zodiacs on the high seas, on ice floes dying the coats of seal pups to render their fur worthless, and in the Pacific caught in the cross-hairs of Russian ships firing harpoons at whales.

On a 1975 expedition, as the 80-foot *Greenpeace V* dropped anchor near Masset to undertake an archeological exploration of abandoned whaling stations in the southern Queen Charlotte Islands, Hunter wrote in *The Sun* that "crew members also succeeded in getting so close to Pacific gray whales that they could reach out and touch the giant creatures, looking them directly in the eye."

Hunter's last column for *The Sun* was published in August 1975.

Often called the original Rainbow Warrior, Hunter left Greenpeace in the late 1980s but remained a supporter, especially of direct-action anti-whaling warrior Watson and his Sea Shepherd Society.

Hunter wrote several books, including *Warriors of the Rainbow*, and became a television reporter in Toronto.

In 2001, he ran unsuccessfully for a Liberal seat in Toronto.

A father of four, he died of prostate cancer in 2005 at the age of 63, his journalistic legacy living on in his daughter Justine, a respected journalist who, for several years, was also a *Vancouver Sun* reporter.

Prime Minister Pierre Trudeau married 22-year-old Margaret Sinclair on March 4, 1971 in North Vancouver.

The bachelor takes a wife

In what may have been the best-kept secret of his prime ministership, 51-year-old perennial bachelor Pierre Trudeau married 22-year-old Margaret Sinclair in a secret romantic wedding on March 4, 1971, at St. Stephen's Church in North Vancouver. The luminous young bride was pictured by *The Sun* in a white cowled coat beaming under a cloud of rice confetti, clutching the arm of her new husband. The wedding, followed by a six-course dinner and reception at the Capilano Golf Club, was such a well-kept secret that the priest who performed the Catholic marriage didn't know the groom's identity until the week before.

The Sun of March 5 – the paper had once again excised Vancouver from its nameplate – featured a Moira Farrow interview with Margaret's mother, Kathleen, who gushed that her new son-in-law "may be old but he's young at heart." The dashing couple, who had met three years earlier in Tahiti, would have three sons before divorcing in 1980 after a tumultuous nine years.

RCMP officers rode into a crowd of more than 1,000 pro-marijuana demonstrators on Aug. 7, 1971 in what became known as the Gastown Riot.
Glenn Baglo/Vancouver Sun

The young and the restless: Part one

As it had in many a decade before, youth unrest simmered throughout the 1970s.

In what came to be called the Battle of Jericho, 150 bullet-proof-vested RCMP brandishing riot sticks smashed their way into a hostel encampment on the Jericho army base in October 1970, evicting 200 transient squatters who had set up residence in one of the base's buildings after being evicted from the Beatty Street Armory.

In May 1971, anti-development activists tore down a fence at the entrance to Stanley Park and occupied the site, but the boiling point for both protesters and police came on Aug. 7 when riot-equipped mounted police rode into a crowd of more than 1,000 pro-marijuana demonstrators in Gastown, arresting 79 and

sending 12 to hospital. Dubbed the Battle of Maple Tree Square, the melee became known as the Gastown Riot.

Sun photographer Glenn Baglo, carrying a camera and flash and wearing a *Sun*-labelled helmet, was in the thick of things in the Gastown brawl, capturing dozens of graphic images of police and protesters, along with a shot of an eight-foot-long mock marijuana joint. In an interview for the paper, Baglo said police officers shoved him with their sticks and threatened to take away his equipment. One mounted officer who confronted him said: "Do you want that camera smashed?"

Following public outrage over police brutality, Mayor Tom Campbell asked the attorney-general to appoint an impartial inquiry. The Vancouver police, meantime, advised *Sun* management that future press passes brandished by reporters and photographers would require photo identification.

Celebrating the shooters: Glenn Baglo

If *The Sun*'s reputation had been built on its writers, it was no less renowned for its news photography. The eye of the photographer is like the ear of the writer, and the best newspaper photographers, like the best newspaper writers, are both reporters and craftsmen, using their innate sense of the story to freeze a moment in time, even when that requires wading into angry mobs, dangling from bridge decks, corralling unruly rock stars or capturing that glorious iconic frame of the winning goal in an Olympic gold medal hockey game.

When Glenn Baglo joined the *Sun* photo department in the summer of 1970, he was a new recruit among a seasoned troop of shooters that included George Diack, Deni Eagland, Charlie Warner, Dave Buchan, Brian Kent, Ray

On Aug. 14, 1974, native Indians blocked the Bonaparte Reserve entrance near Cache Creek and told *Sun* photographer Glenn Baglo his camera would be smashed if he took more photos. One of them pointed his gun directly at Baglo, who snapped the photo. *Glenn Baglo/Vancouver Sun*

Allan and Dan Scott.

It didn't take long for Baglo to measure up. He won two National Newspaper Awards right out of the gate: one in 1970 for a photograph of an older woman with a cane trying to see and hear what she could through a crack between doors at a faith healing event at the Pacific Coliseum, and another in 1971, in which he discreetly depicted a family enjoying an unclothed outing at Vancouver's nudity hot spot, Wreck Beach.

Baglo also received an NNA nomination in 1993 for what might well be his most famous shot, one that evoked an age-old view of a daily newspaper's disposability. When he was assigned to photograph media baron Conrad Black, his future boss, Baglo recalled that "for some reason 'fish' popped into my mind. I checked for fish mongers near the office and found one on Fourth Avenue, and bought a small whole salmon.

"I was photographing Conrad in the office so I had placed the salmon inside a newspaper and had it to hand him. He entered with all his regal bearing and we were introduced. I said, 'I'd like to shoot a picture that contains a surprise for the reader.' And I produced the salmon wrapped in *The Vancouver Sun*. I added that I wanted him to hold it like he would a sheaf of briefing papers, so the salmon didn't readily come to view, but would be discovered by the viewer. He took the prop and adopted the pose. He allowed me to shoot three frames.

"The editors wrote a headline, a caption and a pull-quote that all said the same thing: 'The future of newspapers is not fish wrap.'"

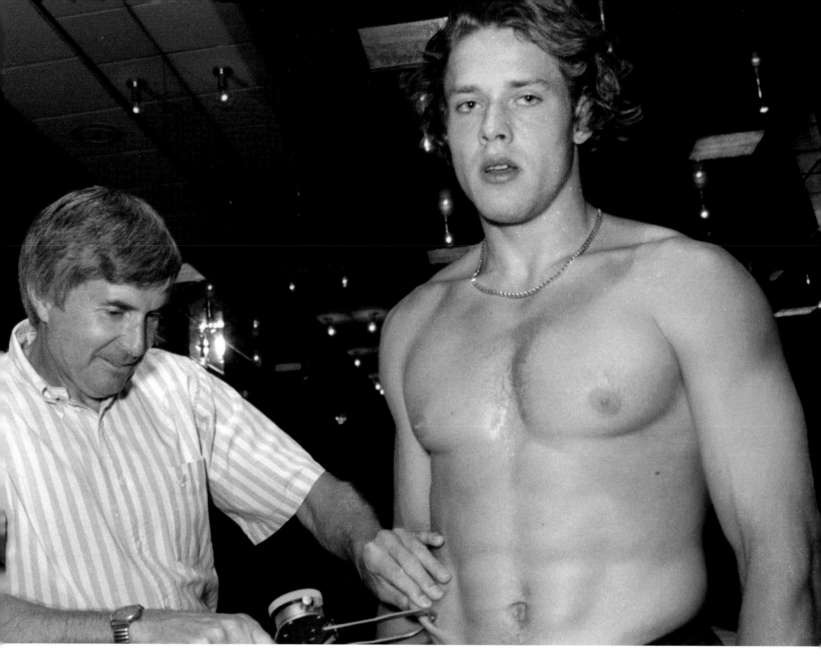

Of all the photographs he took during his long *Sun* career, Ralph Bower's most famous shot may be this image of Vancouver Canuck Pavel Bure, naked from the waist up, getting a physical test from Dr. Ted Rhodes in 1994. *Ralph Bower/Vancouver Sun*

Celebrating the shooters: Ralph Bower

One of Glenn Baglo's peers was Ralph Bower, who started as a *Sun* copy boy assigned to the photo department in 1955. In his ensuing 41 years at *The Sun*, Bower took 10,000 photographs with 20 different cameras, most of them Nikons, which was *The Sun*'s camera of choice. Each new camera heralded a new age of technology, from a Speed Graphic 4x5 to a Mamiya twin-lens reflex to 35-mm Nikons to digital Nikons, all complemented by dozens of lenses.

Tapping into the Bower vault of *Sun* stories, which are legion and legend, is to find oneself at the intersection where history and happenstance meet who's who. When he was sent to photograph Russian ballet star Rudolf Nureyev, for instance, Bower had no idea what the famed dancer looked like, so he walked up to someone in the Hotel Georgia and asked for help. It was Nureyev.

"I went up to him and said 'I'm looking for the Mad Russian,'" Bower recounts. "I thought it

was a ballet! He turned and looked at me, and could have punched me right in the nose. But he sort of grinned. I said, 'Oh, have I said something wrong?' And he kept glaring at me. 'I said, I'm sorry, I hope I didn't offend you.' But he posed for me, right in the lobby of the Georgia Hotel."

His most photographed political subject was Pierre Trudeau. One shot, taken at the Bayshore Hotel, almost didn't happen, as Bower arrived just as the prime minister was diving into the hotel pool. "I was just walking in with my camera and he goes up and does a jack-knife. I'm like, oh God, I missed that! Well, knowing Trudeau, he went back up again, waited until my camera was cocked, and away he went again. He was a performer."

In 1985, Bower won a National Newspaper Award for a spot news photograph of an agitated father, involved in a child custody dispute, wielding a knife and dangling his baby son by the ankle out the window of a third-floor apartment in Vancouver.

His most celebrated sports shot was the 1994 beefcake portrait of Russian Rocket

Pavel Bure of the Vancouver Canucks. Dressing-room photos were banned by the NHL after someone had snapped Wayne Gretzky in the shower, so when Bower saw Bure getting a shirtless checkup in another room, he popped in and took the photo. Not surprisingly, it was published on page one the next day, the shaggy-haired Bure looking more like a ripped Adonis than a Russian right winger.

"They tell me it sold 4,000 extra papers," recalled Bower. "I got letters from housewives saying, 'You made my day.' Then the phone rings, and the Canucks are mad as hell at me. Steve Tambellini said, 'You'd better see Pat Quinn! You're in trouble. You broke the rule.' I told Pat I wasn't in the dressing room when I shot it."

Bure asked Bower for a few prints and, when he delivered them, the hockey hunk said: "Hey, Ralph, you workin' for *Playboy* now?"

By the time he retired in 1996, Bower had snapped "prime ministers, the Queen, the collapse of the Second Narrows Bridge, the Pope, Elvis Presley, the Lions, the Canucks and everything in between."

Heavyweight champ Muhammad Ali scored a convincing win over Canadian George Chuvalo on May 1, 1972 at the Pacific Coliseum. *Ralph Bower/ Vancouver Sun*

A billionaire, two boxers and a band

Juxtaposing the 1970s social movement that focused on serious environmental and political change was the diversionary insouciance found in pop culture – *Annie Hall* and *The Godfather* were packing theatres, while disco music was battling soft pop on the charts. As the world said goodbye in August 1977 to Elvis Presley, the best-selling singer of all time, Swedish band ABBA was selling more records than any other musical act in the decade.

Vancouver theatres and nightclubs were jammed with partygoers, big-ticket concerts were packing them in, and the city was a magnet for all manner of celebrity.

A March 15, 1972 headline in *The Sun* announced that reclusive billionaire "Howard Hughes arrives here" and revealed that Hughes had checked into the Bayshore and was "alive and well." He would stay for six months, but reportedly never left his blacked-out penthouse suite.

Two months later, on May 1, boxing demigod Muhammad Ali beat Canadian heavyweight George Chuvalo in a North American Boxing Federation championship at the Pacific Coliseum. The match was arranged by local stock promoter Murray Pezim, a colourful character whose financial dealings often landed him in *The Sun*'s business section headlines.

Reporter Larry Still's front-page story on the lead up to the boxing match, accompanied by a Dan Scott photograph of the two fighters standing on scales, noted that "Ali, looking suitably mean and snarly in a black and white silk dressing gown, tipped the scales at 217-1/2 pounds" while "Chuvalo, less flamboyant in a tattered blue bath robe, weighed in at a hefty 221 pounds." The fight itself, according to reporter Hal Sigurdson, was really decided in the sixth round when "Ali sliced open George Chuvalo's forehead like an over-ripe grape."

The following month, a Rolling Stones concert at the Coliseum provoked a riot, in which a mob reportedly lobbed Molotov cocktails, stink bombs and rocks at police, injuring 31 officers. *The Sun* news story by Scott Honeyman and Bill Bachop began with: "The Rolling Stones and an ecstatic crowd of 17,000 were inside, flying stones and an unruly mob of 2,500 were outside." Wandering through the melee, according to the report, were scalpers trying to sell the $6 face-value tickets for $20.

The March 15, 1972 *Sun* front page heralds the arrival in Vancouver of reclusive tycoon Howard Hughes.

Politics and partisanship

The day after B.C.'s new premier Bill Bennett was celebrating his decisive Dec. 11, 1975 victory with his father, W.A.C. Bennett, *The Sun*'s editorialists were suggesting he work quickly for "a bridging first, then a closing of the partisan valleys torn through this province's social landscape in past weeks."

Editorials are not bylined – traditionally they are considered the voice of the newspaper and not that of a single journalist – but the names gracing the editorial page provided a hierarchical clue, from the top down: Stuart

Keate, vice-president and publisher; Bruce Hutchison, editorial director; David Ablett and Allan Fotheringham, senior editors; Bruce Larsen, managing editor; Eric Downton, Lisa Hobbs, Mac Reynolds and Tim Traynor, associate editors.

The Len Norris cartoon beside the editorial depicted a frustrated man sitting on his sofa, holding the newspaper's election results, while his harried wife, surrounded by 11 children and a dog, asks: "D'you mind? They've never seen anyone eat their hat."

Homing in on Habitat

In May 1976, hundreds of delegates converged on Vancouver for the Habitat conference, a United Nations forum on human settlement convened to address the global challenge of sheltering the poor. Attendees included Margaret Mead, Mother Teresa and Buckminster Fuller. Prime Minister Pierre Trudeau, who arrived in town with his wife Margaret, told the conference that the change necessary to adjust to the planet's soaring population will require a "conspiracy of love." Local activist Alan Clapp held a parallel Habitat Forum in the unused Second World War aircraft hangars at Jericho Beach, a well-attended music and talk fest that was a rank-and-file alternative to the official discussions being held downtown.

A full-page ad in *The Sun*, placed by the International Meditation Society, welcomed the Maharishi Mahesh Yogi to Habitat, promoting his May 31st address and the Yogi's self-proclaimed "age of enlightenment" as reasons that local crime had dropped and "citizens in Vancouver have experienced a growing sense of social orderliness and harmony in their environment."

Meantime, the landfill in Langley was so full that it had to be closed.

Awards 'r' us

With two coveted National Newspaper Awards newly filling its trophy cabinet, the paper geared up for another acceptance speech in 1976, when the prestigious Michener Award for Journalism, the Canadian newspaper industry's top honour for public service journalism, went to *Sun* Ottawa bureau chief John Sawatsky for a series of stories on cover-ups of illegal practices by the RCMP and Quebec police forces.

Publisher Stuart Keate and managing editor Bruce Larsen had given Sawatsky a year to work on the story, not unusual in an era when *The Sun* was known for its investigative reporting and when its management was generous with its pocketbook, and reporters' time. The Michener would be just one of dozens of provincial, national and international awards *The Vancouver Sun* would frame and hang on its newsroom and office walls over the years, an

Columnist Pete McMartin, pictured with photographer Glenn Baglo, joined *The Sun* in 1976 and would become one of the paper's most popular columnists. *Vancouver Sun*

acknowledgment of excellence in every journalistic discipline from reporting and cartooning to design and photography. Among them: a total of 43 National Newspaper Awards won between 1951 and 2011.

Strike two

While *The Vancouver Sun* was busy covering the news of the day, things were boiling over internally.

On Nov. 1, 1978, Clark Davey was named publisher, succeeding the much-respected and retiring Stuart Keate. On the same day, the 1,400 employees of *The Sun* and *The Province* went on strike.

The Pacific Press dispute, once again, centred on the pressmen, but all eight unions went out, shutting down the plant.

While picket lines girded the building day after day, for eight long months, inside the 100 or so non-union workers still collecting a salary and coming to work every day had little to do, beyond congregating in the top floor cafeteria and catching up on backlogged work.

It was a testy time, and would only exacerbate long-standing employee/management tension.

It also resulted in the loss of *Sun* editorial staffers, including controversial columnist Doug Collins, who defected to the *Vancouver Courier*. Collins' right-wing tirades had long ruffled feathers, both inside and outside the newsroom, including those of trade unions when he

was the paper's labour reporter. He was fired at one point for freelancing – which was verboten – but when he sued for wrongful dismissal, he won and returned to work.

Pacific Press strikers, as they had done in 1970, dusted off the *Vancouver Express*, which published an editorial on Nov. 3 headlined "Press ganged." It slammed the intractability of management and its "Eastern interests," the potential loss of jobs through automation and noted that "we are no longer dealing with newspaper people; we are confronted by cost accountants who wouldn't recognize a good newspaper even if they cared to produce one."

A letter appearing in the *Express* from *Sun* publisher Davey and *Province* publisher Paddy Sherman took the 180 pressmen and mailers to task for shutting down the operation and putting more than 1,000 co-workers out of work, including "another 8,000 carrier girls and boys and contractors."

It was the strike that also introduced to readers the notion of "featherbedding," whereby management asserted that the generous manning clauses controlled by the pressmen and mailers unions, under special contract clauses, were being abused to the detriment of the company's bottom line.

The strike ended on June 26, 1979, but it had dealt an irreversible financial blow to Pacific Press. Many of the advertisers whose flyers had routinely stuffed the papers and contributed significantly to the business's bottom line had moved their business to the community weeklies – and they never came back.

THE OPENING CEREMONIES Friday night may have been the only time Vancouver Canucks will get this close to the Stanley Cup for many years. The cup was flown here—it took a full seat on a regular flight—especially for the NHL opener. Up near the bowl part are the names of Vancouver Millionaires, who won it in 1915. Canucks' debut brought 15,062 fans into Pacific Coliseum.

NHL HISTORY MADE

Vancouver's debut
—a night of firsts

It was a historic night for Vancouver hockey Friday, a night when the Canucks played their first-ever National Hockey League game and a night when the Pacific Coliseum was so full of dignitaries there was hardly an unstuffed shirt to be found.

Unfortunately for the Canucks and the 15,062 who came to urge them on, the Los Angeles Kings turned up too and became the death of the party. The Kings won 3-1, but it was still a memorable night—a night of firsts.

These were some of them:

● First man introduced — Bob McCusker, representing the Canucks of the sixties.

● First prolonged ovation — for Fred (Cyclone) Taylor, who helped Vancouver win the 1915 Stanley Cup.

● First national anthem — Juliette, who sung it admirably.

● First boos — for the people's mayor, Tom Terrific.

● First ceremonial face-off victory — Tom

SPORTS
Duncan Stewart · Editor

BARRY WILKINS
. . . Canucks' first

Terrific again, over federal public works minister Art Laing.

● First gaffe — neglecting to have a speaker representing the NHL, followed closely thereafter by neglecting to introduce the Kings.

● First official face-off victory—Canucks' Andre Boudrias over Kings' Bob Pulford.

● First shot on goal — King's Ed Joyal at 3:17 of first period.

● First save—Canucks' George Gardner.

● First Canucks' shot on goal — Boudrias at 3:32.

● First penalty — to Pulford for delaying the game at 4:26 of the first period.

● First fight — Canucks' Orland Kurtenbach and Kings' Dale Hoganson at 5:37 (no decision).

● First misconduct — Canucks' Pat Quinn at 11:28.

● First goal — King's Ross Lonsberry, 9:26, second period.

● First Vancouver goal — Barry Wilkins, 2:14, third period.

● First victory — the Kings, 3-1.

● First sore loser—the guy who yelled, "Give the ball to Leroy."

And as the 15,062 filed out, there were the first grumblings of a winter of discontent.

ONE OF DALE TALLON'S shots was so hard it knocked Los Angeles Kings goalie Dennis DeJordy on his butt, which did nothing more than prove that Tallon has a big-league shot. He was on target, but the rebound went to Gilles Marotte, bringing up the rear.

Photos by
Ralph Bower and Brian Kent

IT WASN'T MEANT to be the woodchoppers' ball but there were times Friday night when the lumber was lifted a little higher than regulations allow. Like the time (left) when Kings' Barry Cahan (3) sent Canucks' Mike Corrigan reeling out of goalie Dennis DeJordy's crease. And the other time (right) when Vancouver's Pat Quinn didn't like the way Gilles Marotte barred him from that same crease.

The Vancouver Canucks played their first regular season NHL game on Friday, Oct. 9, 1970 at the Pacific Coliseum. A sellout crowd of 15,062 watched the home team fall 3-1 to the Los Angeles Kings, with Barry Wilkins scoring the Canucks' lone goal.

Bob Dirakowski reads the paper in his taxi on a slow night following the end of the transit strike in March 1978. *Glenn Baglo/Vancouver Sun*

A photographer's net worth

While hockey fans were buzzing about the Oct. 9, 1970 Pacific Coliseum debut of the Vancouver Canucks – *Sun* sports editor Duncan Stewart's story noted that NHL history had been made with "a night of firsts" that included the Canucks' first goal by Barry Wilkins in the third period and the first fight, between Orland Kurtenbach and the Kings' Dale Hoganson – *Sun* photographer Ralph Bower was tinkering with a new invention: the net cam.

He wanted to put a camera right in the goaltender's net, to provide a different perspective on the action, and asked the *Sun* carpenters to help out. They built him "a bird cage-like wooden box with a folding safety hinge to protect the players and the 35-mm lens and the cameras." To operate the Nikon's motor drive, an under-ice cable – connected to a doorbell switch – was laid from the goal to Bower, sitting near the goal judge. After convincing the NHL of its efficacy, Bower took his first "net-cam" shot on Dec. 12, 1970 at the Pacific Coliseum – just two months after the Canucks first took to the ice – a "puck-view" save by Canucks goalie Charlie Hodge of a head-on shot by Golden Seal forward Ernie Hicke. Bower used his homemade net cam several times after that, but it wouldn't become a hockey standard until the onset of digital photography in the 1990s.

Wooing back readers

It took several days after the strike to get the paper back on readers' doorsteps. The first issue, on June 29, 1979, included a full-page promotional ad – Now, *The Sun* shines brighter than ever! – reminding readers of *The Sun*'s virtues in a blatant appeal to home subscribers: new home and real estate sections; a revamped You feature section; a Saturday travel section; three "capital" columnists (Michael Valpy in Ottawa, Marjorie Nichols in Victoria and Bruce Hutchison in Vancouver); a new bridge column; three new comic strips (*Star Wars, Pop Idols* and *Pavlov*); enhanced television listings in Friday's TV Week; and the addition to the front page of a new Focus feature and the Herman cartoon panel.

The Sun's writers, long recognized for their talent and strong opinions, also helped bring readers back, and *Sun* managing editor Bruce Larsen was quick to add to the staff, attracting subscribers with the hiring of a new consumer columnist, Nicole Parton.

Her self-titled column reprised the institution that was Penny Wise, the name of the consumer column penned decades earlier by Evelyn Caldwell. Parton's breezy style and zeal for fighting on behalf of readers' consumer rights made her one of the paper's best-read columnists, so much so that *The Sun* had to hire an

The Sun's fashion pages published this photo of a model wearing fall fashions in front of a newspaper kiosk in 1975. *Vancouver Sun*

The Sun newsroom in February 1972. *Ray Allan/Vancouver Sun*

assistant to help her field the nearly 1,000 letters she received each week, along with the hundreds of reader phone calls that came in every day on the two lines in her office. When Parton urged readers to petition the Canadian Radio-television and Telecommunications Commission to ban tampon ads during the dinner hour, more than 100,000 *Sun* readers responded and the campaign later spread to newspapers across Canada. While *Sun* readers won that battle, they ultimately lost the war as times changed and such impropriety became more acceptable. In addition to her weekly columns (which often required a legal once-over, especially when she was taking on a big retailer or *Sun* advertiser), Parton wrote three books during her 17 years at the paper and six more after leaving *The Sun* in 1996, selling close to 300,000 copies.

The daily miracle

Labour relations would remain tender throughout the plant following the strike, even as things returned to relative normalcy in *The Sun* newsroom.

Hot type had yet to give way to cold type, technology in the form of computers had yet to transform the filing process, and the paper was still being produced the old-fashioned way.

It was, and is, the daily miracle, a round-the-clock process that starts before dawn with the gathering of local, national and international news, photographs and graphic material from a variety of sources – including staff and numerous wire services – all of it distilled from hundreds of choices to an eclectic selection of the several dozen that fill the pages of the average newspaper, along with the advertising and promotional content initiated by those departments.

Columnist Stephen Hume has estimated that *The Sun* gathers, edits and delivers to readers "more than 125,000 news items a year . . . an encyclopedia's-worth of current information every 12 months" and "your typical large-market daily newspaper contains somewhere between 60,000 and 130,000 words, about the count for a standard paperback." *The Sun* staff of 175 putting it all together in the 1970s included reporters in the city, sports, business and arts departments, the editors in charge of those sections, an art editor, wire editors, a national editor, news editors, an assortment of copy editors and the senior editors who ultimately made the final decisions during the several news meetings held every day.

The paper was "laid out" by the makeup department, an adjunct to advertising, using a complicated formula that ensured the proper ratio of advertising to editorial content and the proper placement of ads. The six-day-a-week paper averaged 60 to 100-plus pages, with the advertising content ranging from 30 to 70 per cent, depending on the day of the week and the size of the paper.

In the early 1970s, the paper's "home edition" – the paper delivered to subscribers by dinner time – had a noon deadline. It would be "chased" with late-breaking news until the 2:15 p.m. deadline, when the final buff edition with its tan/peach-coloured front page went to press.

Reporters punched out their stories on manual typewriters, Underwoods mostly, using carbon-copied folio paper. The top copy was hand-edited by a phalanx of copy editors, then slipped into a plastic leather-strapped Zip Tube and sent out through pneumatic tubes to the composing room – or the backshop, as it was called – tucked in a corner on the same floor.

Once there, stories were given to linotype machine operators, who would set the type. Compositors would lay out the page and then make a proof for proof-reading by the editorial department. Stereotypers would then make the cardboard mould, and the hot metal press plate. The engravers would scan pictures and make plates to be used by the compositors putting the pages together. The finished plates, which weighed close to 50 pounds and were curved in a half-moon shape with "stand-up"

The paper's new publisher, Clark Davey, greets the newsroom on Oct. 31, 1978.
Glenn Baglo/Vancouver Sun

lettering, were then sent down a conveyor track to the basement and mounted on the presses. Once they had been used to print the pages, the plates went back on the conveyor into a big melting pot at the end of the line, to be recycled as hot metal.

The rumbling to life of the giant workhorse presses in the basement caused *The Sun* newsroom floor to shake and signalled the start of the daily run, as comforting a sound as any journalist could hope to hear.

The young and the restless: Part two

The Sun was in the midst of a generational shift, its newsroom a spicy stew of hard-bitten experienced veterans, such as political pundit Marjorie Nichols, and a new crop of freshly recruited graduates from journalism schools across the country.

As with every passing of the torch, the young learned by example. In a June 29, 1979 editorial page column, Nichols noted with her trademark clarity that "in theory, Bill Bennett should be a happy man. He is rich, handsome, in apparent robust health and has just been awarded a shiny new mandate in the premier's office, good for up to five years." But, she wrote, a Liberal revival was afoot and "if

the standoff continues, Socreds will be immediately recognizable by their chair-shaped posteriors."

Among the newbies was wordsmith Pete McMartin, who was hired in 1976 and who would work variously as a harbour reporter, cityside reporter and sports columnist before taking up residence as the paper's general columnist on Sept. 1, 1981, with a stirring piece on fatherhood and the birth of his son, David.

McMartin's storytelling capabilities and human take on everything from politics to posies – often described as a thrice-weekly master class in writing – would fittingly install him in the company of the paper's most feted writers.

His memorable dispatch from the October 1989 earthquake that struck the San Francisco Bay area, killing 63 and causing $3 billion in damage, showed not only his writerly flair but his intuitive reportorial skills.

Then a sports columnist, McMartin was in Candlestick Park when the quake hit, covering the third game in the World Series between the Oakland Athletics and the San Francisco Giants.

He immediately went into news mode, filing stories by candlelight, including this passage: "When the shock hit, we were in an upper level concourse of Candlestick Park, shouldering through happy fans. It rolled over us – not a violent jerking, but a rhythmic muscular swaying that knocked people off-balance. No one fell down. No one screamed. Above us, the stadium's huge steel light standards swayed like car aerials. The upper concrete rim of Candlestick – a boomerang-shaped baffle designed to deflect the park's notorious winds – rippled like a shaken bedsheet."

A heart-rending series by McMartin on 43-year-old palliative care nurse Helena Tang – from her diagnosis with stomach cancer to her death 10 months later in November 2002 – was published over a period of eight months, 15 stories in all, and won a National Newspaper Award for McMartin and *Sun* photographer Ian Smith, whose intimate portraits of Tang helped humanize the agonizing toll of terminal cancer.

The art of the office romance

The 1970s were a great time to be a reporter in *The Sun* newsroom, a wide open space that was noisy with clatter and chatter, with shouting editors, constantly ringing phones and bustling copy runners, over-flowing with ideas and attitude. The place was electric, full of energy and expectations. Company spending was free-wheeling, assignments never-ending, writing opportunities boundless. Many of the paper's single reporters were also involved romantically, with one another or with staff at *The Sun*'s sister paper, *The Province*, down the hall. The Pacific Press library separated the two newsrooms but you could stand in one newsroom and see, and yell, into the other. And, every once in a while, management had to remind staff that cross-border canoodling during working hours was frowned upon and that while *The Sun* may have been in bed, at least corporately, with *The Province*, it was still the competition. Despite their efforts, there would be seven marriages between library staff and newsroom staff, and many more romances and weddings involving staffers in both newsrooms.

The young and the feckless

Despite his free-wheeling workplace, Clark Davey was a stickler of a publisher, an old-school journalist who expected his employees to represent his paper appropriately. At a 1979 luncheon to welcome the 14 summer reporting interns hired to replace vacationing veterans, Davey looked around the big coffin-shaped table in his boardroom while the youngbloods tucked into their steamed salmon and said, sternly: "I couldn't send a single one of you to cover the courts. A judge would take one look at you and kick you out." He was right. Everyone in the room, except Davey, who was wearing a suit and tie, was dressed for a day at the beach, including one Langara graduate who was clad in skin-tight kelly green jeans with a loud, matching Hawaiian shirt.

The Vancouver Press Club, the private watering hole of local newsies, was conveniently located on Granville across the street from *The Sun*'s offices and printing plant. *Colleen Kidd/Vancouver Sun*

Vancouver Whitecaps goalie Phil Parkes, holding the NASL championship trophy, and team captain John Craven (right) celebrate with fans following the team's 1979 Soccer Bowl victory. *Ralph Bower/Vancouver Sun*

The local watering hole

On Aug. 12, 1979, *The Province* began publishing on Sundays, leaving the advertising-lucrative Saturday market to its rival roommate, *The Vancouver Sun*. The bold move, which had involved months of negotiations with the pressmen, was the topic of the hour, among other items of news-centric gossip, at The Vancouver Press Club.

The nondescript club was tucked into a storefront right across the street from the Granville Street plant and was, in the tradition of reporter-frequented booze joints throughout history, a dank smoky hole-in-the-wall, bereft of character but for the occasional front page or cartoon stuck on the wall and the people who occupied the bar stools. Wedged between a cheesecake cafe and an art gallery, the members-only club entertained hundreds of PacPressers over the decades, its walls a toe-curling repository of industry conspiracies and secrets.

A stuffed moose presided over the club's bar, the beer was cheap and the food hearty, and it was the haunt of respected veterans like Patrick Nagle, who had been a Southam correspondent during apartheid in South Africa, and Larry Still, the paper's superb legal reporter, both of whom would often hold court after their shifts, spinning tales of their hair-raising exploits and captivating the tyros lining up to buy them jugs of suds.

Queen Elizabeth speaks with a Prince Rupert woman on her royal visit to that city in 1971. *Deni Eagland/Vancouver Sun*

The club was also a popular drop-in for the pressmen and other production folks who worked the Pacific Press night shift. While most news reporters typically worked the early morning shift to file on deadline, or a 2 p.m. to 9 p.m. shift writing for the next day's paper, the mechanical unions worked graveyard shifts and the Press Club, for many of them, filled in the down times.

Such was the foot traffic jaywalking back and forth across busy Granville Street between the club and the plant at all hours of the day and night that the city installed a traffic light at Granville and 7th.

THE 1980s

The 1980s:
Heroes, villains and heading for the Hills

After a thorny, unsettling eight-month strike in 1979 that shut down Pacific Press, The Vancouver Sun was working hard to find its way back into readers' hearts, delivering a 25-cent package of local and international news, business and sports, lifestyle and advertising, along with the daily and weekend comics pages, crossword puzzles and a variety of weekly feature sections – everything the 1980s reader needed to stay informed, intrigued and entertained.

The decade would bring a roller-coaster roster of news, captivating readers with stories of Air India and Expo 86, of a moonwalking pop star, of the evil darkness that was Clifford Olson, and the shining lights that were Terry Fox and Rick Hansen.

With another change of ownership at The Vancouver Sun, and the arrival of irrepressible editor Nick Hills, the paper's unofficial motto du jour was holding true: Never a dull day.

ABOVE: Cloaked in a traditional native Indian blanket, hereditary Gitxsan Chief Art Wilson surveys the damage of clearcut logging in Kispiox in 1988. *Steve Bosch/Vancouver Sun*

PRECEDING PAGE: The first Vancouver Sun Run attracted 5,000 runners in 1985 and has grown every year since, with close to one million runners, joggers and walkers having donned the run's trademark T-shirts through 2012. *Peter Battistoni/Vancouver Sun*

The making of a national hero

In Port Coquitlam, a young cancer survivor who had lost his right leg to osteogenic sarcoma in 1977 was contemplating an ambitious dream: a cross-Canada fundraising run for cancer. Terry Fox began training rigorously, developing what would become his trademark hop/stride, and telling *Sun* reporter Elizabeth Godley in a March 18, 1980 story that "I ran with the flu, with shin splints, losing toenails. In order to do this trip, I felt I'd have to get used to that sort of thing."

His reasons, he said, were simple: "When I was going through the treatments, I didn't know what would happen to me. I was fortunate, so I feel with running I'm carrying on a battle for the people I left behind in the cancer ward."

On April 12, 1980, Terry Fox dipped his artificial leg in the cool Atlantic waters in St. John's, Nfld., then turned west to begin his Marathon of Hope. Accompanied by his friend Doug Alward and, later, his brother Darrell, Fox had minimal financial support to get him started. He had written letters to various companies and agencies, including the Canadian Cancer Society, and had received a limited amount of cash as well as gas and running shoes. Running alongside the small camper donated by Ford, the tousle-haired 21-year-old started his quest to have every Canadian donate $1 to cancer research.

"It takes more courage to fight cancer than it does for me to run," he told reporters.

The start of his run garnered only a small mention, and photograph, on page A11 of the April 14 *Sun*, but his story would gain momentum, and media attention, with every mile he covered. Roadside crowds began turning out to cheer him on, including 10,000 in Toronto, donating to his cause at every stop on the route. For a time, it seemed that he was unstoppable.

But things did not turn out as Fox had planned. Doctors determined his cancer had spread to his lungs and, on Sept. 2, 1980 in Thunder Bay, Ontario, Fox tearfully announced that he had to give up on his dream, ending his run after 5,342 kilometres in 143 days, having raised $1.8 million.

Back home, *Sun* photographers captured Fox, sitting with his mom Betty and dad Rolly, at Royal Columbian Hospital, his familiar mop of curls framing a tired, dejected demeanour. He was wearing his ubiquitous white Marathon of Hope T-shirt, emblazoned with the Canadian flag. "I said the only way I was going to come back to Vancouver was to run in," he told *The Sun*. "But I tried as hard as I could. I don't think you can ask any more of me."

Less than two weeks after his return, as a still-green reporter who had been on the job for only a year, Shelley Fralic was sent to the Vancouver airport to report on a Sept. 12 meeting between Fox and Bob Richards, an Olympian turned minister whose sermons Fox had listened to while running. Fralic spotted Fox walking alone in a corridor and approached him, asking if he would agree to sit down and

Port Coquitlam's Terry Fox had already run more than halfway across the country on one leg to raise money for cancer when he was forced to halt his Marathon of Hope on Sept. 2, 1980. At an emotional press conference back home with his mother Betty, Fox announced his cancer had metastasized to his lungs. *Glenn Baglo/Vancouver Sun*

talk about all that had happened. The interview, one of his last, focused on his worry that the media had some of the story wrong, and he wanted readers to understand exactly how much ground he had covered during his run.

"This is something I want to get straight. It's important to me. Everybody said I had run halfway across Canada. Geographically, I was half way, but mileage-wise, I was 700 miles past halfway."

Fox also corrected the notion that he had been running the equivalent of 26 kilometres a day, when in fact he was averaging a marathon a day: 26 miles. On some days, he said, he ran as many as 30 miles, in an effort to accommodate a route designed for stopovers in the major cities between St. John's and Vancouver. He also revealed that the longer he was on the road, the more uncomfortable it became to run because he was losing weight and his artificial leg no longer fitted properly.

The details were important to him, but there was no question that Terry Fox's bigger goal had galvanized the nation. His death on June 28, 1981, at the age of 22, marked the start of the annual Terry Fox Run, which now takes place in more than 60 countries and has raised close to $600 million, vastly exceeding his modest dream.

Among Fox's many accolades are the Lou Marsh Award as Canada's top sportsman in 1980, an Order of Canada and a special Canadian coin and stamp. His name graces numerous statues, streets and buildings across the country, as well as a B.C. mountain, a Canadian icebreaker, 14 schools (including his own secondary school in Port Coquitlam) and a Rod Stewart song – *Never Give Up On A Dream*. He also received a stirring tribute at the 2010 Paralympic Games in Vancouver, which honoured not only his legacy as an athlete but as a fundraiser. Many of the athletes taking part in the Games lost limbs during battles with cancer; without Fox's efforts, and the research it fostered, there is no telling how differently their lives may have turned out.

In 2011, an unpopular arched statue dedicated to Fox in 1984 and placed in the Terry Fox Plaza outside BC Place Stadium was replaced with four bronze statues of Fox in various stages of running. The works were designed by artist and author Douglas Coupland, who in 2005 had published a book about Fox, titled *Terry*.

Fox's quiet fortitude, steadfast determination and strength of character continue to inspire not only his country, but the world.

There was a rush to buy street editions of *The Sun* on the afternoon of Jan. 28, 1986, after the U.S. space shuttle *Challenger* exploded, killing all seven astronauts aboard. *Deni Eagland/ Vancouver Sun*

giving their growing children a certain amount of freedom. The serial killer's plea bargain with the RCMP, in which he was paid $100,000 to help police locate the bodies of seven missing victims, further underscored the growing sense that Vancouver was no longer a safe town.

The Sun's award-winning coverage, which involved a team of dedicated reporters filing countless stories, was a disturbing chronology of recovered bodies, community fear and perceived police bungling.

In the Olson File special of *The Sun*'s Jan. 14, 1982 edition – under the banner headline "Olson was paid to locate bodies" and alongside the down-page story "Olson given life for 11 murders" – it was revealed that before Olson was arrested and pleaded guilty he had been in custody four times, and that B.C. Attorney-General Allan Williams did not regret the "smelly" payoff. Williams said the deal allowed police to gather the evidence for conviction and enabled parents to bury their dead children, perhaps giving them some kind of closure.

One day, *Sun* reporter Rick Ouston, who had been covering the case, answered his phone in the newsroom, only to hear: "Rick. It's Cliff. Cliff Olson." Ouston had reached out to Olson through the killer's wife Joan, whom Ouston had interviewed several times previously; she'd talked of life with their young son in Kitsilano after news of the murders and her husband's involvement became public. On the phone, a glib Olson told Ouston he wanted to set the record straight on some media reports. He also wanted to complain about his treatment in Oakalla Prison.

Ouston recalled his first thoughts after picking up the phone. "The man on the

Southam takes the west

The Vancouver Sun changed hands once again when, on Aug. 27, 1980, Southam Inc. bought the paper from Thomson Newspapers, which had purchased *The Sun* only months before from FP Publications. Southam, which already owned *The Province*, was expanding a newspaper empire that included dailies in major cities across Canada, among them the *Ottawa Citizen*, *Montreal Gazette*, *Edmonton Journal* and *Calgary Herald*.

The purchase further cemented the Pacific Press joint operating agreement, allowing the single owner to consider opportunities for amalgamating platforms across the country while striving to maintain the editorial independence of each title.

In August 1981, the Royal Commission on Newspapers – known as the Kent Commission and created to address concerns over the growing concentration of media ownership in

Canada – released a report that took aim at the Southam and Thomson chains for their recent transactions in Vancouver, which coincided with the closing of the *Ottawa Journal* and *Winnipeg Tribune*, known as Black Wednesday. The report, a followup to the 1970 Davey Report, which examined similar issues, did not recommend changes to Pacific Press but did suggest that a federal Newspaper Act would help control media concentration. Such an act failed to materialize.

The Olson file

In the summer of 1981, darkness would descend on Vancouver with the Aug. 21 court appearance of Clifford Olson, who would eventually be charged with the murders of 11 local children, aged nine to 18. The horrific case cast a pall over the region, an unsettling feeling, especially for parents who had been used to

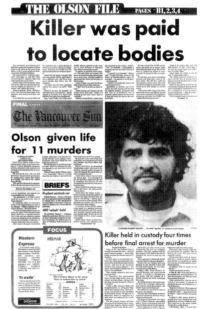

A special report on serial killer Clifford Olson, published Jan. 14, 1982, won a National Newspaper Award for a team of *Sun* reporters.

phone identifying himself as Olson could have been anyone, from the alleged killer to a prankster trying to get a fake story into the newspaper. I had to determine it was Olson, so I asked him how he could prove he was. Olson proceeded to give me chilling details on where he said two as-yet unrecovered bodies had been stashed.

"After the call I called the two top Mounties in charge of the investigation. They asked me how I knew it had been Olson. I gave them the directions. They were quiet. Then one asked: 'What are you going to do with the interview?' Frankly, I didn't know. Olson had been charged but not convicted and deserved a fair trial the same as any other accused. I wrote a story containing some of the information and *Sun* editors, justifiably worried about being found in contempt of court, huddled with the newspaper's lawyers into the night. My story ran the next day with a rare copyright. The full story of the interview couldn't be told until after Olson pleaded guilty 11 times."

Olson, who would join the ranks of the world's most reviled serial killers, was sentenced to 11 life terms and would serve 29 years before dying of cancer in a Quebec prison hospital in September 2011 at the age of 71.

The city, some said, was never the same.

Management by brothers-in-law

With *The Sun* retaining its broadsheet format, its little sister, *The Province,* switched over to a tabloid format in August 1983, making it an easier, more portable read for the growing number of commuters taking transit every day from the suburbs into downtown Vancouver.

And in a tacit acknowledgement that its moniker did not reflect the sprawling geographic population it served, *The Vancouver Sun* once again changed its nameplate to *The Sun*, but it was a short-lived attempt at inclusivity and "Vancouver" would soon reappear in the nameplate.

A few months after the new broadsheet/tabloid split at Pacific Press, *The Columbian* newspaper in New Westminster ceased publication, forced into bankruptcy after 122 years. Although a sad loss for the local industry, many of its first-rate reporters migrated to other newspapers, including Bruce Smillie, Douglas Todd, Clive Mostyn, Chris Rose and Gerry Bellett, all hired by *The Sun.*

The spring of 1983 also brought a changing of the management guard in *The Sun* newsroom.

Gordon Fisher arrived from the *Ottawa Citizen,* a lateral move that would have him come to the paper as the night assistant managing editor and, in 1985, move into the managing editor's office.

Fisher was attracted to the paper's history, its strong stable of columnists like Denny Boyd and Marjorie Nichols in news and James Lawton

The boys' club: *Sun* managers (left to right): Michael McRanor, Gordon Fisher, Ian Haysom and Nicholas Palmer in 1986. *Bill Keay/Vancouver Sun*

in sports, its emphasis on strong design and photography and its legendary personality – "I really did feel it had in its DNA a sense of the power of the writer and of opinion" – but his enthusiasm was soon tested by *The Sun*'s other legacy: the perpetual rancor between management and unions.

Another draw for Fisher was the opportunity to work with brother-in-law Michael McRanor, the legendary Tartan Terror known for thundering about the newsroom, shouting blustery orders across the editorial floor and striking fear in the hearts of more than a few rookies. McRanor had already been at the paper for 15 years, his wiry energy and take-no-prisoners style forging a management ethos that was as far from coddling as one could imagine.

McRanor was as respected a writer and mentor as he was an editor, and his recent recollection of the day he joined the paper demonstrates his skill with language. "I was hired in *The Sun*'s executive parking lot in August 1968 when, having left a Volkswagen bug there, vacationing *Edmonton Journal* newsdesker Ben Tierney and I decided to explore job prospects. On the editorial floor we encountered the newsroom's resident wit Archie Rollo who – in remarkably-sweet Glasgow accent – said managing editor Bill Galt was at lunch but expected 'possibly within the hour, perhaps later this afternoon or maybe sometime tomorrow.'

"Back at the car, we faced a portly man reminiscent of Bluto who, braced on stout legs and brandishing what appeared to be a sawed-off two-by-four, declared he was in charge of security, that we'd violated such by parking in an area sanctified for management employees, that he'd called a tow truck and was now barring our exit.

"Just as the situation became combustible, Mr. Galt – I never then or afterwards referred

to this lovely man familiarly – exited the passenger side of a car that appeared to enter the lot under the right arm of the agitated Bluto. Appraised of the situation and our mission, he invited us to the newsroom, grasped my hand and announced: "This man's an employee; I just hired him.

"I started a month later (Tierney declined a *Sun* job, opting to join Southam News Bureau in Ottawa and forging a long career as foreign correspondent) and worked every position on the newsdesk until recruited by the peerless Alex MacGillivray in 1972 as book/travel/copy editor in the old *Leisure* magazine; succeeded him as *Leisure* editor in 1974; appointed assistant managing editor in 1979; executive editor in 1989 and was still functioning until sidelined in 1993 by what sublime colleague David Wright described as an 'unpronounceable malady.'"

The great divide

It didn't take long for Gordon Fisher to discover *The Sun* had a different definition of political news than did its eastern sisters. He was used to the work of the Southam News Service, whose political columnists, like Charles Lynch, focused most of their attention on Ottawa. When he wondered why deskers were routinely spiking Southam News copy – literally spiking the hard copy printouts – without even reading them, one of the desk's more colourful and outspoken editors, Larry Emrick, told him it was "snooze news."

That was seconded by editor Bruce Larsen when, while standing in his office one day and gazing out the windows to the mountains beyond, said to Fisher: "You need to understand that our readers don't give a shit what happens beyond those mountains."

Dusting off the pickets

On March 28, 1984, five years after its longest shutdown, picket lines once again encircled the Pacific Press building. Issues for the now six unions producing *The Sun* and *Province*, all of which served strike notice, focused on wages and the company's proposal of a three-year contract with a wage freeze in the first year. The unions' 1982 contract had given workers a 33-per-cent raise over two years. It was a dispute that also saw the Newspaper Guild – representing 950 of the 1,350 unionized workers at Pacific Press in the newsrooms, advertising, circulation and promotion departments – withdraw from the joint council and seek independent mediation.

Two months later, with the ink drying on a new contract, *Sun* publisher E.H. (Bill) Wheatley's re-entry message to readers – published on Thursday, May 24, 1984 in a press run of 250,000 papers – apologized to readers that the paper wouldn't be as large as usual for a few days, nor was there time to produce the popular glossy *TV Times* magazine for Friday, "but it is a great feeling to once again have a newspaper to present."

A pope, a preacher and a pop star

For two days in September 1984, hundreds of thousands of followers turned out to worship Pope John Paul II at masses in Abbotsford and at BC Place Stadium, less than a year after the Teflon roof was inflated over the new 60,000-seat arena. It was the first papal visit to Canada and the 19-hour Vancouver itinerary was a whirlwind, according to *Sun* coverage, including motorcades with the holy father waving from his Popemobile, meetings with the young and disabled, impromptu blessings and stopovers at local churches for papal catnaps.

Sun columnist Denny Boyd had been following the Pope's Canadian tour and, in his column on the day of the Vancouver departure, he said the 63-year-old pontiff radiated stamina and magnetism and left "not so much an impression of piety as of astonishing strength . . . clearly, he preaches nothing he cannot practise."

In October, the jam-packed dome welcomed evangelical preacher Billy Graham and, a month later, 126,000 screaming locals paid up to $40 a ticket to watch pop idol Michael Jackson moonwalk through three shows at the stadium.

Reporter Neal Hall's review in *Leisure* called the Jacksons' Victory Tour show an "awesome spectacle" of lasers, smoke machines and mechanical monsters, "the likes of which has never been seen before."

Michael Jackson's 1984 Victory Tour drew record crowds over three nights to BC Place.
Steve Bosch/Vancouver Sun

The tragedy of Air India

Shingara Cheema was thrilled to be heading home to his wife and three children on the family farm in the Punjab after spending several months visiting his mother Reshaw and attending his younger brother's wedding in Vancouver. But the 30-year-old never made it home – he was among the 329 who died on June 23, 1985 when Air India Flight 182 exploded over the Irish sea enroute from London to Delhi. Of those who died in the terrorist bombing, 280 were Canadians of Indian origin. Eighty-two were children.

It was a story that would define the career of *Sun* reporter Kim Bolan, who interviewed the Cheemas and other Vancouver-area relatives of the dead in the days following the crash, and would follow the complicated case with tireless due diligence as it unravelled over the next few decades.

The 1985 bombing – which included a related incident at Tokyo's Narita airport, in which a bomb exploded before it could be placed on another Air India flight, killing two baggage handlers – was the work of militant Sikhs linked to Vancouver.

In 1991, after an extensive investigation and controversial trials, the only person ever convicted in the bombing, Inderjit Singh Reyat, was sentenced to 10 years in prison for his part in the Narita bombings. He was given another five years in 2003 after admitting guilt in the Flight 182 bombing and was also found guilty of perjury in September 2010 for lying 19 times at the 2003 Air India trial that acquitted Ajaib Singh Bagri and Ripudaman Singh Malik. Reyat was subsequently sentenced to another nine years in prison.

Over the years, Bolan's unrelenting work on Air India has taken her to India and Pakistan, where she tracked alleged mastermind Talwinder Singh Parmar, and to England, where she covered the extradition hearing of Reyat, held in the Old Bailey. She also travelled to Ireland to interview first responders and those who helped the victims' families deal with the tragedy.

The story would seldom fall off Bolan's radar, with *Sun* files showing she has written close to 1,000 stories on the subject of Air India since the fateful crash in the Atlantic.

Her reportorial laser beam was no less focused in November 1998 when Tara Singh Hayer, publisher of the Surrey-based *Indo-Canadian Times* and an Air India Crown witness who had been paralysed in a previous shooting, was assassinated in his driveway. Hayer's still unsolved murder was considered retaliation for his editorials condemning the growing violence in the local Sikh community.

Bolan's investigative coverage of the Hayer slaying and complex politics of Sikh militancy also attracted threats on her life, beginning in 1997 and as recently as 2011, prompting the newspaper to provide her with security when it was deemed necessary by authorities.

Her Air India work has earned numerous awards, including a Courage in Journalism Award from the International Women's Media Foundation. Her book on the bombing, *Loss of Faith*, won the 2006 Dafoe Prize.

Sadly, the Air India case left other innumerable scars, for Vancouver-area Sikhs and beyond, unfairly tarnishing an entire community and adding to the growing perception that the Canadian legal system too often allows killers to get away with murder.

For Bolan, it brought newfound conviction to a reporter already renowned for her dogged determination to get the story, and right the wrong. Today, her *Sun* work covering local crime, from the Hells Angels to gang warfare, is unmatchable.

The Air India crash dominated *The Sun*'s front page on June 24, 1985, with reporters covering both the human tragedy and the criminal link to Vancouver.

Reporter Kim Bolan won the 2006 Dafoe Prize for her book, *Loss of Faith*.
Steve Bosch/Vancouver Sun

75 cents minimum outside Lower Mainland   TV TIMES   60 CENTS (Coin Box 75¢)

THE PARTY'S ON!

FRIDAY, MAY 2, 1986

The EXPO Vancouver Sun

WE WELCOME WORLD

ROYAL IN RED: Diana, Princess of Wales, makes entrance at Crystal Pavilion

ROYAL DISPLAY: sheltered from the rain, Prince Charles, Diana and Mila Mulroney take in the fireworks display

Royalty and rain share fair's opening

By BRIAN KIERAN
and DAVE SMITH

Expo 86 opened today on twin fronts as exuberant earlybirds surged through the gates at False Creek and Prince Charles and Diana, Princess of Wales, opened the Canadian pavilion at Canada Place on the harbor.

As the Stadium Gate opened at 8:30 a.m., the first 200 visitors rushed through the turnstiles with a wild cheer.

By 10 a.m., when the first pavilions opened, crowd control officials estimated 5,000 people were on the site. One of the most popular attractions was the monorail, where a lineup of several hundred people formed quickly.

Expo spokesman George Madden referred to the 8:30 a.m. start as a "soft opening" designed to get visitors into large holding areas inside the three main gates to reduce congestion and lineups outside the gates.

Despite intermittent rain the mood at the Stadium Gate was one of unrestrained excitement.

"I feel like a proud father," said Premier Bill Bennett, who was chatting up visitors.

"People have lined up . . . even in this unusual weather. You bet I am excited. You could feel it on the site

all last week as everyone was getting ready for today and I know it will last all summer," Bennett said.

Among those who lined up to get in early today was Elaine Degaris, 29, of Richmond, who said she and

three friends had been waiting since 3 a.m.

The first official day for Prince Charles and Diana began with a 10:30 a.m. date with Prime Minister Brian Mulroney and his wife Mila at Canada Place.

- Mayor Mike Harcourt dropped from welcoming party, A3
- Dinner guests stand on chairs to glimpse Diana's tiara, B1
- Denny Boyd sneaks into cruiser's royal bunk room, B2
- Jim Pattison welcomes Expo's first paying customers, B3.
- Editorial; Roy Peterson cartoon; Vaughn Palmer; B4
- Mingling; Marjorie Nichols; Election; Pete McMartin; B5
- Expo calendar for today and Saturday, D10
- Spirit of Chemainus makes inaugural run, G3

Transport Minister Don Mazankowski, provincial Tourism Minister Claude Richmond, Expo commissioner Patrick Reid and Canada Pavilion commissioner Bruce Howe also greeted the royal couple before Prince Charles cut a ribbon to open the pavilion.

Eighteen-year-old Annaliese Hunt of Langley left home at 5 a.m. to make sure she had a good view of the royal couple.

Clutching a yellow rose she stood in the front row in the pelting rain.

"I've waited five years for this," she said. "I don't care how hard it rains. I've wanted to see them since their engagement," she said.

Also in the crowd was Ruth Schell, a senior citizen from Newport Beach, Calif.

"What an attractive pair they are. I saw them last night and I just had to come back for another glimpse," she said.

For the royal couple, there was a little comic relief after the pavilion opening ceremony, as they watched the antics of pavilion mascots Goose and Beaver, actors dressed in huge costumes, representing Canada's best-known creatures.

Next, the royal couple strolled along the pavilion's western walk.

Please see EXPO, A2

Want to keep an eye on your investments while you're visiting Vancouver? Puzzled by the metric system? Want to know what's on about town? This index will help visitors to the city find that information — and much more — in the newspaper.

EXPO for our VISITORS

U.S. Dollar
= $1.3720 Cdn

Yen: 124.70
= $1 Cdn

Foreign Exchange	H6
Entertainment Guide	D10
Metric Conversion	E1
New York Stocks	H9
Handy numbers	H2
Classified Guide	E3

PREVIEW SECTION PROVES POPULAR

The Vancouver Sun scored in a big way with its colorful Expo preview section Tuesday.

We sold 27,000 extra copies on the street and by mail. Requests have been so strong that that day's paper is sold out.

We're expecting similar response Saturday, as editors, reporters and photographers work through tonight on a weekend edition packed with colorful Royal tour and Expo coverage.

And then we'll go to work on producing yet another bumper Expo special, which will be part of your Saturday, May 31, paper.

FALL-OUT: Radiation from the site of the Chernobyl nuclear power plant disaster was reported to be diminishing today, but world concern continues to mount. A12-15

WEATHER   E1

SUNNY PERIODS

"My personal computer just told me to mind my own business!"

INDEX

Bridge	E6	Letters B4	G4
Business	H5	Names	D2
Classified	E1	Restaurants	D4
Comics	C5		
Crossword	E7	Sports	H1
Editorials	B4	Theatres	D5
Entertainment	D1	Weather	E1
Garden C2	E6	What's On	D6
Home	C1		
Horoscope	E5	Wheels	F1

Classified 736-2211 Circulation 736-2201

★★★★ FOUNDED 1886 • VOL.99 • No. 452   132 PAGES

The Vancouver Sun's front page on May 2, 1986 welcomes Expo 86.

Diana, Princess of Wales – accompanied by B.C. Premier Bill Bennett – greets a crowd in Kelowna during her visit to B.C. for the opening of Expo 86. *Craig Hodge/Vancouver Sun*

The fairest of them all

"The party's on!" and "We Welcome World" announced *The Expo 86 Vancouver Sun* on May 2, 1986, as thousands of locals turned out in the rain for the official opening of Expo 86 by Prince Charles and his "royal in red" wife, Diana.

"The Prince and Princess of Wales were the stars of Expo Friday, but the fair belonged to Jimmy," reporter Gordon Hamilton wrote of the standing ovation given by 65,000 fair-goers to honour chairman Jimmy Pattison at the fair's opening ceremonies.

The Sun's daily coverage was extensive and included numerous special sections – such as a preview supplement that sold 27,000 extra copies – keeping *Sun* reporters and photographers hopping to adequately cover all the fair's comings and goings as 22 million visitors, along with 10,000 journalists from 60 countries, crowded the displays and events offered by 54 participating nations. More than 1,000 *Sun* stories were written and 50,000 photographs taken over the fair's nearly six-month course, until the gates closed on Oct. 13.

Readers, aided by *The Sun*'s daily Expo 86 calendar, were captivated by First Nations performances, concerts and cuisine from all over the world. Dozens of acts – Roy Orbison, Johnny Cash, Ray Charles, Bryan Adams, Annie Lennox and Lena Horne among them – lit up the various Expo stages, and one of the longest lineups could be found regularly outside the Saskatchewan pavilion, which served huge portions of country comfort food.

The legacy of the fair, originally called Transpo 86, included SkyTrain and Expo Centre, the unique silver "golf-ball" building that would become Science World, along with a stirring of national pride that would be rekindled more than two decades later when the 2010 Olympics came to town.

The fair also prompted a mini-makeover of *The Sun*, which reinstated the word Vancouver in its nameplate after an absence of three years, and boasted to readers that they now had "the whole world in your hands." Following the lead of the newly popular *USA Today* south of the border, *Sun* section fronts began sporting full colour.

Entertainer Liberace poses atop the Highway 86 sculpture at Expo 86.
Ian Smith/Vancouver Sun

Man in Motion Rick Hansen on the road from McBride to Prince George in March 1987. *Ian Lindsay/Vancouver Sun*

Queen Elizabeth and Prince Philip dine with Premier Bill Vander Zalm in 1987, during the royal couple's visit to Vancouver for the Commonwealth Conference. *Mark van Manen/Vancouver Sun*

The man in motion

Echoing the historic feat of his late friend Terry Fox, paralympic athlete Rick Hansen embarked on his own world fundraising tour from Vancouver's Oakridge Mall on March 21, 1985. His wheelchair prowess and muscular pumping arms became a familiar image during his Man in Motion journey, which amassed millions for spinal cord research and raised universal awareness on issues facing the disabled.

Twenty-six months and 40,000 kilometres later, on May 22, 1987, the Man in Motion wheeled back into the mall to a hero's welcome. The next day, 50,000 locals turned out to fete Hansen at BC Place Stadium. He had raised $24 million and heightened awareness throughout 34 countries, and his Legacy Fund would become his new life's work. Victoria's Grammy-winning producer and composer David Foster wrote a song in tribute: *St. Elmo's Fire (Man in Motion)* was a number one hit.

In a special eight-page Souvenir Edition, published the day of his return, *The Vancouver Sun* celebrated Hansen's triumphant achievement with photographs and gushing stories that equated the historic feat to the Ulysses odyssey in the Homer epic, and also told the "road to romance" love story of Hansen and Amanda Reid, the physiotherapist who accompanied him on the tour. They would marry that October.

The Queen's secrets

That same month, Queen Elizabeth visited Vancouver – her 22nd trip to Canada since 1957 – prompting *The Sun* to send columnist Nicole Parton to the official cocktail party. Although much of Parton's brief audience with the monarch was off the record, sticking to official protocol, the long-retired Parton would let some of the secrets slip years later.

"Everything was off the record," Parton recalled. "Those are the royal rules, but a lot of time has passed. The Queen – who drank Dubonnet with a twist – told me Charles and Diana were very happy and the nasty rumors had been trumped up by the media.

"The media is never supposed to divulge what the Queen says in private, so I never have. I absolutely loved her. She was a pip. Those were the days when her hair was dyed in a shade that my media memory recalls as Chocolate Kiss. The Queen wore an uncut, deep blue sapphire the size of three of my knuckles across. Her eyes were almost as blue, and revealed how inquisitive she was about everyone and everything. Even the most mundane detail of my job seemed to interest her. Other members of the media awaited their turn. Total estimated time for our private audience: two minutes. No photos were permitted. I spent ages learning how to curtsy (a lady-in-waiting taught me). I had nothing to wear and had to borrow a hat and buy a gaudy suit jacket for the occasion. I later donated it to some charity, which – because of its history – put it up for auction . . . (but) I will never part with my Royal Tour Media Pass."

Lawyering up

At one time, lawyer Jack Potter was a fixture on the newsdesk, his job to vet the stories of the day, and although he would eventually be replaced by a local law firm and the incomparable libel lawyer Barry Gibson, *The Vancouver Sun*'s long history of legal battles would continue unabated, not a few of them connected to business reporter David Baines.

Hired in 1988 to replace stock market reporter Peter O'Neil, who would go on to become *The Sun*'s Ottawa correspondent, Baines' target was Howe Street. His watchdog coverage and investigative skills so earned the ire of promoters, brokers and regulators that, in 1992, Vancouver police advised him they had learned through an informant that somebody was shopping a contract on his life. The Exchange, anxious to neutralize the bad publicity, offered a $100,000 reward for information leading to the arrest of the alleged plotter. No arrest was ever made.

Baines' unwavering determination to peel back the unsavory layers of the Vancouver Stock Exchange not only changed the industry, but readers' perspectives on stock markets. In his 23 years at *The Sun*, his thousands of stories about securities fraud triggered countless police and regulatory investigations, resulting in scurrilous promoters being kicked out of the market or put behind bars. A story he wrote in 1990 exposing a pyramid scheme called Dial-a-Purchase prompted promoters and about three dozen investors – who didn't yet realize they were victims – to rent a bus and storm *The Sun* newsroom in protest, scattering notes and files and scuffling with *Sun* staff before police arrived and cleared them out. In the aftermath, *Sun* management tightened security, restricting the once-open access to the newsroom.

Over the years, Baines has been sued 19 times, more than any other *Sun* journalist. He's also won four National Newspaper Awards, more than any other reporter or columnist in Western Canada. But he is not yet ready to declare victory. "No matter how many battles we win, we will never win the war. There are just too many confidence men out there, and too many investors who, when presented with too-good-to-be-true investment deals, are willing to suspend their disbelief."

The mark of merchandise

A century of daily publishing has left not only a journalistic legacy in *The Vancouver Sun*'s wake, but a mountain of merchandise, from hats (oh so many hats) and jackets to Christmas cards, badges, backpacks, shoelaces, bowling shirts, paperweights, calculators, memo pads, posters, workout gear, drinking glasses, door pulls, pen sets, coffee mugs, watches, key chains, clocks, pants, computer cases, bumper stickers, aprons, umbrellas, golf balls, sports bags and calendars. And then there are the nearly one million T-shirts filling local closets, all of them

Stock market columnist David Baines keeps an eye on Brian Slobogian, the former president of Eron Mortgage Corp., at B.C. Supreme Court. Slobogian pleaded guilty to fraud and theft and was sentenced to six years. Baines won a 2005 National Newspaper Award for his special series on the Eron scandal. *Mark van Manen/Vancouver Sun*

Cookbooks have been bestsellers for *The Sun* since the 1920s.

worn by the runners and walkers who have been pounding 10 kilometres of downtown Vancouver pavement every spring since 1985 as part of The Vancouver Sun Run. Not to be left out: books, thousands of them, from the cookbooks published by Edith Adams Cottage over 75 years to the hundreds of titles written by *The Sun*'s cartoonists, photographers, reporters and columnists, including Simma Holt, Stuart Keate, Denny Boyd, Bruce Hutchison, Barry Broadfoot, Jack Scott and, in recent years, Nicole Parton, Gary Mason, Keith Baldrey, Mike Grenby, Marjorie

Nichols, Brenda Thompson, Ruth Phelan, Kim Bolan, Jonathan Manthorpe, Bill Keay, Stephen Hume, Daphne Bramham, Neal Hall, Kevin Griffin, Ian Mulgrew, Lori Culbert, Steve Whysall and Douglas Todd.

Revolution by cheesecake

The mid-1980s brought more unrest to *The Vancouver Sun* newsroom. Many staffers felt the redesign and cost-cutting initiatives by publisher Gerald Haslam, acting on orders from the Southam head office in Toronto, had undermined the paper's integrity. They were concerned about the paper's lack of an Ottawa bureau, the decision to no longer staff suburban council meetings and the year-long delay in appointing a sports editor.

When long-time marquee writers such as the much-respected political columnist Marjorie Nichols left the paper for greener pastures, a group of reporters got together in a dessert cafe across the street from Pacific Press in the summer of 1987 to plan their strategy. Later dubbed the Cheesecake Revolution, it involved respected writers Denny Boyd and Moira Farrow, along with union activists, and would prompt managing editor Gordon Fisher to write a memo to the group offering to sit down and talk about their issues. Fifty-five reporters and editors signed a letter accepting his proposal and, when a meeting was finally held, some 70 staffers showed up to air their grievances with Fisher, Haslam and editor Bruce Larsen. Most of the issues were eventually resolved, including the naming of both a sports editor and an Ottawa correspondent.

Our Vaughn-ted political heavyweight

When the vacant 80-hectare Expo 86 site was sold to Hong Kong billionaire Li Ka-shing in 1988 for $320 million, it was a controversy that dominated headlines. Li's Concord Pacific firm planned to build housing and offices as part of a $2-billion Pacific Place development, but detractors argued it had been sold for a song and other bidders had been given the cold shoulder.

Vaughn Palmer, *The Sun*'s venerable Victoria columnist, followed the story closely, and detailed the pros and cons of the financial machinations that showed the deal made some sense for the provincial government, which had paid $60 million for the site in 1980. "In the long run, the bottom line on the sale is less important than other benefits that will accrue to the province as the site is developed." The sale, Palmer also noted, would ultimately pay off for Vancouver, with benefits that included jobs and revenue in a showcase development.

Palmer's tenure at *The Sun* has mirrored the path of many of its writers. He started as a summer intern in April 1973, recruited from the *Ubyssey*, and worked part-time until he landed a full-time reporting job the following year.

Long before he became the respected elder of the Victoria press gallery, he was *The Sun*'s rock critic. Palmer once wrote a negative review of pop singer Peter Frampton, joking that the star wore a wig, false leg and glass eye, and received so many threats that he had to write a retraction.

His music critic career lasted from 1977 through 1980 when, to the newsroom's surprise and delight, he was named city editor, a position he would leave in 1982 for a one-year journalism fellowship at Stanford. Palmer returned to the paper as an editorial writer and, in January 1984, moved to Victoria and *The Sun*'s always hopping provincial bureau, becoming one of the most prolific columnists in the paper's history, producing five columns a week delving into the political shenanigans of the legislature. His accolades include a 1988 Jack Webster award for reporting, the Bruce Hutchison Award for Lifetime Achievement (given by the Jack Webster Foundation), and the Hyman Solomon Award for excellence in public policy journalism.

Long-time political columnist Vaughn Palmer at his office in Victoria. *John McKay/Victoria Times-Colonist*

Coupland and the caveman

The demographic bulge known as the Baby Boom was giving way to Generation X, a label for those born between the early 1960s and early 1980s and popularized by local writer Douglas Coupland in an article for *Vancouver* magazine. Coupland had freelanced for *The Vancouver Sun* for a time, supplementing his income by $75 a week with his contributions to the Budget Gourmet column. But the fledgling writer bristled at *The Sun*'s editing of his work and, in a 2007 piece for *Vancouver*, remembered that "I quit the *Sun* job because I described the portions at some long-gone restaurant as being not unlike the bronto-ribs that tip over the Flintstones' car during the closing credits of that show. My then editor, Daphne Gray-Grant, crossed that out and put 'caveman-like.' . . . I quit after the Flintstone edit." *Generation X* would not only become a best-selling book for Coupland in 1991, it would become part of the international lexicon.

China syndrome

On June 4, 1989, the world was glued to the drama unfolding in Tiananmen Square in Beijing, where an estimated 240 pro-democracy protesters were killed by Chinese military troops who opened fire on civilians. Of all the disturbing and graphic footage beamed around the world, the image that came to symbolize the horror was the heart-stopping sight of a lone man in a white shirt facing down a column of advancing tanks.

The Sun's China in Crisis series, especially relevant in a city with one of the largest populations of Chinese outside Asia, featured files from news agencies such as Reuters and Associated Press, and provided local perspective with dispatches from Ben Tierney, filing for Southam News from the chain's Hong Kong bureau. "Leaders are living on borrowed time" headlined one Tierney column, which mused on the hypocrisy of Chinese leader Deng Xiaoping's talk of reform while maintaining a brutal police state. Tierney posited that China had been "plunged into a bloody turmoil that is likely to last for months, perhaps years."

The British invasion

After three years as *The Sun*'s tenacious editor, Bruce Larsen retired in 1988. His 43 years in the news business had seen him work at *The Winnipeg Tribune* and *The Province* before being hired as *The Sun*'s city editor in 1959. Larsen would hold a number of positions at *The Sun*, including sports editor and 11 years as managing editor before settling into the editor's chair in 1985.

In February 1989, Nick Hills was appointed as Larsen's replacement. The former general manager of Southam News was a diminutive, moustachioed, spark plug of a man and his arrival was a reminder of the long tradition of British influence in the newsroom, in which legions of cheeky Brit transplants had long lent the paper an edgy, humour-tinged, Fleet Street air. Their ranks over the years included Jack Brooks, Moira Farrow, Nicholas Palmer (who after numerous posts at the paper would become senior editor, overseeing much of the paper's future technological change), Michael McRanor, Larry Still, Dave Wright, Max Wyman, Steve Whysall, Gerry Bellett, Jonathan Manthorpe and Ian Haysom.

Among them was the proper Ann Barling, who had shown up in 1955 wearing a hat and gloves to interview for the secretary position for managing editor Hal Straight. She eventually became the paper's Life editor, a position she would hold until her early retirement in 1995.

Barling was petite but tough, known for her steadfast adherence to proper English. Her staff of a dozen or so writers, deskers and columnists produced an average of 45 pages a week on food, fashion, health, homes and lifestyles, with a dozen or more extra pages on weekends when New Homes was added to the mix. And while more women were working on the news side, more men had jumped over the potted plants: Phil Hanson and Peter Wilson were among Barling's feature writers.

Fashion was an advertising money-maker for the paper, and while Barling was known for being mindful of her budget, she routinely sent fashion reporter Virginia Leeming to the annual runway shows in Milan, Paris and New York to report on the latest style trends. Models were brought in to *The Sun* photo studio for layout shoots, and Leeming would spend much of her

Popular *Sun* gardening columnist Steve Whysall with hundreds of entries received for a bulb contest in 1994. *Ian Lindsay/Vancouver Sun*

The ever-stylish Virginia Leeming, pictured here in 1996, covered the world's biggest runway shows during her career as fashion writer for *The Sun*. *Ian Lindsay/Vancouver Sun*

Allan Fotheringham (second from left) leaves court Dec. 17, 1985 during a recess in his Supreme Court libel trial. Accompanying him, from left, are *Maclean's* magazine managing editor Robert Lewis, Marjorie Nichols, and Jack Webster. *Brian Kent/Vancouver Sun*

Nick Hills spent just two years as editor of *The Sun*, but the stories he left behind are legendary. *Mark van Manen/Vancouver Sun*

week dropping in on local haute couture boutiques to gather clothes and accessories for the week's ad-packed section.

It was a time when the feature pages, like other sections in the paper, routinely changed its name in an attempt to be current and to reflect cultural shifts: Life became You, Fashion became Style, *Week-End* became *Leisure* became Review became Mix.

A Hills of beans

The leadership style of the energetic and capricious Nick Hills would prove a stark contrast to the stoic, assiduous helming of the newsroom by his brush-cut predecessor Bruce Larsen.

While Hills' investiture as *Sun* editor was brief – he would last only two years – it included many an excellent adventure, most involving copious consumption of alcohol and the profligate spending of company profits. One such escapade

involved a now legendary visit to the paper's Victoria bureau. Hills, city editor Scott Macrae and managing editor Gordon Fisher (who left *The Sun* in 1989 to return to the *Citizen* as editor and would eventually become publisher and then president of *National Post*) treated bureau staffers Gary Mason and Keith Baldrey to dinner at the upscale Deep Cove Chalet. The three bosses had an 8 p.m. flight back to Vancouver, but one expensive bottle of wine turned into another and the flight time came and went. When Hills explained their pressing dilemma to the restaurant owner, stressing that they simply had to get back to Vancouver that night, the accommodating host had a solution: he chartered them a plane and piled them into his white Rolls-Royce for the trip to the airport. In what was later described as a scene out of *Casablanca*, the three soused editors boarded the fog-shrouded plane on the tarmac as the plane's engines roared. The tab for the restaurant alone was $2,000.

Nick Hills, they would say forever after, was one high-flying newspaper editor.

This dramatic 1985 photo of a distraught knife-wielding father dangling his son from a third-floor floor apartment in Vancouver earned photographer **Ralph Bower a National Newspaper Award**. *Ralph Bower/Vancouver Sun*

THE 1990s

The 1990s: Back to the future

After a decade of turmoil and change for The Vancouver Sun, the 1990s brought more of the same. Amid a shuffling of deck chairs in Canadian newspaper ownership, radical technological and readership shifts would not only rock the nearly century-old daily, but force a reinvention that included another move, new presses, a switch to morning publication and a reinvigorated design. After 85 years, the paper's Olde English nameplate was retired in favour of a more streamlined look, and the revolving door at the top continued, as a series of editors and managing editors came and went while The Sun struggled to retain its once-strong foothold in Vancouver's newspaper market.

ABOVE: Players and spectators celebrate with B.C. Lions place kicker Lui Passaglia after he led the Lions to the Grey Cup victory on Nov. 27, 1994. *Mark van Manen/Vancouver Sun*

PRECEDING PAGE: Staff at the printing plant, including (from left) Andy Bezanson, Don Shaw (glasses) and Ken Klecker (foreground), check out *The Vancouver Sun*'s new morning edition, which hit the streets on Sept. 16, 1991. *Craig Hodge/Vancouver Sun*

Out with the old, in with the new: *Vancouver Sun* newspaper boxes from 1997 (above) and 2009 (above right). *Nick Didlick/Ian Smith/Vancouver Sun*

Editor-in-Chief John Cruickshank introduces the newsroom to the new-and-improved *Vancouver Sun* in October 1997. *Ward Perrin/Vancouver Sun*

Synergy and the literate acquisitors

In 1990, freshly hired *Sun* editor Nick Hills was intent on taking his new charge up-market, partly by downplaying crime stories and making more room for international coverage, and partly by contracting professionals to determine where improvements could be made inside and outside the newsroom.

Most major-market newspapers routinely conduct readership surveys to stay on top of market trends, but Hills' own journalistic leanings were reinforced when he commissioned a $100,000 Angus Reid readership poll. It determined *The Sun* should focus its resources on the 21 per cent of readers dubbed "literate acquisitors" by the pollsters, a nonsense descriptive of the city's monied and educated upper-middle-class demographic, most of whom lived on the city's west side or on its north shore. Hills and his management team were encouraged to ignore the "insular forlorn," who were a lost cause, and not to fret about annoying the "middle-class joiners," who were the majority of *Sun* readers and who would stay with the paper no matter what it did. Another category, the "post-literate hedonists," didn't matter because they were otherwise engaged with alternative media like *Utne Reader*.

While Hills and his team were sorting out how to translate the findings into circulation numbers, *Sun* employees were being "synergized" by consultants hired to probe the psychological health of the staff, and perhaps stem the tide of newsroom discontent. For weeks, senior editors could be found huddled together outside meeting rooms, valiantly trying to get in touch with their feelings. In a profession where insecurity-meets-ego is a good thing – those twin traits are the hallmarks of any journalist worth his or her salt – the process proved a failure. Most participants spent their self-improvement sessions making fun of the wasteful spending on navel-gazing or resenting their absence from the newsroom.

The Nisga'a Treaty took effect on May 12, 2000, four years after an agreement-in-principle had been reached and following years of negotiations. B.C. Premier Ujjal Dosanjh, who marked the occasion with Nisga'a Chief Joe Gosnell, said: "The suffocating weight and shackles of the Indian Act are gone, and gone forever." *Steve Bosch/Vancouver Sun*

The beat reporter and Stockholm Syndrome

The long-standing impasse between Canada's First Nations and the government continued to fester throughout the decade.

An Aug. 1, 1990 *Sun* front page featured a photograph of a nattily-suited Premier Bill Vander Zalm speaking to a group of Kitwancool native Indians, his news of a just-signed federal/provincial land claims pact signalling a move in the age-old chess game between caretaker governments and aboriginals pushing for self-government.

But in a followup Weekend Special feature, *Sun* native affairs reporter Terry Glavin wrote of the growing frustration of Indian bands who were mustering forces for a long, even violent, direct-action campaign to resolve their long-standing grievances. In the story, the Musqueam's Wendy Grant, after expressing condolences to the family of a police officer shot the previous week at a native standoff in Oka, Quebec, told Glavin: "Let there be no mistake as to who pulled the trigger. The assassins were the federal and provincial governments, whose policies of ignoring and trampling on the rights of aboriginal people finally and predictably forced the Mohawk to the wall."

Native rights had been covered by *The Sun* as a matter of course for years, but when the situation began heating up in the 1980s, reporter Glavin was given the native Indian affairs beat full time. A consummate tale-spinner,

***Sun* native affairs reporter Terry Glavin.**
Vancouver Sun

***The Sun*'s July 31, 1998 editorial cartoon by Roy Peterson.**

he explored both sides of the issues, talked to bureaucrats, visited reserves, and wrote stories of the shocking social and economic plight of B.C.'s native Indian bands. His knowledgeable and sympathetic reports offered readers a new behind-the-scenes point of view, usually from the perspective of the First Nations. So immersed was he in the beat that he once filed a memo to the city desk in the Chilcotin language, prompting a profane earful from assistant city editor John Olding.

Glavin's increasingly partisan coverage,

however, represented a dilemma that editors often face: while beat immersion fosters better sources, more in-depth stories and regular scoops, the danger is that reporters can become too involved in the subject to maintain non-partisan perspective, which is the definition of reporting. To ensure impartiality, editors often rotate beats, but reporters who have spent years learning about a subject can be resistant to abandoning their field of expertise. Glavin would leave the newspaper several years later for a career as a freelance journalist and author.

Don Babick had grand visions for *The Sun* when he was named president of Pacific Press, and then *Sun* publisher, in 1992. *Glenn Baglo/ Vancouver Sun*

The Sun rises in the morning. Again.

GOOD MORNING B.C. was *The Sun*'s above-the-nameplate greeting on Monday, Sept. 16, 1991, heralding the paper's switch back to morning publication after decades of afternoon publication. The move, mirrored by daily papers all over North America, was a reflection of a demographic shift: more women were joining the workforce and families simply had less leisure time in the evening. Readers, many of them commuters, wanted their news on the doorstep by 6 a.m.

The revamped morning paper, produced under the stewardship of genial new editor-in-chief Ian Haysom, included his page-one message to readers extolling the paper's latest attributes: better story labelling, a Best of B.C. series seeking reader feedback and an A3 Voices column for public submissions. On the paper's new Sunrise page – which included the New York Times Crossword, the weather report, winning lottery numbers and quips and quotes – gifted *Sun* scribe Douglas Sagi wrote in his Diary that

Hot off the presses: the new morning *Sun*, Sept. 16, 1991.

"the whole world needs an editor," especially the ministry of transportation and highways, which had erected signs on the Coquihalla highway that read "Visability Limited."

Up Parryscope

Also new to the columnist ranks was freelancer Malcolm Parry, the charming and rather aristocratic former editor and publisher of *Vancouver* magazine. Parry's gossipy, photo-laden, three-times-a-week *Sun* offerings covered the local elite in arts and industry. His style was often compared to the breezy, inside-baseball musings of *The Sun*'s late great "saloon reporter" Jack Wasserman, and Parry soon become a fixture at every major social event in the city, often showing up for mere minutes to press the flesh, get the item and snap a few shots with his palm-sized digital camera. He became known as the master of the "cleavage cam" – overhead shots of female decolletage – and was known to boast that he could get into any event, without an invitation, simply by donning a tuxedo.

NDP premier-elect Mike Harcourt holds a copy of the Oct. 18, 1991 *Vancouver Sun* with the headline declaring his election victory. Fortunately, editors had picked the right headline earlier in the evening before results had been tallied. *Denise Howard/Vancouver Sun*

Deadlines and commitments

In one of those election-night deadline dilemmas that recalls the infamous 1948 *Chicago Tribune* headline Dewey Defeats Truman – published the day after Truman won the U.S. presidency – the Oct. 17, 1991 B.C. provincial election was a nail-biter for editor Ian Haysom and his newsroom crew.

As Haysom tells the story, "*The Sun* had just become a morning paper, and the deadline for the first edition was pushed to 8:30 p.m., which meant we had to call the election results ourselves before the TV stations. So, to prepare for various outcome scenarios, I wrote five stories (big NDP win/narrow NDP win/NDP minority/ B.C. Liberal win/B.C. Liberal minority) using results we had up to that time. We wrote five different headlines. Vaughn Palmer wrote five different columns. At about 8:25, everyone was bugging us about which one to go with, and we said: 'NDP romps to historic majority' and luckily we turned out to be correct. Big gamble."

Then Haysom and Victoria bureau chief Keith Baldrey had a clever idea. The first edition came off the presses before 10 p.m. and was delivered to the newsroom. When Haysom and Baldrey looked at it, Haysom turned to Baldrey and said: "Are you thinking what I'm thinking?" Baldrey was, so he grabbed six copies and hopped in a cab to Robson Square, where new premier-elect Mike Harcourt was about to give his victory speech.

"I could hear him on the car radio and was praying he wouldn't finish before I was there," Baldrey recalled. "I rushed in, pushed my way through the crowd (no small feat) and made my way to the side of the stage and thrust a copy into Harcourt's hands. He just looked at it. I yelled 'Hold it up! Hold it up!' He did just that. Our photog (Denise Howard) got the shot and I seem to remember she threw the film to one of the other photog crew who raced back to the newsroom. That shot became the main art on page one for subsequent editions."

Don Babick to the rescue

After a series of Pacific Press publishers and presidents had come and gone in the nine years since Clark Davey's reign – his replacements included Bill Wheatley, Gerald Haslam and Stuart Noble – Don Babick was appointed president of Pacific Press in January 1992 and, a month later, was named the new publisher of *The Sun* and *Province*. An accomplished and respected businessman with strong daily newspaper roots, Babick would steer the paper through difficult financial waters during a time when revenues were suffering and cost-cutting included the loss of dozens of employees let go as part of a larger downsizing initiative that included early retirement buyouts.

Babick's newspaper career began in 1959 selling ads for the *Montreal Gazette*, and he would become a driving force in most of the major markets across the country, serving as publisher of four Canadian dailies during his career, among them *The Vancouver Sun*, *Province* and *National Post*, before retiring in 2003 to sit on numerous boards, including the *Toronto Star*'s.

Babick considered his time at Pacific Press – seven years though 1999 – a career highlight, a challenge that saw him guiding the papers back into the black, overseeing the hiring of a new *Sun* editor and a move back downtown to the Granville Street waterfront.

Among Babick's biggest undertakings was the resolution of the press problem. In May 1990, Pacific Press had opened a $50-million printing plant in the Newton area of Surrey, its Manroland Flexographic presses designed to print both *The Sun* and *Province*. The Flexo presses used water-based inks, a welcome change for readers who had long complained that traditional oil-based ink left black smudges on their clothes and furniture. But the press was limited in its printing capabilities and when *The Sun* went to morning publication, it became clear both papers could not be produced at the Newton plant. *The Sun* printing would move back to the 2250 Granville Street plant until six years later, when a new printing plant would make its debut in Surrey.

Pat Pederson (left) and Brenda Thompson were among the many "Edith Adams" home economists who kept *Sun* readers cooking over the years. *Jeff Vinnick/Vancouver Sun*

Saying goodbye to Hutch, Don, Penny and Edith

The B.C. newspaper world was mourning one of its own in September 1992 with the death of Bruce Hutchison. The revered *Sun* journalist had been the paper's editor (also called an editorial director) from 1963 to 1979, and then its editor emeritus until his death at the age of 91. He produced many books during his career, earned numerous awards – including three NNAs – and was writing columns right to the end. His last column, filed a month before his death, was on Bill Clinton's bid for the U.S. presidency. For many, Hutch's death signalled the end of an era, but his indefatigable work ethic and impressive journalistic legacy would live on through the many journalists he mentored.

The Vancouver Sun also marked the passing in March 1993 of Don Cromie, the memorable publisher who had overseen the paper for 22 years as an independent owner, having inherited the paper at age 26 from his father Robert in 1942. Cromie reigned during what many consider the golden era of newspapering, when a sign in the Sun Tower noted "there will be no drinking on the premises during working hours" and when publishers thought nothing of throwing an impromptu party to celebrate circulation gains or sending reporters globetrotting in pursuit of a good story.

When Cromie sold the paper in 1964, *Sun* columnist Jack Scott reflected on his tenure, writing that "his columnists rode off violently in all directions, brandishing their tiny lances. And when that didn't seem enough, he instituted our Page Five so that the opinions of heretics, dissidents, scholars, propagandists and controversialists might challenge the reader to reach his own conclusions."

In May 1998, the death of Evelyn Caldwell marked another transition of the old *Sun* into the new era of newspapering. By the time of her 1974 retirement, Caldwell had written nearly 8,000 consumer columns over 30 years under the pseudonym Penny Wise. Working in an age when newswomen were relegated to the society pages, Caldwell covered the Korean War in 1951, met Nikita Khrushchev in 1955, interviewed Elvis Presley in the 1960s and covered both the Queen's coronation and Grace Kelly's wedding. In an interview a few years before her death, at 89, Caldwell said she was her "readers' eyes and ear. I took them everywhere."

A year later, *The Sun* quietly removed Edith Adams from its pages. The fictitious Martha Stewart of the day, Edith Adams (who, for 34 years, was Winnipeg-born etiquette expert Eileen Norman but otherwise a consortium of home economists such as Marianne Linnell, Barbara McQuade and Brenda Thompson) had ruled the paper's domestic roost since 1924, pumping out non-stop household guidance and

Bruce Hutchison's long, legendary career at *The Vancouver Sun* began in 1963 and ended with his death in 1992 at age 91. He filed his final column a month before he died. *John Yanyshyn/Vancouver Sun*

producing thousands of recipes from an on-site test kitchen. The kitchen, one of only two operating in North American newspapers, was quietly shuttered less than a decade later.

THANKS!

The Vancouver Sun

BRITISH · COLUMBIA'S · NEWSPAPER

75 CENTS MINIMUM OUTSIDE LOWER MAINLAND

WEDNESDAY, JUNE 15, 1994 **C**

✦ **FINAL EDITION** 50 CENTS

GARY HERSHORN/Reuter

RANGERS captain Mark Messier (right) and Esa Tikkanen hoist the Stanley cup

Canucks: you did us proud

PETE McMARTIN
Vancouver Sun

One goal.

It's a cruel way to end a 108-game season. The New York Rangers won a hockey game 3-2 Tuesday and ended a 54-year-old drought. Last night, they sipped from the Stanley Cup.

The Vancouver Canucks lost, but in the process got a thirst for winning. This is a team with a future.

"It was a battle," said Canucks captain Trevor Linden as he sat on a chair against the wall in the Canucks' dressing room, the blood-stained towel hanging over his right shoulder. It was Linden who scored both Canucks' goals.

"I don't think we got beat by a better team. It could have gone either way."

There were moments when it seemed possible. In the second period, Cliff Ronning came close, dancing around the Rangers' net, but he couldn't get off a proper shot. He had broken a bone in his right hand, the result of a Joey Kocur hit in Game 6. He had to have the hand frozen for Game 7.

"I can't shoot," said Ronning, his damaged hand wrapped in bandages. "I just tried to be as effective as I could.

"But I couldn't even feel the end of my stick. I couldn't raise the puck."

Nathan LaFayette came close, too, hitting the crossbar with a shot that would have tied the game up in the third period. But in this game of inches, the Rangers got the breaks.

Vancouver Canuck coach Pat Quinn said the Rangers simply got too far ahead for his team to catch up.

"I thought going into this game we were destined to win," said Quinn. But Quinn said the Rangers capitalized on a number of Canuck penalties.

And other than Linden, Quinn said his team didn't get scoring from his team's big guns.

"Our goal scorers started to stretch out again and when you do that against this team you tend to get lost."

Not that it mattered all that much. If it was a bandwagon that Vancouver fans jumped on at the end of the season, it's not one they were ready to abandon after the game.

Fans spilled out of the Robson Street bars and chanted "Go Canucks go!" and "Rangers suck!" SkyTrain filled with fans from Surrey and New Westminster heading into Vancouver after the game, and they chanted "We won! We won!"

Maybe we did. We had two front pages made up for this issue of *The Sun*, depending on the outcome of the game. They came with two different headlines.

Our second choice is the one you read here. We decided on, simply, "Thanks!" with the idea that, even in defeat, the Canucks not only entertained and excited us, they embodied the qualities we most like to see in sport: grace, tenacity, toughness, purpose. They did themselves and their city proud.

The other front page, the one that we did not run, read "Champions!"

We ran the wrong headline.

DOUBLE TROUBLE: The New York Rangers celebrate Adam Graves' goal to go ahead 2-0, as Canuck goalkeeper Kirk McLean hangs his head.

PAUL CHIASSON/CP

CANUCKS

- ■ The Vancouver Canucks want to say thanks, and will hold a Fan Appreciation Day on Thursday, A2
- ■ The New York Rangers' curse has been exorcised. Alex Strachan in the Big Apple, A3
- ■ Lord Stanley's precious cup may be gone, but the pride of a province survives, D1
- ■ He took us all on one heck of a ride, but Pat Quinn won't be back as coach. Mike Beamish, D3

Early editions of the June 15, 1994 *Sun* – thanking the Canucks for a thrilling run-up to game 7 of the Stanley Cup final – were soon replaced by pages reporting on the "Robson rowdies" who were rioting in the streets.

Downtown Vancouver was a disaster zone on June 14, 1994 after the New York Rangers beat the Canucks 3-2 in Game 7 of the Stanley Cup final. The scene would play out again 17 years later, after the Canucks lost another Game 7, this time to the Boston Bruins. *Steve Bosch/Vancouver Sun*

The good, the bad and the ugly of hockey fever

Canucks fans, meanwhile, were being dazzled by their new Russian rocket, Pavel Bure. As skilful *Sun* sports writer Iain MacIntyre wrote of Bure's Nov. 5, 1991 debut, "It's the biggest premiere since the Phantom opened at the Queen Elizabeth. Or Schwarzkopf opened in the Middle East."

But fans showed their ugly side on June 14, 1994, when the downtown core erupted in violent chaos as hockey fans began rioting in the streets after the Canucks lost the seventh game of the Stanley Cup final to the New York Rangers. Page one banner headlines – from THANKS! to CURSES! – soon turned to reports of hooliganism as 60,000 "Robson rowdies" smashed windows, looted stores and attacked police.

The paper's new managing editor, Scott Honeyman, went from walking the paper through a celebratory first edition with a front-page photo of Canucks goalie Kirk McLean, to a final edition filled with riot coverage and little mention of the actual game. As often happens when news breaks on deadline, reporters and photographers were pulled from every part of the newsroom and dispatched to cover the riot. *Sun* photographer Steve Bosch's photos of tear-gassed rioters and smoke-filled streets would be eerily similar to those published in *The Sun* 17 years later, when another hockey riot tarnished the city's reputation following the Canucks' loss in another Stanley Cup final.

Back inside the newsroom in the midst of the chaos, Honeyman couldn't find a compositor to take reporter dictation over the phone, something required by the Pacific Press contracts, so he stormed into the composing room and told the foreman that if they didn't come up with someone right away, he would do the job himself. Minutes later, the compositor showed up. He was deaf.

The Sun would later be required by a court order to relinquish all the night's negatives to Vancouver police spokeswoman Anne Drennan. It was a portfolio, Honeyman recalled, that included Malcolm Parry's latest cleavage-cam shots.

Walking softly, with a big stick

In Scott Honeyman's four years at *The Sun*, he earned a reputation as a hard-nosed leader – and an unabashed regular visitor to the nudist enclave of Wreck Beach – despite his soft-spoken demeanour and calm approach to conflict.

One of his first acts as managing editor was to let go more than two dozen temporary employees, which caused a union ruckus and months of arbitration, and would eventually result in some of those temps being hired back as regular staffers. Honeyman also faced an arbitration board hearing over the paper publishing freelance photos by Parry, instead of having them shot by a staff photographer. Parry, and the paper, won that scrap. And when union reps complained that *The Sun* ran a piece by Vaughn Palmer, a non-union columnist, as the line story on page one, Honeyman suggested to the union delegation in his office that the paper had more important matters to worry about than "this petty bullshit." Within minutes of the meeting's end, an email message from one of the shop stewards went out to all staff, repeating Honeyman's words. Not long after, union supporters began wearing badges that said "No more petty bullshit."

You can't make this stuff up

One thing never seemed to change in *The Sun* newsroom: the characters who came and went over the years. There was the entertainment reporter who killed off his grandmother several times as an excuse to call in sick, and then decided he had a phobia that prevented him from going across the Granville Street Bridge, where most of his assignments took place. Union grievances occurred routinely, often for the oddest reasons. One employee formally complained that the person sitting next to her chewed his sandwich too loudly. Others fought over desk assignments, some wanting window seats, others preferring a quiet corner, others demanding the drapes be closed to shut out the glaring afternoon sun. After the 1997 move downtown, one reporter insisted management speak to waterfront authorities about the cruise ship and sea plane noise. One summer intern had her desk phone ripped from the wall when the senior reporter whose desk she was sitting in showed up for work. And stress leave became popular, with more than a few employees opting out for months at a time to deal with various afflictions, psychological and otherwise. And in a profession where drinking, smoking and carousing had not only been long-accepted, almost mandatory, pastimes, the company's in-house employee assistance program was working overtime to discreetly aid staffers in kicking their various addictions.

In 1992, Canadian media baron Conrad Black bought 23 per cent of Southam but his newspaper visions, as this cheeky 1993 photo implies, were far more than fish wrap.
Glenn Baglo/Vancouver Sun

Into the Black

Changes at *The Sun*, especially at the top, just kept coming. In November 1992, Conrad Black's Hollinger Inc. bought 23 per cent of Southam Inc. for $259 million, the first move in the chess game that would see many more strategic moves before the decade's end.

But the more things changed, the more they seemed to stay the same. For eight days, from Nov. 1 to Nov. 8, 1994, *The Vancouver Sun* was once again on strike due to a labour dispute, this time a dust-up over plans for new presses and backshop technology that required fewer staff to operate, as well as a buyout offer that would reduce Pacific Press staff numbers by 200.

While their picket-signed colleagues circled the building, non-union employees tackled janitorial duties inside and occasionally embarked on "forbidden" tours into parts of the plant they had never seen, like the pink-tiled men's washroom on the second floor and the lunch room

in the basement pressroom, where the work chart had spots for employees who were on vacation, leave of absence, extended sick leave or "in jail." The inside staff also spent a great deal of time in the fourth-floor cafeteria, cooking up the perishables left behind. While the head of advertising flipped pancakes for breakfast, other administration staffers were busy tucking into leftover frozen ice cream treats.

When the new contract was signed, it included a $500 signing bonus.

In a letter to readers in the returning paper of Monday, Nov. 14, publisher Don Babick thanked customers for their patience and apologized for the disruption, promising to provide readers with their missing crosswords and ensure that, in the absence of their coveted *TV Times* magazine, complete television listings could be found in the daily. And he urged readers to check out the paper's new comic strip, *Mutts*.

It wouldn't be the end of labour unrest that decade. On July 7, 1999, *The Vancouver Sun* was

Manual typewriters had made way for desktop computers by the 1990s, but the promise of a paperless newsroom clearly never materialized.
Ian Lindsay/Vancouver Sun

once again on strike, this time for the mere 2.25 hours it took 1,000 workers to reach a contract agreement with Pacific Press management.

Out with the new, in with the new

In 1995, four years after both had assumed the newsroom's leadership, editor Ian Haysom and managing editor Scott Honeyman were gone, eventually replaced by the erudite John Cruickshank, from the *Globe and Mail*, and managing editor Paul Sullivan. Theirs, too, would be a rocky tenure, marked by a major re-design and an upscale editorial tenor.

Those weren't the only changes. After 33 memorable and award-winning years as a *Vancouver Sun* cityside reporter, the much admired Moira Farrow retired in 1995. She was adamant, however, that there be none of the fuss made of late for other outgoing staffers, and that wish was granted. At the end of her shift on her last day, she quietly gathered her things, said goodbye to a few nearby colleagues, and began walking toward the newsroom exit. As she did, every single person on the floor rose to their feet and began clapping. It was a fitting tribute to a classy, hard-working journalist. Sadly, Farrow died only two years later.

Three months after Farrow's retirement, Denny Boyd, whose lyrical writing had graced *The Sun*'s pages for nearly 40 years as a sports reporter and city columnist, also retired. As

Getting ready for *The Sun*'s annual fundraising garage sale in December 1988 are writers (clockwise from front) Denny Boyd, Nicole Parton, Shelley Fralic, Gillian Shaw, Jenny Lee, Virginia Leeming and Susan Balcom. *Chris Helgren/Vancouver Sun*

Wasserman's successor, Boyd's must-read daily takes on Vancouver, its growing pains and its increasingly eclectic citizenry are now a treasured historical legacy. He would write, too, about his own shortcomings, his alcoholism and his propensity for beautiful redheads, so endearing him to readers that hundreds turned out for his funeral 11 years later.

Boyd, who was 27 when he first walked into

the Sun Tower, once wrote how working for *The Sun* was like "going to the big time. I had heard about it from afar, as pilgrims hear about Lourdes." He soon developed the Sun Strut, as he called it, "the cocky walk of reporters who worked for a cheeky, independent, chainless newspaper. It was a circus and there was a new act and new clowns every day. I wouldn't have missed it for the world."

Copies of *The Vancouver Sun* make their way through the new, world-class presses at Surrey's Kennedy Heights printing plant and into the mailroom before being trucked out to readers. *Steve Bosch /Vancouver Sun*

The old girl lands a new guy

The summer of 1997 found Conrad Black once again expanding his media empire.

The year before, his Vancouver-based Hollinger Inc. had upped its stake in Southam, which included *The Vancouver Sun*, to 50.7 per cent. Then, in July 1997, Hollinger added to its newspaper stable with the purchase of 19 Canadian newspapers from Thomson, slowly building a portfolio that by the end of the decade would include full ownership of the 33 papers in the Southam chain.

Amid all the change, *The Vancouver Sun*'s once robust circulation of 200,000-plus was starting to decline, a phenomenon experienced by many major-market daily newspapers on the continent.

A combination of environmental awareness and more competition, much of it related to the twin diversions of home computers and cable television, were being held responsible for a troubling decrease in circulation and readership. People simply didn't have time to read, and the eco-friendly among them didn't like the sight of newspapers, fashioned from trees,

piling up in the corner.

To address the problems on the editorial front and send the message that he meant business, Black injected not only cash and capital into the Pacific Press operation, but some new *Sun* blood. Among the new hires were seasoned investigative reporters Stewart Bell and Marina Jimenez.

Sun staff had mixed feelings about Black. While many acknowledged that he was an intellectual powerhouse who loved and understood newspapers and journalism, it was no secret that neither he nor his right-hand man, David Radler, held any love for unions, and it was also no secret that the salaries and benefits of the 800-plus Pacific Press employees were among the most generous on the continent. Or, as Radler described it at the time, "Too many people taking too many slices from a rapidly diminishing pie."

Once again, the old familiar talk of selling or closing one of the Vancouver papers was making employees nervous, but despite its problems, *The Sun* was still profitable and the rumours slowly died down as Hollinger-initiated buyouts and attrition helped the bottom line.

Moving on up, downtown

After three decades of physical stability at 6th and Granville, Pacific Press upped stakes on July 18, 1997 and relocated to the Granville Square waterfront office tower at 200 Granville Street, returning to its downtown roots of 1912.

In the July 19 Saturday Review section, which was the latest incarnation of *The Sun*'s weekend feature package, a photograph of *Sun* staffers in the old newsroom showed editor John Cruickshank and dozens of employees waving adieu to the dusty past. Inside the section, stories about the Pacific Press building included the time Miss Nude Vancouver walked through the newsroom wearing just a smile, the day Prime Minister Pierre Trudeau interrupted the deadline frenzy while weaving through reporters' work stations on his way to the editorial pages boardroom, the cafeteria cook who made cheeseburgers with the cheese under the patty, the cache of 500 empty rye and scotch bottles found during a renovation in the photo lab and, of course, the bound collection of cringe-inducing headlines holding gems

The carpet was mottled gray, resembling vintage hot metal plates, and the lobby featured a wall of plate-like metal panels and a reception desk designed in a half circle like an old press drum. Along with *Sun* staff of more than 200 – a number that was growing and would prompt publisher Don Babick to build in extra desks - came 350 truckloads carrying Pacific Press computers, work stations, chairs and boxes for all 852 relocating employees.

Elsewhere in the building, the non-mechanical departments such as advertising, promotions and human resources took up entire floors, so much so that Pacific Press soon dominated the office tower.

Pressing news

For the second time in *The Vancouver Sun*'s modern history, it was now printed off-site, on new presses in a purpose-built Surrey facility. Situated more centrally for the increasingly suburban readership, Kennedy Heights was designed to house the mechanical production and distribution of the paper.

The physical distance between the two plants was facilitated by yet another new technology in the newspaper industry: pagination. The four new German-made Manroland Colorman web offset presses at Kennedy Heights replaced the generation-old Goss Headliner letter presses in the old Pacific Press building at 2250 Granville and the Flexographic presses being used to print the *Province* (and, briefly, *The Sun*) at the Surrey Newton plant. They were the foundation of a $180-million, highly automated, printing press operation designed to run off 400,000 copies (the broadsheet *Sun* and the tabloid *Province* combined) every day.

The new system, operating today, was as complex as it was simple. Seven AGVs, or autoguided vehicles, were designed to lift 1,200-kilogram rolls of newsprint from the building's basement stockpile and deliver them to reel stands feeding the paper up to the presses above, which would be prepped with the aluminum printing plates made by the prepress department.

Those plates are made from the virtual pages prepared by the editorial and advertising departments and sent electronically over a 42-kilometre-long fibre optic cable by the Granville Street's then-named Output department.

Once off the press, the papers move on a conveyor to the mailing room, where they may be stuffed with flyers, bundled, bar coded with delivery details, and sent on to the appropriate trucks for delivery to customers.

As for the newsprint, it's now recyclable, a concern for environmentally conscious British Columbians. Gone from this sleek, new scenario are the composing room and the vintage, hand-operated, linotype machine – which today has a place of honour in the Kennedy press hall – both reminders of an era when type was fashioned with molten lead.

Today, the computer-generated process that is pagination means pages arrive electronically at Kennedy complete with stories, photographs, headlines, display copy and advertising, all of it designed on a computer screen in the newsroom instead of being pieced together in the backshop by compositors and engravers.

The state-of-the-art Kennedy Heights operation was billed as the most modern newspaper plant on the planet when it was created, the new presses promising not only speed, increased colour capabilities and quality reproduction but, just as importantly, the ability to print a 10-section, 160-page paper in one pass, something no other press in the world could boast.

The new presses were tested for only six weeks before they began printing *The Sun* live, and today they are cranked up a few hours before midnight with the average run lasting through 2 a.m. or so, depending on the day of the week and the size of the paper.

And while the pressmen's inky footprints used to leave their mark all over 2250 Granville – they had their own table in the cafeteria to prevent ink transfer to fancy white collar clothes – one thing didn't change.

A pressman still takes a copy or two right off the presses shortly after they start rolling, to ensure that colour, registration and page folds are up to standard and acceptable for customers.

such as "Ballet Beauty Mounted in Pool" and "Dwarfs discussed at length."

There was also a nostalgic reminiscence by columnist Trevor Lautens, who worked in the original Sun Tower in 1963. Lautens recalled THE SUN sign illuminated by 540 lights around the building's landmark cupola, "which along with pulsating jolts of neon-created lightning were sufficient to awaken the sleepiest citizen to the importance of a proud, lively, tough paper that dominated the Vancouver media business."

The Sun's new splashy downtown digs were in a specially designed 25,000-square-foot space on the building's mezzanine, shared with the Pacific Press library; its sister paper, *The Province*, was a floor above in a somewhat smaller space.

(The newsrooms would move again — to different floors in the building — with *The Sun* relocating to the 8th floor in 2012.)

The huge west and north-facing newsroom, with open sight lines and floor-to-ceiling glass windows, overlooked the cruise ship terminal and had lost none of the breathtaking ocean and mountain views of its previous home.

At Kennedy Heights, pressman Gary Crews checks inking levels on his computer.
Steve Bosch/Vancouver Sun

In a case of art imitating life, *The Sun* newsroom at 2250 Granville Street was taken over by director Robert Klane in 1993, for filming of *The Odd Couple* with Tony Randall (centre) and Jack Klugman. *Jeff Vinnick/Vancouver Sun*

From Underwoods to the big Macs

Back at 200 Granville, the technological shift wasn't just confined to production. The once busy darkroom in the old building (10,000 rolls of film a year) had been rendered redundant by film-less cameras.

While many newspapers were experimenting with digital cameras, especially for sports, *The Sun* (and *Province*) became the first newspapers in North America to go all-digital in 1995. The cameras could hold 76 images, which could then be transmitted to the newsroom via laptop, eliminating several steps and, some feared, opening the door to photo manipulation. And writers were by now working on sophisticated desktop computers.

The manual typewriter had fallen victim, in the 1980s, to a rudimentary computer system called Tal-Star, but the new, high-powered Macintosh computers were loaded with a newspaper-specific publishing program called Quark Xpress, which used CopyDesk as its primary word processor.

While pagination had eliminated many steps in the traditional printing process, it still required skilled copy editors, who no longer just polished copy and interrogated reporters, but who were required to do page layout, place photos, and write headlines, decks and photo captions.

You say news research library, I say morgue

Whether you were an old-time newsie who still called it, with much fondness, the morgue, or a new recruit who preferred the nicety of its modern appellation, News Research Library, the paper's in-house library was long a vital and integral part of the business, setting up shop alongside *The Sun* newsroom in its new downtown home.

While technology would bring much change to the work of newspaper librarians over the decades, the shared *Sun* and *Province* library provided invaluable information and research while cataloguing and archiving stories and photos for quick and easy access when required.

The numbers tell the story: a total of three million *Sun* articles have been indexed since the 1930s, along with 1.8 million photographs (on negatives and prints) since the 1940s, close to 300,000 digital images since 1994, and 3,912 reels of microfilm preserving every page of *The Vancouver Sun* from 1912 to 2012.

As well as information searching and fact checking, for data such as demographic statistics, property ownership and court records, the library also serviced the public, selling reprints of photographs of quintessentially B.C. images, such as ducks and their ducklings, snow-covered mountains, soaring eagles and, one of the most requested photographs of all, a charming 1968 Ken Oakes shot of five Siamese kittens drinking milk out of champagne glasses.

With the launch of its public Infoline service in 1992, the library also generated revenue through the sale and licensing of content.

The advent of web-based research through Infomart – a Canada-wide newspaper archive that saw librarians training editors and reporters on how to conduct their own research – changed the way reporters researched their stories and, in the spring of 2012, the library closed, its remaining staff and librarian duties, such as Infoline and the sale of material to the public, integrated into *The Sun* (and *Province*) editorial departments.

PRECEDING PAGE: The legendary Tina Turner rocks it out at GM Place in 1997. *Peter Battistoni/Vancouver Sun*

In July 1997, Canadian fishing boats protesting the American sockeye salmon fishery blockaded the Alaska State ferry *Malaspina*, preventing it from leaving the dock in Prince Rupert. *Ian Smith/Vancouver Sun*

Out with the Olde, in with the new nameplate

Charged with reinventing the paper, under the watchful eyes of Conrad Black and Don Babick, were editor John Cruickshank and managing editor Paul Sullivan (and, after Sullivan's brief stint, managing editor Vivienne Sosnowski). They faced not only issues of content but the prospect of reinvigorating a mostly aging baby boomer staff, which had become complacent and disengaged after years in the trenches.

The directive, however, was clear: Institutional reporting, like political scrums and regurgitated press releases, were out. Investigative stories, breaking news, contextual analyses and conversational storytelling were in, as were small news bites and "quick takes" designed for readers on the run.

Under Cruickshank, the thinking man's newspaperman, *The Sun* was completely redesigned by long-time graphics guru Jim Emerson.

Controversially, the Olde English nameplate that had been introduced with the paper's debut in 1912 was ditched. The change was hotly debated among staffers who cited newspapers like *The New York Times*, which never changed its nameplate, but Cruickshank insisted it was time for something fresh and he was adamant that the original font made the paper look old-fashioned. Results from reader focus groups

Debbie Millward, former manager of PNG's News Research Library, takes Canadian author Margaret Atwood on a tour of the library in 2011. *Les Bazso/PNG*

were mixed, but Cruickshank prevailed. After 85 years, *The Vancouver Sun* had a new nameplate in the clean, streamlined Poynter font, a modern look for a modern time.

Such was the chaos around the redesign that management neglected to buy the rights to the Poynter font, prompting the threat of action from a copyright lawyer, followed by a hastily FedExed cheque to settle the matter.

The revamp introduced a hierarchical vertical layout format, accompanied by value-added fact bars and introductory subheads, as well as more suburban coverage, which had long been spotty despite the exodus of readers east and south of the city.

There was also talk of sharing stories and photos with the growing number of ethnic community papers, an initiative that had been attempted with limited success in the past and would prove more successful some years later with the 2011 launch of a Chinese-language *Sun* website.

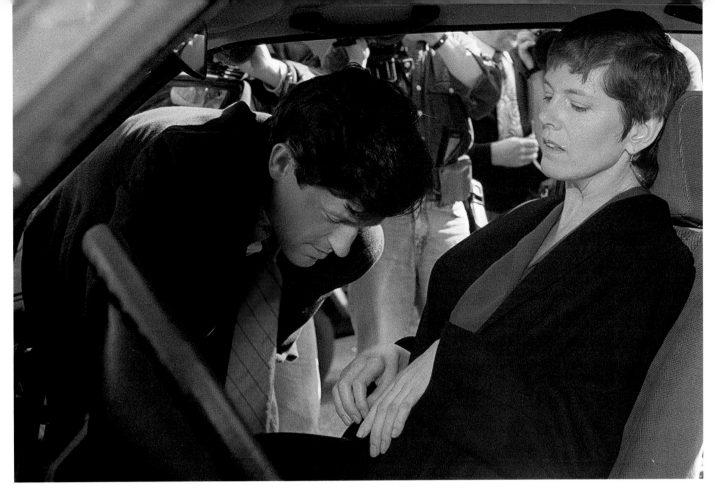

B.C. MP Svend Robinson helped ALS sufferer Sue Rodriguez prepare to attend a press conference following the 1993 Supreme Court right-to-die decision. *John Yanyshyn/Vancouver Sun*

On the comeback trail. But not for long.

The new and improved *Vancouver Sun* was all about delivering a smart and informative news package by marrying design and content, making the paper easier to read - and more interesting.

On Nov. 5, 1997, in a special 24-page section introducing readers to the new presses and new-look *Sun*, columnist Pete McMartin wrote of the changes and the reasons for them, noting that while his talent was being able to "rub two adjectives together to create a little warmth," modern journalism ultimately is more than just asking uncomfortable questions and "turning over stones to find the bugs underneath."

The Vancouver Sun, he wrote, with its clean nameplate and renewed commitment to journalistic excellence and integrity – not to mention an extensive and expensive marketing campaign – had its mojo back.

And readers seemed to agree. Circulation stabilized, the paper was once again the talk of the town, and one had only to listen to morning radio to know that most stories reported on air had been borrowed shamelessly from *The Sun*'s pages, a practice long referred to as rip and read.

And then along came Conrad Black's vanity project, a new national daily that hit newspaper boxes across the country on Oct. 27, 1998. *National Post* espoused a politically conservative voice, and was Black's way of firing a shot across the bow of the national *Globe and Mail* and the big papers in Toronto, a city without a Hollinger daily.

Black threw his considerable financial weight behind his new pet project, hiring away some of his other papers' best people, including Stewart Bell and Marina Jimenez from *The Sun*.

The Post's expensive and relentless promotional and marketing campaigns, as well as local distribution, consumed much of the resources and attention of Pacific Press staff, prompting a great deal of resentment throughout the building.

The same story would play out with varying degrees in all the markets – Calgary, Edmonton, Montreal and Ottawa – where Black also owned the metro dailies.

Staff began to worry, with good reason, that Black's bottom-line business imperative and no-expenses-spared affection for the *National Post* would continue to adversely affect *The Vancouver Sun*.

The Sun's circulation, which had hit record press runs of close to 300,000 on weekends during the 1980s, was once again suffering, hovering in the low 200,000s, a significant concern when it came to determining how much to charge advertisers, whose rates had always been based on readership; the more eyes on the paper, the more an ad costs.

The Sun was also required to run full-page ads urging readers to buy its new sister paper, *National Post*. "For only $6 more a month, the *National Post*, combined with your leading local newspaper, *The Vancouver Sun*, will make you a totally informed reader." Another *Sun* ad read: "If you are not currently a *Vancouver Sun* subscriber, but would like to subscribe to *National Post*, please call the number above for an introductory offer."

Newsroom nerves were starting to jangle, as staffers contemplated newspaper cannibalism and what looked like a wobbly future.

Passing the notebook, and the torch

Like the newspaper itself, the modern-day reporter was evolving from the gutsy street-smart newshound of the early 1900s, those (mostly) men who learned on the job and partied hard and were nothing like the young diploma-rich hires of the 1990s. The new generation of *Sun* reporters was recruited from among the thousands of applications that landed on the desks of senior editors from university journalism programs across the country.

There were certainly more women in *The Sun* newsroom, and not just in the features pages, and more minorities, too. But as the new decade loomed, it was clear another generation of journalists was entering the game, their academic credentials bolstered by critical multimedia skills. Being web savvy was becoming as much a requirement of the job as the instinctive nose for news and the Underwood typewriter had once been.

The old newsroom guard was giving way to the new.

THE 2000s

The 2000s: The world spins a widening web

Fireworks explode over BC Place Stadium at the end of the closing ceremony for the 2010 Winter Olympics on Sunday.

ABOVE: The March 1, 2010 front page celebrates hockey gold for Canada and the spectacular fireworks that marked the closing of the Vancouver 2010 Winter Olympics.

PRECEDING PAGE: "Yes!" Rejoicing readers – and *The Vancouver Sun*'s special July 2, 2003 edition celebrating the city's naming as host of the 2010 Winter Olympic Games – say it all. *Mark van Manen/Vancouver Sun*

The new millennium found The Vancouver Sun revelling in its shiny new presses, snappy redesign and refreshed commitment as the region's paper of record, but the near future would soon find the venerable daily facing yet another blow to its longevity: the world wide web.

The dreaded Y2K bug had proven harmless – or as the Jan. 1, 2000 Sun put it, "Apocalypse Not" – but the reality that humanity was connecting more and more through a pervasive virtual network was becoming ever more apparent.

Where global communication had long been confined to the basics – newspapers, mail, periodicals, telephones, televisions and old-fashioned conversations – the astounding growth of the Internet in the late 1990s was changing not only the newspaper landscape, but the world, forever.

Cyberspace was the new wild west of information dissemination, and The Vancouver Sun was on the cusp of yet another reinvention.

As the centenarian prepared to celebrate her 100th birthday, regaling readers with a century of stories and nostalgic memories of the paper that had grown up with them and their city, it unveiled an appropriate new motto: Seriously Westcoast Since 1912.

To accommodate its "digital-first" initiatives, *The Sun* reorganized its newsroom around a television-topped hub that brings together traditional section editors and a new generation of web editors. Second from left is Harold Munro, appointed *Sun* editor-in-chief in the spring of 2012.
Ward Perrin/Vancouver Sun

Introducing the virtual titans

The Internet was redefining journalism: what it was, who delivered it and how and when it was received. Suddenly, people didn't need to read the newspaper to get their news, not when what they wanted to know was a keystroke away and available in real time, not when smart phones, YouTube, Facebook, Twitter and search engines like Google provided instant access to a world of information.

The growth of online usage for everything from research and shopping to dating and photo sharing was astounding: in 1993, one per cent of information was flowing through keyboards; by 2000 it was 51 per cent and by decade's end it was estimated that 97 per cent of all global communication was web-based.

For newspapers and their readers, the journalistic line began to blur. Bloggers and so-called citizen journalists – self-appointed reporters by decree of their keyboard access – often worked outside the boundaries of industry standards, eschewing issues of plagiarism, copyright and other legal considerations such as libel and publication bans, time-honoured distinctions often lost on the customer.

The web was also altering the language, as the wired generation eagerly bared its collective soul in 140-character tweets and spontaneous personal snapshots, chatting around the world in the shorthand of OMG and LOL and IMO.

Networking, social and otherwise, was now soundly in the hands of a subculture of cool nerds, unlikely billionaires such as Apple's Steve Jobs, Facebook's Mark Zuckerberg, Google's Larry Page and Sergey Brin and, of course, Microsoft's Bill Gates, who were clearly charting this new virtual territory.

If newspapers were the bedrock of modern communication, the Internet was creating a new high water mark, and it was only somewhat comforting to hear 27-year-old wunderkind Zuckerberg publicly remind his 845 million users of just that on the eve of taking his $75-billion-plus company public in 2012.

"At Facebook, we're inspired by technologies that have revolutionized how people spread and consume information. We often talk about inventions like the printing press and the television — by simply making communication more efficient, they led to a complete transformation of many important parts of society. They gave more people a voice. They encouraged progress. They changed the way society was organized. They brought us closer together."

And now they needed a different strategy.

For the love of sports

In a century of distinguished publishing, much of *The Vancouver Sun*'s reputation as a writers' paper could be found in the calibre of its sports pages. From the early stylings of writers like Jim Taylor, Denny Boyd, James Lawton and Archie McDonald to the modern-day storytelling of Elliott Pap, Gary Kingston, Brad Ziemer, Mike Beamish and inimitable columnists Iain MacIntyre and Cam Cole, *Sun* scribes have preserved the art of sports writing as a vital, vivid part of a daily's lineup. The sports reporter is a different breed, dedicated to a life on the road and a head full of statistics, to late-night deadlines and draughty press boxes. Their learned and descriptive depictions of Grey Cups and nail-biting Stanley Cups, of golf and soccer, baseball and basketball, of Olympics and Paralympics, of the professional sprinter and the high school hoopster, comprise a lively 24-hour package that masterfully takes readers into the heart of the action.

When former *Sun* legislative reporter turned city editor turned sports columnist Gary Mason picked up a coveted National Newspaper Award for sports reporting in 2000, he joined a stellar *Sun* sports gallery of NNA winners that included Dick Beddoes (1959), Jim Kearney (1966) and McDonald (1980).

Mason had written a compelling profile of Vancouver Grizzlies guard Mahmoud Abdul-Rauf, who had conquered his childhood struggle with Tourette's syndrome to became an NBA star.

Two years later, Mason would win another NNA for a series on the retired players from the 1972 Soviet hockey team, an assignment that saw editor-in-chief Neil Reynolds send his columnist to Moscow for a month to track down and interview the mostly forgotten, destitute players.

After 19 years with the paper, including a stint as deputy managing editor, Mason left *The Sun* and joined *The Globe and Mail* in 2005.

The city and *The Sun*'s sports writers, however, were soon wrapped up in the 2006 Winter Olympic Games in Turin, where Canadian athletes won a national record 24 medals and where speed skater Clara Hughes would bring home a gold and a silver, providing a taste of the Olympic glory that would shine on Vancouver in 2010.

Je t'aime, Papa

Under the headline "An Extraordinary Canadian," a pensive, statesman-like photograph of former Prime Minister Pierre Elliott Trudeau consumed the cover of the Sept. 29, 2000 *Sun*, a tribute to a political titan who had lost his battle with cancer at the age of 80. The extensive package inside included pictures of the charismatic Trudeau with his trademark red rose, while stories spoke to his political legacy and his B.C. links: a snapshot of Trudeau and Vancouver-born wife Margaret swinging

THE VANCOUVER SUN

www.vancouversun.com   SATURDAY, NOVEMBER 9, 2002   FINAL

THE SUMMIT SERIES: A VANCOUVER SUN SPECIAL REPORT

'Tell them how we live'

What became of the Russian players who battled Canada for hockey supremacy in 1972? Thirty years later, **Gary Mason** goes to Moscow to find out. Today, he tells their stories.

Few of the players from the Summit Series are as angry as Yevgeny Mishakov. Now living on a military pension of about $80 a month, he says: 'This country has left me behind.'

MOSCOW

Thirty years after the 1972 Summit Series between the then-Soviet Union and Canada, there are still winners and losers. And it is mostly the players who came out on the short end of the epic eight-game hockey clash who lost even more when their playing days were over.

"We are the forgotten ones," said Yevgeny Mishakov, a rugged forward on the Soviet team. "We are forgotten by our own people and by our own government.

"They have left us to live on nothing. It is a disgrace what happened to the great veterans of hockey here. Tell them in North America how we live."

In September, on the 30th anniversary of the series, I travelled to Russia to track down as many members of the Soviet team as I could. I wasn't interested in quick reflections on the series itself as much as I was the story of their lives. What were they doing now? How did they live? What, if any, benefits did they derive from being part of one of the greatest hockey encounters in history? Moreover, how were they coping in the New Russia,

the one with the dog-eat-dog, capitalist sensibilities?

For almost a month I travelled around Moscow and the surrounding countryside looking for the players and their stories. I found them in arenas and coffee shops, met them in their homes and on street corners. In the end, I tracked down nearly all of them. Those I couldn't meet in person I talked to over the phone, through my interpreter Denis Neznanov, to see what they were now doing.

See BITTERNESS A3

THE FORGOTTEN ONES MIX E1

New NPA ads target COPE-NDP

Trailing badly in Sun poll, the party gets aggressive for final week of civic campaign

By DAVID REEVELY

The Non-Partisan Association is set to launch a fierce advertising campaign today, directly targeting the opposition Coalition of Progressive Electors as the municipal election campaign heads into its final week.

"No more pissing around," said Grant Longhurst, the NPA's campaign coordinator, after watching three new television ads in a back room at NPA headquarters on West Broadway. He smiled grimly and cupped an unshaven cheek in one hand.

"We're behind," Longhurst

said, shrugging. "If we want to win, we have to be aggressive. The message is that we do not want the NDP to have control of our city council, our school board, or our park board."

One television ad shows a fast ferry cruising down the coast while warnings of "Fudget Budgets" and other alleged fiascos of the provincial NDP flash on the screen.

"If the city of Vancouver is determined to elect the NDP to run the city, through COPE, it's incumbent upon us to make sure that connection is clear to the voters," Longhurst said.

INSIDE
- Who The Sun endorses in Vancouver, and why, A21
- An oasis of calm in Victoria, B1
- Drug addiction on the west side: four families tell their stories, B5
- Vancouver Island's hot button issues, B7
- No wrong or right in drug debate: Pete McMartin, B8
- Development in White Rock, F5

A *Vancouver Sun* poll, published Friday, showed NPA mayoral candidate Jennifer Clarke trailing Coalition of Progressive Electors candidate Larry Camp-

bell — 56 per cent to 29 among decided voters. Valerie MacLean of vcaTEAM was third with 14 per cent.

Ken Bayne, the City of Vancouver's director of financial services, said a clause in the municipal charter would make real fiscal vandalism difficult.

"The Vancouver charter, and other municipal legislation in British Columbia . . . is very clear that municipal governments can't run a deficit," Bayne said.

The NPA's headquarters, in a former furniture warehouse, was nearly empty a little before 1 p.m. Friday. Here a campaign worker sat at a card table with a telephone; there another picked up a campaign sign blown off the wall

See THE NPA A4

INSIDE

B.C.'S FIRST MILITARY VOLUNTEERS
A23

Cloudy, showers
Full report, G7

$1.40 RETAIL
$1.50 COIN BOX

David Raines	F5
Births & Deaths	B10
Bridge	D17
Paula Brook	F2
Business	F1
Michael Campbell	F3
Careers	C1
Classified	C6
Comics	G8, G9
Crossword	D15, D18, E21
Editorials	A22
Ferry Schedule	A7
Horoscope	D19
Insight	A31
Letters	A35, B8, E23
Lotteries	A2

Pete McMartin	
Mix	
Movies	
Vaughn Palmer	
Malcolm Parry	
Michael Sanger	
Sports	
TV	
Theatre	
West Coast Home	
Barbara Yaffe	

canada.c

Over 11,300 prizes to over 10,000 winne

THE WEB: MillionaireLottery.c

Call 604-602-584 or toll free 1.888 445.5825

ANY LONDON DRU
Also at the Vancouver Gener and UBC Hospital

LONDON DRUGS

BETTER THAN 1 IN 12 TO WIN

WOW!...

We're already 50% sold!

...after just 1 month! Here's why...
Two 8-in-1 Grand Prizes with everything you see here. Take the prizes and live the millionaire lifestyle, or *take the money* and be a millionaire!

BC GAMING #847123

Columnist Gary Mason's 2002 series on the impoverished and forgotten 1972 Russian hockey stars earned him a second National Newspaper Award for sports reporting.

two-year-old son Sacha down a corridor at the Vancouver airport, an interview with the Salmon Arm man on the receiving end of the infamous Trudeau middle-finger salute. *Sun* columnist Stephen Hume wrote that the cultured, enigmatic Frenchman and his "flower power" appeal "blew into public consciousness like some kind of electrical storm. He was a man

made for the times and his arrival put him right into the sweet, slick seam where one political and social culture was yielding to another."

At the state funeral, Justin Trudeau immortalized his father with a moving eulogy that ended with a touching tribute: "The woods are lovely, dark and deep. He has kept his promises and earned his sleep. Je t'aime, Papa."

Justin Trudeau, carrying an iconic rose at the 2000 funeral of his father, former Prime Minister Pierre Trudeau, is flanked by his brother Sacha, his aunt Suzette Rouleau and his mother Margaret Kemper. *Pierre Obendrauf/Montreal Gazette*

The Vancouver Sun and its sister papers across the country had a new owner in November 2000: Izzy Asper and his Canwest Global Communications Corp. *Peter Battistoni/Vancouver Sun*

New century, new ownership

In what was becoming a familiar pattern, the millennium brought yet another ownership shuffle for *The Vancouver Sun* (and *Province*) when Canwest Global Communications Corp., a media empire run by the Asper family of Winnipeg, bought Southam Inc. and other Hollinger holdings for $3.2 billion.

The Nov. 15, 2000 transaction included 14 dailies, 126 weeklies and half interest in *National Post*.

Canwest already owned 17 television stations in Canada, including BCTV, which would soon become Global, but the blockbuster deal made it the country's largest media company.

The deal also gave rise to the term convergence, the bespoke initiative that had Canwest's considerable print, broadcast and Internet properties sharing their bounties with one another, creating an integrated media consortium aimed at content and advertising dominance in the wildly competitive marketplace.

"The power of our traditional media combining with leadership in the new media will be an unprecedented force and will create exciting changes in the media scene," Canwest chief executive Leonard Asper told reporters.

For long-time staff at *The Vancouver Sun*, it was just another twisting turn on the unpredictable amusement park ride that had been the paper's masthead history over the previous few decades, as a series of owners, editors and publishers had come and gone, mostly outsiders who'd left their mark in ways that were both progressive and regressive. Talk in the newsroom after the Canwest takeover was that you just never knew what to expect when you showed up for work.

In *The Sun*'s mezzanine lobby, a large framed portrait of Conrad Black was quietly removed.

Terror in the towers

On the morning of Sept. 11, 2001, the world watched stunned and in disbelief as terrorists hijacked four commercial planes in the air over the eastern U.S, flying two of them directly into the iconic Twin Towers of the World Trade Center in Manhattan, and turning the metropolis into an ash-covered hell. As the unspeakable tragedy unfolded live on television, another plane hit the Pentagon, while another crashed in a field in Shanksville, Pennsylvania.

A same-day special 32-page section, Catastrophe in America, was overseen by editor Neil Reynolds and managing editor Patricia Graham. Then assignment editor Harold Munro was on his way to work that morning when he heard the news on the radio. Arriving in the newsroom, his first call was to columnist Pete McMartin, who was sent to the Peace Arch so he could get across the border before the U.S. government shut it down. Then Munro started calling reporters, those on shift and off, and when it was decided *The Sun* would put out an afternoon edition that day, everyone switched into high gear.

"By mid-morning," Munro recalled, "we were told to produce an afternoon edition, which meant rounding up early files from as many local reporters as possible, grabbing wire stories and photos. The pages were designed, edited and shipped to Kennedy Heights to be printed and delivered to street hawkers in downtown Vancouver in time for the afternoon commute.

"I remember walking outside to look up Granville Street and seeing office workers crowded around hawkers to buy the special edition. After dispatching the special edition, we started over again with content for the next day's paper."

The coverage provided a wrenchingly descriptive diorama of disturbing images and heart-rending stories of shell-shocked survivors, many of whom had lost loved ones or had fled for their lives from the collapsing towers. "The worst was seeing people jump," was one witness's vivid recollection, while another recalled the moment "the sky went black." The special section's cover did not have a headline, just a photo of the first tower engulfed in smoke and flames in the seconds after the plane hit, along with two quotes, the first from U.S. President George W. Bush – "Freedom itself was attacked this morning and I assure you freedom will be defended" – and the second from New York Mayor Rudolph Giuliani – "I have a sense it's a horrendous number of lives lost."

"Thousands perish" was *The Sun*'s sombre headline on its next-day edition of Sept. 12, above a photograph of the ash-shrouded remains of the World Trade Center, crushed vehicles and mounds of debris in the foreground.

The 9/11 attacks, attributed to Islamic extremist Osama bin Laden and al Qaida, killed nearly 3,000 people and gave rise to the NATO-backed invasion of Afghanistan and a protracted and controversial 10-year war that would take the lives of 158 Canadian soldiers.

CATASTROPHE IN AMERICA

THE VANCOUVER SUN

www.vancouversun.com   TUESDAY, SEPTEMBER 11, 2001   SPECIAL EDITION

SPECIAL EDITION

"**Freedom itself was attacked this morning and I assure you freedom will be defended.**"
President George W. Bush

"**I have a sense it's a horrendous number of lives lost.**"
Mayor Rudolph Giuliani

Terrorism at the World Trade Center, New York City 8:45 a.m. EST Tuesday, September 11, 2001

70 CENTS RETAIL
75 CENTS COIN BOX

$1 MINIMUM
OUTSIDE LOWER MAINLAND

When terrorists struck the World Trade Center in New York on Sept. 11, 2001, *The Sun* newsroom swung into action, publishing a rare extra edition within hours of the attacks.

Tears for a fallen comrade

When junior Vancouver firefighter Alex Noke-Smith flew to New York in the fall of 2001, he took with him a cheque for $675,000, raised in a boot drive, and a heavy heart. He was among a small group of Vancouver firefighters attending the funeral of Christian Regenhard, one of hundreds of New York firefighters and first responders killed a month earlier in the Sept. 11, 2001 terrorist attacks on the World Trade Center.

Sun photographer Ian Smith was also in New York, assigned to cover the Vancouver contingent.

"When firefighter Alex Noke-Smith came out

Photographer Ian Smith won a National Newspaper Award for his heart-wrenching photo of Vancouver firefighter Alex Noke-Smith. It was taken in New York at the funeral procession of Christian Regenhard, one of hundreds of firefighters killed in the Twin Towers attacks on Sept. 11, 2001. *Ian Smith/Vancouver Sun*

with the procession, I could see how attending the funeral had left him saddened," Smith recalled. "I followed him along until he got to a spot on the street outside the church, where he would stand in line as the funeral procession passed. As it did, two big tears rolled down his cheeks. I was across from him and captured the moment. I knew I had exactly the picture I had gone to New York to capture."

In a later interview with *The Sun*, Noke-Smith said that even though he didn't know Regenhard, he felt a personal connection. The two were the same age, 29, had young children and were rock climbing hobbyists.

"In firefighting," Noke-Smith said, "there's this brotherhood, this camaraderie. It didn't matter if it happened across the continent and it didn't matter if it wasn't one of the guys from our crew; it was almost like it was in our backyard."

Smith's touching picture earned him a National Newspaper Award for spot news photography.

A monster unearthed

In a city that would never recover from the murderous spree of Clifford Olson, convicted of killing 11 Vancouver-area children in the early 1980s, it seemed inconceivable that such evil could strike twice.

But two decades after Olson, police began digging for evidence on a Port Coquitlam pig farm and *Sun* readers were learning what many had suspected for some time: Robert Pickton had been preying on prostitutes, luring them to his slovenly suburban acreage where he murdered them.

Women had, in fact, started disappearing from the Downtown Eastside in the 1980s, with the frequency increasing through the 1990s. When relatives started complaining that police were putting little priority on what turned out to be dozens of missing women, *The Vancouver Sun* began publishing a series of stories in the fall of 2001, revealing the police investigation did not have adequate resources and was ignoring evidence suggesting Pickton might be a suspect in the case of the "forgotten" women. On Feb. 5, 2002, the Missing Women Task Force, which had been formed the previous year by the RCMP and Vancouver police, began a firearms search of the Pickton farm, uncovering personal items and, ultimately, the remains of many women.

The Sun's page one story on Feb. 8, by reporters Lindsay Kines and Kim Bolan, was startling: "Police searching for firearms on a Port Coquitlam farm found personal identification and other items linked to at least two of the 50 prostitutes missing from Vancouver's Downtown Eastside, *The Vancouver Sun* has learned."

It would be the first hint of the devastating and disturbing narrative that would unfold over the next decade, a litany of disenfranchised women discarded by society, murdered by a

monster and ignored by authorities indifferent to their disappearance.

Month after month, a *Sun* investigative team began peeling back the layers of the Pickton case, assiduously covering the lengthy and complicated court proceedings while putting a human face on the story, with numerous profiles and photographs of the missing and murdered women.

Pickton, who would eventually confess to killing as many as 49 women, was initially charged with 27 murders and, in December 2007, was convicted on seven counts of second-degree murder and sentenced to life without parole

for 25 years. Two years later, the B.C. Court of Appeal denied his bid for a new trial and ruled that trying Pickton on the remaining 20 charges would "impose further enormous demands on financial and judicial resources."

A Missing Women Commission of Inquiry was created after the legal options were exhausted, amid lobbying from frustrated relatives and charges of police inertia and mishandling. It began hearing testimony in 2011, including an admission that Pickton had, indeed, been on the police radar in 1998.

The Pickton case, which took years to complete and cost $70 million, was the kind of

THE VANCOUVER SUN

www.vancouversun.com   FINAL   FRIDAY, FEBRUARY 8, 2002

Search of pig farm yields missing women's ID

Robert William Pickton a person of interest since 1998

Lindsay Kines   Kim Bolan

Police searching for firearms on a Port Coquitlam farm found personal identification and other items linked to at least two of the 50 prostitutes missing from Vancouver's Downtown Eastside, *The Vancouver Sun* has learned.

Members of the joint RCMP-Vancouver city police missing women task force were present for the firearms search Tuesday night and discovery of the women's ID prompted them to get a second warrant for the property, according to police sources familiar with the investigation.

Officially, however, police weren't saying Thursday what they found during the firearms search that prompted them to get a second warrant.

"We are very confident in our reasons for obtaining the search warrant and as you know, we need to have some really good information in order for a judge to grant us a search warrant," said Constable Catherine Galliford, who speaks for the missing women task force.

Dozens of RCMP officers patrolled the farm Thursday, while neighbours, schoolchildren and curiosity-seekers flocked to the area, jamming traffic and queuing in front of the throng of television cameras from local, national and U.S. media outlets.

But Galliford refused to comment on whether any human remains have been found on the four-hectare (10-acre) site.

"We are not in a position to disclose to the media or the public any physical evidence that we may find here at this property or any other property, because

that may be used as direct evidence in court," Galliford said.

Late Thursday afternoon, however, police forensic identification specialists picked up a small black purse in the entranceway to the property, as well as several other items along a ditch at the edge of the property.

Police sources have identified Robert William Pickton as a person of interest in the case. He is listed on B.C. assessment records as one of three owners of the property being searched.

The farm, which is bordered by new housing developments, has been sealed off since Tuesday, with police stationed at every entrance. On Thursday, police began erecting a chain-link fence to keep

out intruders.

Court records show that after the search, Pickton was charged with possession of a loaded, restricted .22-calibre revolver, unsafe storage of a firearm, and possession of a weapon without licence or registration.

Pickton is no longer in custody and has not been charged with any offences relating to the disappearance of women from the Downtown Eastside. He is due to appear in court on the weapons charges Feb. 28.

Galliford said the missing women task force became interested in the property during its review of all files on prostitu-

See **CITY POLICE RECEIVED** A4

Robert William Pickton (above and right), whose property is being searched by police, heads into a pigpen on his farm in this 1996 still from a Global BCTV News video. The footage was taken during a story about a property tax complaint.

Missing Women

INSIDE

■ How the investigation led to a Port Coquitlam pig farm.   A2

■ At the scene: a steady stream of media and the curious.   A2

■ Stabbing in 1997 led to police interest.   A3

■ The 50 missing women.   A3, 4, 5

■ Port Coquitlam tried to shut down parties at 'Piggy's Palace.'   A5

■ Part of the farm was sold for redevelopment in the early '90s.   A5

INSIDE

Morning showers Full report. E7	At Home E1	Horoscope C9
	Births & Deaths B7	Ann Landers E7
	Bridge C38	Letters A15
	Daphne Bramham A8	Gary Mason D1
	Business D9	Pete McMartin B1
	Classified F12	Movies F2
	Comics/Kids B8	Vaughn Palmer A14
	Crossword C1, C8, C14	Sports D1
	Editorials A34	Theatre F5
	Entertainment F1	Wheels C1
	Ferry Schedule E7	Barbara Yaffe A34

$1.40 RETAIL
$1.50 COIN BOX

canada.com

$1.50 MINIMUM
OUTSIDE LOWER MAINLAND

It's official: We're a have-not province

By CRAIG McINNES

VICTORIA — For the first time, British Columbia officially became a have-not province in 1999-2000, Finance Minister Gary Collins said Thursday.

Federal government figures for the period show B.C. should qualify for $30 million in equalization payments — money paid by Ottawa to the country's poorest provinces — when the final

tally is done, probably in a few months.

Collins said it is likely the spike in energy revenues lifted B.C. back among the have provinces in 2000-2001, but he said the province may have slipped back again since, because of the drop in energy prices.

Collins also revealed at an open cabinet meeting the provincial budget deficit for the coming year will be a record $4.4 billion.

"We are facing huge fiscal challenges in our province," said Premier Gordon Campbell, who blamed the former NDP government for B.C.'s decline into have-not status, along with Newfoundland and six other provinces.

"This is something that's obviously new to British Columbia, it's never happened before. It's a shame it happened a year and a half before the last election, there

was no reason for it to happen, but the incompetence and mismanagement of the previous government."

Ottawa spends about $10 billion each year on equalization payments to help poorer provinces provide services.

Until now, B.C., Alberta and

See **COLLINS CLAIMS** A6

Barbara Yaffe on the shame of it all, A34
Other announcements from cabinet, A6

$2.00 Plus tax
Big Mac and Small Fries

ENDS FEB 28

Not valid with any other offer. See in-restaurant for details.
At participating McDonald's Restaurants. ©2002 McDonald's Restaurants of Canada Limited. For the exclusive use of McDonald's Restaurants of Canada Limited and its franchisees.

The front page of *The Vancouver Sun* on Feb. 8, 2002 realized the city's fears: the Downtown Eastside missing women were traced to Willie Pickton's pig farm.

story that showcased how daily journalism can make a difference: only by holding authorities accountable can the truth of a story be told. *The Sun* has published more than 700 stories since the case broke in 2002, and the paper and its unwavering Pickton team – which also included Lori Culbert, Neal Hall, Jeff Lee and Chad Skelton – have garnered numerous accolades and awards.

Patricia Graham, the *Sun* editor-in-chief who oversaw the Pickton coverage, said it was evident early on that the investigation was stalling because the women were among those easy to ignore.

"An apathy surrounded the investigation, and there was good reason to believe that this apathy was costing more women their lives. It was *The Vancouver Sun* that first revealed that the number of women who had gone missing was much higher than what police had been saying, and this kick-started things into high gear.

"The Pickton trial wasn't just about a man alleged to have committed some gruesome murders. It was about the high cost of a societal attitude that labelled some people as 'throwaway.' It was about a lack of communication and cooperation between two police forces, the RCMP and the Vancouver Police Department. It was about poor investigative techniques. And it was about how these things combined to cause missed opportunities to solve a crime that led to unnecessary loss of life."

Hello sweetheart, get me my blog

The Sun's rapidly growing web presence since the launch of vancouversun.com – which has come a long way since its web debut on Dec. 2, 1995, when the site was offered as a dial-up, subscription-based service for "internetters" in a deal between Southam New Media and IBM Canada – was a brave new world for some staffers, who could see the old days slipping away. After nearly a century of producing the daily the old-fashioned way – on printing presses, the product delivered by truck and carriers to stores and readers' doorsteps - there was suddenly a live parallel universe that required none of the above.

Employees were trained on new web software called SouthParc, and the physical newsroom was altered to bring staff within reach of a giant round hub, a circular desk stocked with big-screen televisions and populated by senior editors and section heads, who in turn were surrounded in a spoke formation by web teams and writers. Unlike previous decades, where editors mostly stayed in offices and editorial meetings were held behind closed doors, the day's news business was now conducted out in the open. The newsroom's complement of digital editors was rivalling, and eventually surpassing , the size of some departments.

The shift in editorial priority was also aided by the Canwest Editorial Service operation in Hamilton, which was paginating an average of 130 print pages a week for *The Sun* – eventually increasing to all but a handful of special pages – freeing up precious time for *Sun* staff to create their own digital content.

Reporters and columnists were encouraged to post daily blogs, to take video and participate in real-time online forums on everything from elections to gang murders. Breaking news, celebrity photo galleries and Canucks coverage were beginning to attract thousands of page hits a day, as were popular daily blogs updated frequently by reporters such as Kim Bolan (The Real Scoop) and education writer Janet Steffenhagen (Report Card).

Like most newsrooms in North America, *The Sun* was also contracting, getting smaller, its numbers reduced by attrition. Reporters used to filing a single story for the next day's paper now found themselves filing updates to the website throughout the day, holidays and weekends included.

But translating all that impressive virtual circulation – amounting to hundreds of millions of page hits a year – into advertising dollars would prove frustrating for *The Sun*, along with daily newspapers all over the continent.

From database to Fatabase

When reporter Chad Skelton joined *The Sun* in 1998, his affinity for using Internet resources to break investigative stories by searching government databases sparked *The Sun*'s emergence as a national leader in the fledgling field of computer-assisted reporting. The paper's inaugural project, in 2008, allowed readers for the first time to search safety ratings for thousands of local daycare centres and nursing homes. Since then, the paper has produced dozens of online maps, interactive graphics and searchable databases on everything from parking tickets to parolees. The projects, including a database of public-sector salaries that has attracted more than six million page views to date, have won awards and generated enormous reader interest. In 2010, another *Sun* news-you-can-use online project – the Fatabase – logged 500,000 page views on its first weekend as readers browsed the nutritional information for dozens of local restaurants.

News on the go: *The Vancouver Sun* is available today on desktop computers, smart phones and tablets. *Ward Perrin/PNG*

Moving the mountain

After five years of holding its collective breath, the moment B.C. had been waiting for had arrived: Vancouver/Whistler was selected as the host city for the 2010 Winter Olympic and Paralympic Games, narrowly beating out Pyeongchang, South Korea. Thousands of supporters cheered and waved Canadian flags as they watched the photo finish live on the big screen at GM Place on July 2, 2003.

"YES!" screamed *The Sun*'s front page, with a note to readers that staff had worked through the night to produce a 24-page special section on the Games to complement the 16 pages of Olympic news.

A photograph of the Canadian contingent at the Prague news conference included bid president and soon-to-be Vancouver Games CEO John Furlong, Prime Minister Jean Chretien, B.C. Premier Gordon Campbell, Vancouver mayor Larry Campbell, hockey legend Wayne Gretzky and Olympic speed-skater Catriona Le May Doan.

The following day, *Sun* reporter Jeff Lee shared with readers a private moment between Furlong and bid chairman Jack Poole in a corridor of the Hilton Hotel in Prague. "There is almost nothing that the two men don't know about each other," wrote Lee. "They'd worked together, flown to virtually every continent together, and dined with their families together. So a simple handshake after pulling off an Olympic win might seem like a trivial thing. But in an act that left him close to crying and which was not meant for public consumption, Furlong reached over and gave Poole a bear-strong handshake. 'Today, we have absolutely moved a mountain,'" he told his friend.

Furlong and his team could only imagine how big that mountain would be over the years leading to February 2010.

Trailblazer

In August 2003, a new editor – the first woman to hold the position – was appointed to lead *The Vancouver Sun*. Patricia Graham gave up her law career for journalism in 1980, finding her way to *The Province* in 1986 and then moving to *The Sun* newsroom in 1991, where she rose to the position of managing editor and, ultimately, editor-in-chief.

A hard-nosed newsie, Graham set out to make *The Sun* more visual, more local and more analytical, with an emphasis on contextual journalism. With the help of her senior team – managing editor Kirk LaPointe, deputy managing editors Harold Munro and Paul Bucci, senior editor Nicholas Palmer, executive editor Valerie Casselton and editorial pages editor Fazil Mihlar – Graham introduced an updated code of ethics, bolstered the paper's already strong roster of columnists, reorganized local news beats and developed *The Sun*'s increasingly popular website into one of the most-viewed among Canadian newspapers.

For the next eight years, Graham would

2010 Olympic Bid Committee President John Furlong (left) is congratulated by B.C.Premier Gordon Campbell and IOC Member Charmaine Crooks at the 'Yes' Campaign party in 2003. *Richard Lam/Vancouver Sun*

Editor-in-chief of *The Vancouver Sun* for eight years, Patricia Graham emphasized contextual news, digital journalism and community engagement. One of the projects launched under her tenure was a Teens Against Gangs video contest. *Les Bazso/PNG*

preside over some of the toughest belt-tightening in the newsroom's history while stick handling the big stories, like the Olympics and the Bountiful polygamist saga, and the small, including a nasty outbreak of bed bugs in the city.

Graham was succeeded in April 2012 by newly appointed editor Harold Munro, a 26-year *Sun* veteran known for his hard news bent and strategic leadership skills.

Carrying the torch

As athletes Rick Hansen, Wayne Gretzky, Steve Nash, Nancy Greene and Catriona Le May Doan prepared to touch their torches to the indoor Olympic Cauldron and ignite a display of patriotism and firepower at the opening ceremonies of the 2010 Vancouver Olympics on Feb. 12, 2010, even the malfunctioning fourth arm of the cauldron failed to dull the roar of the crowd at BC Place.

It would be an extravaganza like nothing the city had ever seen.

The Games were the third Olympics for Canada, undertaken at a time when the province's fortunes had been stalling. The media, not surprisingly, focused a great deal of attention on the staggering costs of staging the Games, estimated by *The Vancouver Sun* to be

NBA star Steve Nash was one of 12,000 people – athletes, celebrities, politicians and others – to take up the torch in the Canada-wide 2010 Olympic torch relay. *Arlen Redekop/PNG*

Five of Canada's top athletes light the (malfunctioning) torch at the 2010 Winter Olympics opening ceremonies at BC Place. Foreground (from left) are Rick Hansen, Catriona Le May Doan, Steve Nash, Nancy Greene and Wayne Gretzky. *Larry Wong/Postmedia News Service*

extensively redesigned in 2008 to include videos and other multimedia components, as well as reader feedback links – offered breaking Olympic news, photographs and results, along with guides and events schedules, a Twitter feed from athletes and observers, a 17-day live blog, and online forums with Canwest journalists from across the country.

"Our Games" declared *The Sun*'s front page on March 1, the celebratory photograph of Canadian men's hockey team captain Sidney Crosby speaking a thousand words following his thrilling overtime goal on the final day of the Games.

When it was all over, when the 2,600 athletes from 82 countries packed up and headed home after 17 days, the Games were deemed an unparalleled success. Hundreds of thousands of tourists and locals had flooded into Whistler and Vancouver, cheerfully celebrating in the streets and snapping up Olympic souvenirs, especially those coveted red maple leaf mittens and the four stuffed Olympic mascots: Quatchi, Sumi, Miga and Mukmuk.

As Vancouver Mayor Gregor Robertson passed the Olympic flag to the mayor of Sochi, Russia, host of the 2014 Winter Games, British Columbia was left not only with structural legacy projects such as a recreation oval in Richmond, a curling centre in Vancouver and a much-improved regional transportation system, but with a profound sense of national pride and accomplishment.

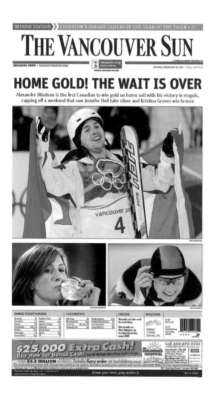

ABOVE: The Feb. 15, 2010 *Sun* shared the news: a Canadian athlete had won Olympic gold on home soil.

FACING PAGE: Canada's Sidney Crosby leaps into hockey history with his overtime goal against the U.S. *John Mahoney/Postmedia News Service*

about $6 billion. It was a figure well beyond the project's on-budget operational costs of close to $2 billion, and included nearly $1 billion for security and billions more for extraneous projects like the Sea-to-Sky highway renovations, a new conference centre to host broadcast media, and the Canada Line from the airport to the downtown core.

The opening day of the Games was marred by the tragic death of 21-year-old Georgian luger Nodar Kumaritashvili, killed in a crash on a training run in Whistler.

But the home-soil Games were a time for Canadian athletes to shine, and they didn't disappoint. Freestyle skier Alex Bilodeau won the country's first-ever Olympic gold medal on home turf, in men's moguls, and the medals just kept piling up throughout the Games, culminating in the heart-stopping men's hockey final between Canada and the U.S., which saw superstar Sidney Crosby score the winning goal in overtime, prompting a roar heard across the country.

Canadians took home 26 medals, including 14 gold – a record at a Winter Games.

The Vancouver Sun's coverage was coordinated by Olympics editor Bev Wake, a former *Sun* sports editor who was also one of three editors assigned to the Games by Canwest. Produced, for the most part, out of the massive Olympic Media Centre in Canada Place, the paper was a daily tableau of joy and despair, of celebration and expectation, with oversize photographs gracing section fronts and inside pages dedicated to dozens of news stories, features, results, graphics and pictures.

The paper had 22 accredited staffers, including six news writers and eight sports writers, five Pacific Newspaper Group photographers (the newly-merged *Sun* and *Province* photo departments) and two computer technicians, plus Wake. The work was supplemented by staff from Canwest's other Canadian papers, including *The Province*, a total contingent of 54 taking up a chunk of the cavernous media centres in Vancouver and Whistler, temporary homes to more than 2,800 accredited press members. Another 7,000 accredited broadcasters worked out of a separate media centre; more than three billion viewers were expected to tune in worldwide.

The Sun's website – which had been

Downtown Vancouver was flooded with thousands of people on the final day of the 2010 Games, after the men's hockey team won gold to give Canada a record 14 Winter Olympic champions. *Stuart Davis/PNG*

Goodbye Asper, hello Godfrey

After months of crippling debt and a winter of uncertainty that included filing for bankruptcy protection in October 2009, *The Sun*'s parent company, Canwest, sold its newspapers to a bondholder group headed by *National Post* CEO Paul Godfrey for $1.1 billion.

In July 2010, the newspapers re-emerged under a new corporate banner: Postmedia Network Inc.

A former helmsman of the *Toronto Sun* and Toronto Blue Jays, Godfrey was considered both an astute business and newspaperman, and there was no question that the company would need to realign itself and become more profitable than it had been in recent years.

Postmedia Inc. now included *National Post*, as well as *The Vancouver Sun*, *Ottawa Citizen*, *Montreal Gazette*, *Victoria Times Colonist* (which it would sell in the fall of 2011 to Glacier Media) and several other Canadian dailies.

In regular company-wide missives, Postmedia conveyed its new strategy, and mantra: Digital first.

Arab Spring and hockey madness

That *Time* magazine declared its 2011 "person of the year" to be The Protestor was utterly appropriate, as violence and unrest were transforming the Middle East and sending the global message that the younger generation was mad as hell and not going to take it any more.

When news came in May 2011 that, 10 years after the 9/11 terrorist attacks, Osama bin Laden had been captured and killed, youthful protesters propelled by the postings of their peers on social media sites took to the streets throughout the Arab countries to fight repression and censorship.

Violence erupted across north Africa as governments and military regimes were overthrown and ousted. Moammar Gadhafi's iron-fisted, 42-year reign in Libya ended on Oct. 20, after months of fighting, when he was killed in a siege.

"Gadhafi's death likely an execution" was the headline on *The Sun*'s CanadaWorld front. Jonathan Manthorpe, the paper's long-time

foreign affairs columnist, noted that "Libya's income from oil exports, estimated at over $30 billion a year, can be both a blessing in the financing of reconstruction and a curse, for the avarice and lust for power it can breed . . . . Within the Middle East and North Africa, what happens now in Libya will influence events in other countries affected by the pro-reform uprisings of the Arab Spring."

In B.C., new Liberal premier Christy Clark was dealing with protests of a different kind when hundreds of people trashed the downtown core on June 15 – breaking windows, looting, setting police cars on fire and taking photos of themselves participating in the melee – in the hours following the Vancouver Canucks' 4-0 loss to the Boston Bruins in Game 7 of the Stanley Cup final. Historians were quick to note that it was the city's 16th riot since 1887, and while most of those early protests had focused on simmering race relations and economic issues like unemployment and homelessness, the modern-day marauders were more often than not trashing the streets after rock concerts and professional sports games.

Sun sports columnist Cam Cole wrote of pride

History repeated itself on June 15, 2011, as rioters took to the streets following another Game 7 loss in the Stanley Cup final. Cars were trashed and burned, windows smashed and stores looted. *Jason Payne/PNG*

The Vancouver Art Gallery was the site of another protest in 2011, this time by followers of the worldwide Occupy movement, directed primarily at economic and social inequalities. *Jason Payne/PNG*

turning to shame for Vancouver, pride that the 40th year of the Canucks saw them in a much-deserved hockey final, shame that "the whole damn city lost its class."

In mid-October, followers of the worldwide Occupy movement camped on the grounds of the Vancouver Art Gallery for five weeks, protesting the tar sands, First Nations injustices, the Enbridge pipeline and Wall Street's capitalist cabal. When a fatal drug overdose and fire safety infractions highlighted troubles in the camp, a court injunction issued in November shut it down.

The Sun, in a story that infuriated readers and prompted dozens of letters to the editor, reported the occupation cost Vancouver taxpayers about $1 million, including nearly $600,000 for policing.

It was indeed a new era of protest, in which foment by Facebook, insurrection by iPhone and turmoil by tweet were the virtual purveyors in a growing wave of public journalism that was increasingly connecting readers in far more expedient fashion than traditional forms of journalism. Like newspapers.

Vancouver Canucks mascot Fin hawks the annual *Vancouver Sun* Raise-a-Reader edition. The successful literacy fundraiser, started by the newspaper in 1997, is one of the legacies of Dennis Skulsky, publisher of *The Sun* from 2001 to 2006. The campaign went national in 2002, and by 2012 had raised close to $20 million for literacy programs across Canada. *Kim Stallknecht/PNG*

Sun publisher Dennis Skulsky carries bundles of newspapers to be sold on a downtown Vancouver street corner for Raise-a-Reader day in 2004. *Ward Perrin/Vancouver Sun*

Vancouver Sun publisher Kevin Bent with students and staff from Thunderbird elementary school, one of the first Vancouver-area schools to benefit from *The Sun*'s Adopt-a-School campaign, which began in the fall of 2011. *Ward Perrin/PNG*

It takes a teacher, a village and a newspaper

When education reporter Janet Steffenhagen wrote a story in the fall of 2011 detailing the frustration of a Vancouver inner-city elementary school teacher whose students were coming into her classroom with empty stomachs and without appropriate warm clothing, it sparked an outpouring of support from *Sun* readers.

It also prompted the paper's 30-year-old charity, The Vancouver Sun Children's Fund, to do what it does best: ask readers to open their hearts and wallets to help the neediest children in B.C. communities.

And so was born the Adopt-a-School campaign.

With the support of Board president, PNG president and *Sun* publisher Kevin Bent, and guided by energetic board member and *Sun* reporter Gillian Shaw, a newsroom team produced a series of compelling stories and photographs that was published through the 2011 Christmas season.

Sun readers – who over the history of the fund have generously donated $11 million to assist 900 children's charities – joined local businesses in providing the identified schools with everything from cash to coats, from iPads to washing machines. By year's end, the campaign had raised close to $300,000, an amount matched by the fund for a total of nearly $600,000, and plans were under way in 2012 to expand the program into a self-sustaining project that would continue to help the region's neediest school children.

Is there an app for that?

In a move that left no question that digital did indeed come first in the Postmedia philosophy, *Sun* editor Patricia Graham was appointed PNG vice-president of digital in October 2011. There was no getting around it: the world, and the newspapers serving it, were now part of a soft-wired social media universe, as millions of sleek high-tech hand-helds like the iPod, the iPad, the iPhone and their smart phone and tablet cousins became palm-sized substitutes for traditional paper and ink.

Graham's daunting challenge: bring revenue to the online product, not an easy undertaking given that an entire generation has been trained to expect free information.

Despite the widespread practice of repurposing and aggregating – whereby websites freely reproduce content without benefit of credit or payment to the original source, and where much of the posted material is pulled from newspapers with highly paid staff – there remains the reality that it costs a significant amount of money to maintain the well-oiled infrastructure and bricks-and-mortar production plant that is the news and information-producing daily newspaper.

It may be that newspapers, in their rush to provide apps and free online content to keep up with the Joneses, have been remiss in educating users that it requires a healthy bottom line to gather and present news professionally, that public bloggers, for instance, don't have access to NHL locker rooms or movie screenings or political press rooms, and that a great deal of the news wafting about in cyberspace still comes from traditional news sources like *The Sun*.

Advertisers have also been slow to follow print's move to the web, and most daily newspapers are finding themselves caught between the proverbial rock and a hard place – having offered their content for free for the past decade or so, it is becoming increasingly difficult to financially sustain those "free" websites without advertising revenue.

Fuelling the dilemma is the phenomenal growth of the *The Sun*'s website, which added a Chinese language version, *Tai Yang Bao*, in late 2011. Overall, page views increased to 456 million in 2011, up from 66.5 million in 2007.

The second hundred years

Venerable brands like *The Vancouver Sun* have long been used to reinventing themselves, adapting over the decades as changing demographics and readership needs dictate.

The next 100 years of *The Sun* should prove no different.

It's widely expected that North American newspaper websites, including *The Vancouver Sun*'s, will begin introducing "metred models," or paywalls, for their online content. Newspaper-by-smart-phone is also growing at a rapid rate, as social commerce and geo-targeting become new buzz words. And all indications are that readers and advertising dollars will continue to migrate from print to digital, even though the hard copy of the paper continues to drive revenue and return on investment.

The promising news is that, despite the myriad diversions at their fingertips, people still like to read newspapers, still cherish that fresh package of news and entertainment delivered to their doorsteps every day.

A Canadian Newspaper Audience Databank survey released early in 2011 showed that readership of *The Sun* in 2010 had, in fact, grown for both the print and web versions, although the biggest jump was for the online edition. The NADbank numbers also revealed that 900,000 Metro Vancouver adults read *The Sun* in print or online at least once a week.

"This is a real good news story," said Kevin Bent, who succeeded Dennis Skulsky as PNG boss in 2006. "*The Vancouver Sun* is retaining its print readers while expanding its online audience, which is precisely what we need to do to position ourselves for a successful future."

In the year of our 100th birthday, the news of our imminent death, it seems, may well be greatly exaggerated.

There are seven billion people on the planet today, millions of them connected by digital devices, and as the definition of news continues on its path of perpetual change, the future of the newspaper industry surely lies in its prodigious capacity to adapt, its legacy of comforting the afflicted and afflicting the comfortable no less an imperative than it has ever been.

Like the city for which it is named, *The Vancouver Sun* has weathered its first 100 years with grace, grit and style, doing what it does best in the writing of history's first draft, a solemn responsibility that it will carry with much pride and obligation into its second century.

RIGHT: *The Vancouver Sun* sign at 200 Granville Street lights up the sky on June 27, 2012. *Ian Lindsay/PNG*

VANCOUVER SUN PUBLISHERS

2006 to present: Kevin Bent

2001 to 2006: Dennis Skulsky

1999 to 2000: David Radler (Pacific Press chairman)

1999: Ken King

1992 to 1999: Don Babick

1988 to 1991: Stuart Noble (president)

1985 to 1989: Gerald Haslam

1983 to 1985: E.H. (Bill) Wheatley

1979 to 1983: Clark Davey

1964 to 1978: Stuart Keate

1942 to 1964: Don Cromie

1936 to 1942: caretaker management

1917 to 1936: Robert Cromie

1912 to 1917: John P. McConnell

VANCOUVER SUN EDITORS-IN-CHIEF

2012 to present: Harold Munro

2003 to 2011: Patricia Graham

2000 to 2003: Neil Reynolds

1995 to 2000: John Cruickshank

1991 to 1995: Ian Haysom

1989 to 1991: Nicholas Hills

1985 to 1988: Bruce Larsen

1979 to 1985: No editor in this period; publishers Davey then Wheatley, and managing editor Bruce Larsen.

1963 to 1979: Bruce Hutchison

Prior to 1963, The Sun had publishers and managing editors, not editors-in-chief.

SELECTED BIBLIOGRAPHY

Bruce, Charles. *News and the Southams*. Toronto: MacMillan of Canada, 1968. Print.

Davis, Chuck. *The Greater Vancouver Book*. Vancouver: The Linkman Press. 1997. Print.

Davis, Chuck, and Mooney, Shirley. *Vancouver: An Illustrated Chronology*. Vancouver: Windsor Publications, 1986. Print.

Edge, Marc. *Pacific Press: The Unauthorized Story of Vancouver's Newspaper Monopoly*. Vancouver: New Star Books, 2001. Print.

Keate, Stuart. *Paper Boy: The Memoirs of Stuart Keate*. Vancouver: Clark, Irwin & Company, 1980. Print.

Lee, Jack, et al. *The Fabulous '50s: Sun / Province Reunion, Pan Pacific Hotel, Feb. 4, 1994*. Vancouver: Pacific Press, 1994. Print.

Nichols, Marjorie, with O'Hara, Jane. *Mark My Words: The Memoirs of a Very Political Reporter*. Vancouver: Douglas & McIntyre, 1992. Print.

Parry, David. *A century of Southam*. Toronto: Southam Press Limited, 1977. Print.

Roy, Patricia E. *Vancouver: An Illustrated History*. Toronto: James Lorimer & Company, 1980. Print.

Rutherford, Paul. *A Victorian Authority: The Daily Press In Late Nineteenth-Century Canada*. Toronto: University of Toronto Press, 1982. Print.

Smith, C. Rhodes, and Carignan, Pierre. *Restrictive Trade Practices Commission: Report Concerning the Production and Supply of Newspapers in the City of Vancouver and Elsewhere in the Province of British Columbia*. Ottawa: Department of Justice, 1960. Print.

Stursberg, Peter. *Extra! When the Papers Had the Only News*. Sound Heritage Series: No. 35. Victoria: Province of British Columbia, 1982. Print.

ACKNOWLEDGEMENTS

*Special thanks to Vancouver Sun Projects Editor Bev Wake,
who edited this book with vigour and a keen eye, and to Peter Merrison
and Joseph Llamzon of the Pacific Newspaper Group's creative department
for their collaboration on layout and design. Former PNG library manager
Debbie Millward was also invaluable with the extensive research required
to tell The Sun's story with accuracy and alacrity.*

*Vancouver Sun Publisher Kevin Bent and Vancouver Sun Editor-in-Chief
Harold Munro were more than generous in providing the resources
necessary to write this book. Former Sun Editor Patricia Graham
was equally generous with her support and inspiration.*

*Thanks, too, to Sun reporter John Mackie, avid Sun historian and fellow keeper
of the flame, for his indefatigable work on the centenary project.*

*Without Kate Bird's patient humour, unflinching attention to detail
and exacting standards, this book would not have been possible.*

*And, of course, there would be no 100 years of The Vancouver Sun
without all those publishers, reporters, columnists, photographers, editors,
artists and assorted characters, in the newsroom and throughout The Sun's
offices and printing plant, who have worked with such journalistic dedication
and professionalism over the decades, or without the readers
and advertisers throughout British Columbia who have chosen us
as their newspaper of record for the past century.*